MARK ROWLANDS was born in Newport, Wales. He is a Professor of Philosophy at the University of Miami and the author of sixteen books, including the bestselling *The Philosopher and the Wolf*, also published by Granta. His books have been translated into more than twenty languages.

Also by Mark Rowlands

The Philosopher and the Wolf:
Lessons from the Wild on Love, Death and Happiness

Running with the Pack:
Thoughts from the Road on Meaning and Mortality

A Good Life

Philosophy from Cradle to Grave

Mark Rowlands

GRANTA

Granta Publications, 12 Addison Avenue, London W11 4QR

First published in Great Britain by Granta Books 2015
This paperback edition published by Granta Books 2016

9 8 7 6 5 4 3 2 1

ISBN 978 1 84708 950 2 (paperback)
ISBN 978 1 84708 951 9 (ebook)

www.grantabooks.com

Typeset in Melior by M Rules

Printed and bound by CPI Group (UK) Ltd, Croydon, CR0 4YY

MIX
Paper from
responsible sources
FSC
www.fsc.org
FSC® C020471

For Emma

'And let me tell you this too, Mother: everyone of us is responsible for everyone else in every way, and I most of all.' Mother could not help smiling at that. She wept and smiled at the same time. 'How are you,' she said, 'most of all responsible for everyone? There are murderers and robbers in the world, and what terrible sin have you committed that you should accuse yourself before everyone else?' 'Mother, my dearest heart,' he said (he had begun using such caressing, such unexpected words just then), 'my dearest heart, my joy, you must realize that everyone is really responsible for everyone and everything.'

Dostoyevsky, *The Brothers Karamazov*

Contents

Annotations

After my mother's death, my father, to see out what remained of his days (his words, not mine), acquired a modest house in Key West, Florida. A bit tattered, a little threadbare, somewhat run-down: definitely seen better days – a description applicable to father and house in equal measures. A suitably ragged place, he decided, to embark on his own personal voyage to the island of erasure. He always used to say – and, I now remember, this goes back to my childhood – that the Keys would go under around the time he did and then Mother Ocean could wash away any trace that either of them were ever here. My father had a fondness for entirely feigned melancholy. But he wasn't wrong. I am here before the waters come to wash away, like footprints in the sand, all that is left of two people who loved me.

I came here by boat, a small motorboat I rented in Islamorada. The Seven Mile Bridge has already gone, swept away by the storms of summer. The Keys are just the beginning, one of the first visible signs of humanity's unwillingness to accept into its heart the realization of brother Alyosha: everyone is really responsible for everyone and everything. South Florida itself is becoming a series of islands – the new Keys. And the new will go the same way as the old. One should dismiss images of the ocean sweeping in, biblically, over the land, wiping away everything in its path. It is true, Hurricane Cristobal did a very good impression of an angry God, turning the lower Keys into the islands they had always been until a mere one hundred and fifty years ago. But the end of my childhood home owes more to T. S. Eliot than to the vengeful deity of Genesis: *it ends with a whimper rather than a bang. The water that wipes us away comes not from the ocean but the land. South Florida is built on coral rock. This is porous. As the seas rise, they seep through the coral and rise up from the ground, from underneath. And all our dams and levees and pumping stations are helpless in the face of this oceanic fifth column. There is an old saying in these parts: you can hide from the wind but you have to run from the water. You can, in fact, gently stroll away from this water. But you can never come back. These towns have been left to ghosts long before they will sink into the sea.*

But sink they will. Few live here any more, only the most resilient, stubborn, stupid or desperate citizens of the Conch Republic – the ones who have nowhere else to go. The streets are flooded most high tides. On a spring tide, the water might remain for weeks. I tied up the boat on what used to be Front Street and walked a short distance to the corner of Simonton and Caroline, where my dad used to live. It's raining – as it does most summer days now – and that is welcome, taking a little of the edge off the acrid redolence of decay.

It is a hard task, sitting in a dead house in a rotting town, sifting through the curdling residue of a life that was once a booming, humming, thrumming presence: as big as the house he was to me once, and with a laugh that could shake the windows. A hard task, it is true: but far from thankless. I didn't know that everything I touched would resurrect memories long dead: memories called to glory, new again, shining and pristine, as if they were born only moments before. That memories could become mountains, resonating, echoing with life: that was a welcome surprise. John McTaggart, a turn-of-the-twentieth-century architect of British Idealism, argued that time is not real. In my father's house, I can almost believe him.

The greatest surprise, however, is that my father has left behind a manuscript. I found it in the upstairs bedroom, wrapped in brown paper and neatly tied with string. I wouldn't say I'd seen him often after his move here. Key West is not the easiest place to get to, especially in recent times. But I'd visited him here a few times a year. Not once did he give me any indication that he was writing. I seem to remember that he spent much of his adult life complaining that he wasn't writing, but when the old man finally got around to it: silence.

His manuscript is difficult to categorize. It is part auto-biography, definitely – but also comprises unpredictable philosophical musings on the nature of morality and the human condition. As far as the philosophy goes, some of it I think is clearly right, some of it is clearly wrong, and some of it could go either way. The autobiography is even stranger. Sometimes, I'm genuinely uncertain whether the events he describes are real ones or imaginary, or a mixture of both. Sometimes he describes his life from a point of view he could not possibly have had. Sometimes he writes from a perspective in which he – the creator of this manuscript – is not sure that he – the subject matter of this manuscript – actually exists. Truth exists cheek by jowl with what can only be something other than truth: not the opposite of truth, perhaps, but, nevertheless, eerily alien to it. Moreover, it is clear my father had problems with time. His viewpoints can shift, sometimes unexpectedly. His tenses change, often erratically. It is as if my father always had one foot in time and one foot out of it, and was never quite sure which foot should bear the weight. His writing is, therefore, indelibly marked by anachronism. This tendency may have been exacerbated by the condition from which, as I later discovered, he suffered towards his end, and in which at least some of this book would have been written. Or it may not. I know enough about memory to know that, even at its best, it can't be trusted, and that the difference between autobiography and fiction is not as marked as one might believe. I still don't really know what this manuscript is. But I do know this: anachronism holds the key to everything my father wrote.

Even better, it appears my mother – editing was in her blood, she remained an editor to her dying breath, bless her – had been making rather copious notes on the manuscript – copious notes and some rather telling criticisms. As my mother died a number of years before my father, this indicates that his literary efforts, rather than being the final, futile spasms of a broken, dying man, had been going on for some years. Some of her notes were contained in a separate book, which I found secreted away in one of the cupboards, but most I discovered on her old, almost but not quite moribund computer. If my father was aware of my mother's criticisms – and, since her notes were in the house, I assume he must have been aware of at least some of them – any appearance they make in his written words is, barring a few explicit exceptions, not immediately obvious.

As it turns out, I can't help myself. I shall put it all together. In fact I have already started. I'm converting everything into electronic form, and piecing it all together in the *best way I can. Perhaps this is a way of keeping them both around a little longer – walking with them, just a little way, through the sunlit, singing mountains of memory. Although I am not, specifically, a moral philosopher, I do have a little more training than they: Where I think they made mistakes, I shall point them out and try to correct them, and then just run with the ideas to see where I end up. Any footnotes you see will all be mine. Apparently, my father didn't believe in them (and I can sympathize with that). If I know or suspect my father has been drawing his ideas from others, I shall cite the likely sources. Where my comments are too substantial to be entered as footnotes, I shall insert them into the text in italics. But, of course, I am profoundly fallible, and it may be that I am mistaken too. Will the resulting work be my father's, my mother's or mine? Or will it belong to all of us? There is no easy answer to that. And, if the product of our collaborative and partly posthumous pen is correct, that is exactly as it should be.*

In my father's bedroom hangs a picture ...

Nicolai M.
Key West, Florida
2054

1

Words

Il n'ya pas de hors-texte.

Jacques Derrida, *Of Grammatology*

In my bedroom hangs a picture. It faces the foot of the bed, and so it's often the first thing I see each morning, when *l'aurore, de ses doigts de rose, ouvre les portes de l'orient et enflamme tout l'horizon.*[1] The picture is an old map of the world, framed in wood, and rendered in a faded patchwork of browns, yellows, greens and greys. It rests there, roseate, in the birth of the new light.

I have always been somewhere. At every moment since I came into this world, I have always been somewhere on this map. A peripatetic existence – some might call it restless – I have called many places home. But this morning I think: soon, I shall be nowhere at all. There is no place on this map that I shall be. I think this? No, not quite a thought: something

---

1 'Dawn, with its rosy fingers, opens the doors of the orient and sets the horizon aflame.' The *Iliad* in French? I think my father just lost half of his imaginary bookstore browsers right there. And don't get me started on Derrida. Sometimes I think Dad learned nothing from me.

in the vicinity of a thought, no doubt – a thought almost born, almost formed, but one that turns to smoke, slips through my grasping, intellective fingers when I try to think it. Rather than a thought, I am left with a formless and dizzying terror. I arm myself, a muttered ward to be turned against the horror: 'It has been a good life'.

A good life: yes. In the end, it is not a man's deeds that are good or bad, and not the rules or principles he believes in. It is not even the man who is good or bad. Only life. There is so much more to a person's life than is contained within the spatial boundaries of his skin, and so much more than is immured within the temporal prison of his birth and death. It is only a life that can be truly good or bad. And the chances of it being wholly one or the other are negligible.

In his final years, long after he had become profoundly deaf, and when he had not written for a considerable time, Beethoven could be heard repeatedly humming a tune. People took this as a sign of his creative mutilation: a sad but certain indication that this greatest of masters had finally succumbed to time's unforgiving arrow. The tune was jarring in its simplicity – a tune that would be mumbled by a child bereft of musical talent. That tune became the choral movement of the Ninth Symphony: something that, even if he had written nothing else, would eternally justify Beethoven's existence. Moral rules, principles, doctrines and theories are the murmured motifs of the callow: on their own they are childish things, risible and easily refutable. But woven into a life, like overlapping strands of a musical composition, they can sometimes – just sometimes – become something more.

*

Literature is about seeing. Its goal is to enable you to see your own limitlessness in the life of another. As such, we might think of literature as the imaginative extension of compassion, one procured by detailed, painstaking methods. The enormous success of this art form speaks volumes about the strength of our desire to see. Consider the well-known 'paradox of fiction' that has exercised – one might say, embarrassed – philosophers for so long. How can we become emotionally invested in characters that we know, without a shadow of doubt, do not exist? Our emotional attachment is clear: a truly great novel can alter one's mood for days, or longer. It might even 'change one's life'. We endure with fictional characters. We care about what happens to them. And we know, all the while, that these characters are not real. No one really knows why this is so: all attempts to solve this paradox are, I think it is fair to say, problematic. Literature can draw us so deeply into paradox only because it exploits the ability to see oneself in the other. That this invitation to compassion is difficult to decline, even though the object of this compassion does not even exist, is testament to literature's colossal power.

It is true, of course, that philosophers issue their invitations too. But these are, in general, comparatively clumsy affairs – the graceless fumbling of a schoolboy asking a girl out on a date for the first time. Perhaps philosophy only becomes truly persuasive when it most closely approximates literature. Some of Schopenhauer's invitations, for example, I find curiously compelling. But for the most part, the novelist's invitation to see is so much more compelling than the philosopher's invitation to think. The ideas dissected in philosophy are dead: items excised for inspection under the harsh light of the mortician's table. In literature, the ideas are living, breathing, respiring, perspiring, woven into the fabric of a person's life, in all of its limitless wonder, and unintelligible apart from that life. That is why literature has always been the more difficult and exacting discipline.

The novelist's most compelling invitations are often not even clothed as such. Milan Kundera once told us that:

> True human goodness, in all its purity and freedom, can come to the fore only when its recipient has no power. Mankind's true moral test, its fundamental test (which lies deeply buried from view), consists of its attitude towards those who are at its mercy: animals. And in this respect mankind has suffered a fundamental debacle, a debacle so fundamental that all others stem from it.[2]

This passage masquerades as a statement, but is really an invitation. It invites you to put yourself, imaginatively, in the shoes of the powerless: to think back to all of those situations in which you stood in a position of power – over a person not as intelligent as you, a person not as strong as you, a person without your contacts or influence – and ask yourself: how did I do? Was I merciful, or was I not? Now I can see it, more compelling than any argument of philosophers' devising: the case for compassion. And, after that, the case for extending this compassion to animals: the moral case for animal rights, as it is sometimes called – the case against eating them, the case for almost entirely changing the ways we treat them – I can see it. It is there in front of me, palpable.

---

2 This passage is from *The Unbearable Lightness of Being* (London: Faber and Faber, 1984) p. 289.

Words

I find myself compelled to conclude, with Kundera, that mercy is the fundamental moral virtue and that here, in our dealings with those less powerful, we find the fundamental failing of humankind.

But suppose these words – these very same words – had appeared as part of a philosophical tract. Their force, I suspect, would have been substantially reduced. Perhaps nothing would have remained of it. The invitation works not because of what it says but because of where it is: it is woven into the life of two characters, Tomas and Teresa, and occurs shortly after the death of Karenin, their dog, whom Teresa loved with a purity she could not replicate in her love for Tomas. It is not an argument that led me here, but a life. I arrived at this point in moral space because this life issued an invitation that I could not resist: an invitation to see things in a certain way, to look at things in a certain light. True human goodness requires that its recipients have no power. And, of course, who is more powerless than the non-existent – the fictional – character?[3]

These nights that remain to me are littered with dreams. In these, it is me that is there – I know this – but the body in which I appear is unfamiliar. Even more telling: in the dream, this incongruence of my psychological and bodily identity is of no consequence. In fact, it is entirely anticipated. These dreams have almost faded by the time I find myself in front of the bathroom mirror. And yet the face that stares back is both unfamiliar and, at the same time, wholly expected. There is a suspicion that takes hold in some, and the older they get the

3 Perhaps this is true but, given my present situation, I would also like to put in a plug for the natural environment.

larger it grows: gestating like a foetus, until one day it springs forth, in the magnificent birth of certainty. It has all been a dream – all of it. The house of memory can hold only so much. And a dream is just a life with too much in it. Soon I shall be nothing more than words on a page. But was I ever anything more than this?

Kundera thought that it is in vain that a writer will try to convince his readers of the reality of his creation. I object: on grounds of unfair burden of proof. I shall not try to convince you that I exist. Instead, try to convince me that I do not. Imagine: there are two characters, closeted inside an impenetrable fortress. This fortress is the past. The only access the world of today has to these characters is through their written pronouncements – diary-like entries, issued on a regular basis. These describe what is going on in the lives and minds of the two figures. However, you are informed – by an authority unimpeachable – that one of these figures is real and the other is merely his or her invention. There are two questions, one far more important than the other. First, how would you know who is the real figure and who is the fiction? The answer to this is simple. If the writer is sufficiently skilled, and any accompanying evidence sufficiently sparse, you need never know which is which. The second question is far more important and even more difficult: what *makes* one figure real and the other a fiction?

One is the creation of the other, you might say. Yes, but we are all, in our way, creations of others – of our parents and the others who shaped us. We are all dependent existences, stitched together and ejected into the domain of the real by a cosmically unlikely sequence of causes, sources and grounds. Nevertheless, you might insist: there was only ever really one person there. The fictional creation was never really there. But you merely offer me tautologies. Something was really there if it was both real and there. What it means to be real is precisely the question. And don't get me started on the subject of there. Where, after all, is there?

'Is this a dagger which I see before me?' asked Macbeth. Apparently it was not. But what makes the dagger unreal? Sartre argued that the dagger's unreality lies in its strictly limited number of appearances.[4] Macbeth reaches for the dagger and his fingers find, precisely, nothing. The series of appearances that led Macbeth to question whether there was a dagger in front of him have come to an abrupt end. This is the defining feature of the unreal: they comprise a limited – strictly finite – series of appearances. The appearances of a real dagger would not abruptly end in this way. If Macbeth reached for the dagger, his fingers would find hard, cool steel. If someone else were to enter the room, they would see the dagger, could hold it. When a thing is real, there is no limit, in principle, to the appearances through which it shows itself.

Is that it? The difference between unreality and reality amounts to the difference between the finite and the infinite. But, if so, the case against my existence seems to rest on something no one really understands: infinity. Mathematicians can't even agree if there is any such thing. Even worse, infinity on its own is not fit for purpose. Nothing lasts forever. A real dagger must be made and will eventually be destroyed,

---

4 Jean-Paul Sartre, *Being and Nothingness*, trans. Hazel Barnes (Methuen, 1957). The argument he is referring to is in the introduction, although there is no mention of Macbeth.

and it is difficult to see how it might manage to conjure up an infinite number of appearances in the finite intervening time. It is not infinity we are dealing with, but something even more obscure: infinity-in-principle. While a real dagger might not exhibit an infinite number of appearances, it can do so 'in principle'.

What does this infinity-in-principle even mean? If I kept looking at the dagger for an infinite period of time, the appearances would keep coming? (But I cannot look at the dagger for an infinite period of time: fate has other plans for both of us. But, if I could?) Or, if there were an infinite number of people looking at the dagger, they would all encounter appearances of the dagger? (But there is not an infinite number of people. But, if there were?) It is not just infinity you need, it is counterfactual infinity: the infinity that is not but might be. Attempts to understand possibility – the counterfactual – have been, at best, salutary exercises in the inconclusive. And infinity – well, no one understands that. Your case against my existence, therefore, rests on a combination of ideas that no one understands and whose own existence is as doubtful as doubt can get. Forgive me if I don't yet roll over.

Perhaps you might try to dispense with both infinity and the counterfactual. Perhaps finitude, concrete and actual, will serve your purposes just as well. The number of appearances that a real dagger can exhibit is greater – perhaps much greater – than the number of appearances that accompanies its illusory counterpart. This idea is not promising. Surely, there could be no greater gulf than that between the real and the merely imagined – a gulf that is vast and unbridgeable. But on this current suggestion, the difference turns out to be a relatively minor one: we are just talking numbers. You manifest n appearances – you are unreal. But $n+1$ appearances – congratulations, you have successfully jumped the chasm between the unreal and the real. If only the unreal – the reality-challenged – could just try a little harder, put themselves out there a little more, put in a few more appearances every now and then. This is, of course, nonsense: if there is a difference between the real and the unreal, it is not going to come down to numbers.

Perhaps you might look to science to build a case against me. Science, you might insist, is the arbiter of the real, and the reality of the dagger is, therefore, to be established through scientific investigation. Protons, neutrons, electrons and the like: real daggers have them, and unreal counterparts do not. Electron microscopes, mass spectrometers and the like: these are the instruments we have for discovering the real. They allow us to see the molecular or atomic reality of things, and if they were directed at me, they would find nothing.

We cannot, however, solve the question of reality by appeal to science. For what is it to see the molecular or atomic reality of the dagger? All this can mean is that there are further appearances – molecular or atomic appearances that now manifest themselves under the scrutiny of the electron microscope or other instruments. And if we go deeper and deeper into these appearances, venturing into the quantum level, then we are simply presented with further appearances: quantum appearances, quark appearances, spin, charm and charge appearances. The question of reality that arises at the level of ordinary objects also arises at the molecular, atomic and quantum level. The appeal to science – to molecular, atomic and sub-atomic reality – has not solved the problem of what makes something real, merely relocated it to another, more diminutive, level. However deep into the rabbit hole we decide to go, we can never get deeper than appearances.[5]

Descartes once responded to (his own) doubts about his existence with a seemingly decisive rebuttal: if I don't exist, then who is it that is doing the doubting? If I doubt that I exist, this proves that I do exist. *Cogito, ergo sum.* I think, therefore I am. I am nothing more than words on a page, you might think. And mere words are never aware of themselves. In this way, my lack of reality is demonstrated.

But, magically, the following words now appear: 'I am, indeed, aware of my existence.' Thus, it appears I am real after all – these very words confirm it. But these are just

---

5 I am going to be charitable to my father here. Either he is guilty of a simple confusion, or he has not been sufficiently clear about which claim he is actually arguing for. The second interpretation is the charitable one. We should distinguish two different questions: (1) What makes something – anything – real? (2) What makes a human real – rather than, say, fictional? It seems my father must be trying to answer the first question. After all, real humans manifest different appearances from fictional characters – the appearances of the latter are confined to the word, to visual depictions, while those of the former are much broader. So, the reality, or lack thereof, of a human is a matter of what *sorts* of appearance they manifest, and not whether they appear or how many appearances they manifest. In other words, my father does not doubt that if he is real then he is human. But he is questioning what it is to be real. My father's obsession with his reality is, of course, a canonical philosophical theme, but may also be a symptom of the condition he was in when he wrote this part of the book. If so, it suggests this was one of the last chapters he wrote. That seems reasonable. Usually, I also write the first chapter last. After all, how can you know the manner in which you should introduce something until you know what it is that needs introduction? And how can you know this unless you have already written it?

words, you might say, signifying nothing. Words can never point outside themselves and demonstrate the truth of what they say. We are slowly arriving at the crux of the matter. I shall see your Descartes and raise you more words, those of David Hume: 'For my part, when I enter most intimately into what I call myself, I always stumble on some particular perception or other, of heat or cold, light or shade, love or hatred, pain or pleasure. I never can catch myself at any time without a perception, and never can observe any thing but the perception.'[6]

When we introspect – enter most intimately into what we call ourselves, as Hume put it – what do we find? What we, precisely, do not find is a self, or ego, or person or soul. You may become aware of thoughts and feelings, of desires and convictions, of sensations of warmth and cold, dark and light, pain and pleasure. You may become aware of emotions, love, hatred, jealousy and anger. You may become aware of hopes, fears, expectations and dreams. You become aware of mental states – states of mind. But you do not become aware of a self, or ego, or person, or mind or soul, not if we under-stand it as something different from these states – something that possesses these states. You never become aware of any-thing underlying these mental states, something to which they attach or belong.

The question of my reality has led inexorably to the deep truth of existence. We are all just words somewhere. It is always just words – all the way down and all the way in. Thoughts and feelings, desires and convictions, love, hatred, jealousy, anger, hopes, expectations and dreams: these are

---

6 David Hume, *A Treatise of Human Nature* (1738), Book I, Part 4, Section 6.

just inscriptions, words written in a brain. But a word is a recognizable inscription on a page? Perhaps, but the page need not be made of paper. A word may be inscribed in a clay tablet, written in the sand of a beach, or stare out from a computer screen. Nor need the page even be flat. One of the earliest forms of written language comprised a system of knots. Words transcend any particular material realization. Nor does 'recognizable' imply recognition. Words may belong to a language you do not understand: a high-level programming language that few understand, or a dead language that no one understands. Nor need a word even be recognized as a word. The word 'barbarian' comes from the Greek *barbaroi*. This word was onomatopoeic: the Greeks regarded foreigners' attempts to speak as akin to the baa-baa clamours of sheep.

A word need not be recognized as a word and a page need not be recognized as a page. And in the beginning and in the end is only the word. Did I know who I was when I woke up to dawn's rosy fingers playing with the picture of my world – the map on which I had always been somewhere? Did I know who I was before I consulted the mirror and saw the entirely expected, but strangely unfamiliar, face staring back at me? If I answer 'yes', then all this can mean is that some or other thought would have occurred: a thought to the effect that I am someone, that I have a name, and this name refers to me. This thought would have occurred, I assure you. There: these very words confirm it.[7]

*

7 So many things that we think of as discoveries are, in fact, merely stipulations. Far from being astonishing, my father's 'deep truth of existence' – that we are all merely words – is, in fact, merely quotidian observation. This is because he has – stipulatively – broadened the

Words

We can never get behind the thoughts to the thinker. We can never get behind the written to the writer. Thoughts can say they are about their thinker, can present themselves as being about their originator: but they are still just thoughts. Words can tell of their writer, can present themselves as being put on a page by a real man or woman: but they are still just words. The belief in the thinker behind

category of the word to include all the mental and physical events that make us who we are. This has the advantage of making my father's claim almost certainly true, and the disadvantage of making it less remarkable than it seems (though still controversial). I am a series of psychophysical events, and there is nothing more to me than this. This is what is known as a 'process' view of persons: I am a series or network of psychophysical processes. Some call it a 'reductionist' view: you and I reduce to a collection of physical, psychical and psychophysical events. This sort of view has its detractors, but I could certainly be convinced.

The same is true of the epigraph with which my father chose to begin this chapter: 'Il n'y a pas de hors-texte.' When Derrida made this claim, so many people – ironically, they were often people who lauded their abilities to engage in what they called 'close reading' of the text – interpreted him as making an outlandish (and, therefore, from their point of view, desirable) metaphysical claim about the nature of reality. Reality is a text, or has a text-like structure. In fact, Derrida didn't even say that there is nothing outside the text. If he had written, 'Il n'y a rien dehors du texte', matters might have been different. But he didn't. He wrote: 'Il n'y a pas de hors-texte.' This means: 'There is no outside-text.' Derrida's claim is, thus, instantly transformed from the metaphysically risible to the utterly mundane. There are no rules from outside life that can tell us how to interpret the events that occur in our lives. Any rules that we might use to understand the meaning or significance of events in our lives are part of those lives. Wittgenstein made the same point in a slightly different way. There are no rules for the interpretation of rules, for these rules would hang together with – are the same sort of thing as – the rules they are supposed to interpret. Any rule for the interpretation of a rule would be just as open to interpretation as the rule it is supposed to interpret.

In short: I'm inclined to believe what my father says. I just think it might be a lot less remarkable than he realizes. But perhaps I am missing something?

the thought, the writer behind the written, is a mythology, an act of faith. Written on a page, or written in a brain, there is only the written. If I am only words, then I am just like you.

Words are the ways we appear, all of us: the scratches and scribbles through which we announce our presence. They are the appearances through which all of us, in our own way, exclaim: 'I am here too!' We are all cut from the same cloth: a fabric of appearances, a cloak made of words. Even if I was never more than words on a page, I am still more real than you were willing to recognize. Or you are less real than you are willing to concede.

When we are young, and spend so much of our time playing the great game of becoming, it is natural to be dazzled by this glittering achievement: this shining product of writing that is the self. When we grow old, however, things can go one of two ways. The first: terrified by our impending nothingness, we hold this self even tighter, and tell ourselves that we will go on, merely in another place, another form. The second: impressed by the hypnagogic quality of our lives, by how improbable it seems that all of these events and experiences should fit into one single track through space and time, we realize that the self was just a transient caprice. There really was no one to become; there was only becoming. It was all just writing somewhere. Perhaps one has to become old to understand this. But the old do not write philosophy. Or if they do, no one reads it. What they write is just so strange.

*

Words

Since no conclusive case against my reality has been established, I believe I deserve a name – one word around which all these other words can coalesce. My name is Myshkin. The rest is simply words. These words begin here.[8]

8   My father's name was not Myshkin. But nor is this a nom de plume. At least, a nom de plume that injects itself into the text is no longer merely a nom de plume. (This may have something to do with the chapter's Derridean epigraph.) Lev Nikolayevich Myshkin, the principal character of Dostoyevsky's *The Idiot*, was simple, naive, but above all a nice person. His fundamental goodness had unfortunate consequences for those dearest to him. I am not certain why my father used this name for himself. My father was by no means simple. He was not always nice. Whatever moral failings (and strengths) he had were quite different from those of Dostoyevsky's Myshkin. I am by no means certain of this, but I lean towards the view that Myshkin was something like an ideal to which my father aspired. Or, perhaps, the name is intended to signify a lack or hiatus that my father detected in himself. It may be that the name is intended to signify a lesson that my father learned somewhere along the way, and wished to communicate through the choice of this appellation. It may, of course, be that all of these are true. Or none of them. Whatever else is true, my father is not Myshkin. And I am not Nicolai. Curiously, however, my mother's name was Aglaya.

2

Silenus

But for humans, the best for them is not to be born at all.

Silenus, from a surviving fragment of Aristotle's *Eudemus*

My father entered the room clad in the armour of a carefully constructed narrative. He would stand at the head of the bed, well away from the action, mopping his wife's brow as she smiled gratefully up at him. Perhaps, occasionally, when he was feeling particularly brave, he might peer out through tremulous fingers at the events unfolding downstream. This armour buckled and broke shortly thereafter, when the midwife told him to grab a leg and count to ten whenever there was a contraction. 'But how will I know when there is a contraction?' he asked. The midwife exited the room behind a noticeable smirk. As the afternoon slowly transformed into night, he was spared nothing. Nothing. Obviously, it was better than being the one on the bed. Nevertheless, the things he saw. Things he never wanted to see, things he didn't even know were possible. Strange bodily warpings, determined assaults on the laws of biological feasibility. The cone head was the worst. Why did no one ever tell him about the cone head? He silently acknowledged that someone – at some point during the exhaustive inventory of pre-natal courses, programs and modules – must have mentioned it, but he probably just hadn't been listening. His poor son, as if some Amazonian head-hunters had been plying their trade in utero.[9]

If anything, however, the hours and days immediately following the birth were worse. Those days saw him being repeatedly assaulted by a strange sense of unreality – of dislocation and disconnection. He could discern, growing inside of him, a nascent and rather unusual sense of determination: now I have to do whatever it takes to look after my son. But this was underpinned by a vague sensation of horror, a sensation whose content was, perhaps, difficult to pinpoint with any real precision but, roughly, might be gestured to thus:

---

9 Anachronism: a thing belonging or appropriate to a period other than that in which it exists. But we might distinguish two forms of anachronism. It is virtually certain that this account of my father's birth is largely fabricated. Obviously, my father was not in a position to know what was going on in his father's mind at this time. He may have based his account on subsequent conversations with his father. However, the evidence suggests this is unlikely. I never met my grandfather, but from everything I've heard about him it seems unlikely he would be talking about events in this way – if at all. Secondly, and more importantly, my grandfather would simply not have been witness to these events. My grandfather wouldn't have been allowed anywhere near a delivery room in those days. Fathers-to-be were allowed in labour rooms from the 1960s. But labour and delivery rooms weren't combined until the 1970s, which was some time after these events transpired. Nor, for that matter, were pregnancies, in those days, accompanied by an exhaustive schedule of pre-natal courses, programs and modules. This, then, is a case of imaginative reconstruction. The anachronism of my grandfather being somewhere he couldn't have been at that time thus stems from an imaginative reconstruction being projected on someone else: projected by my father onto his father. There is, however, another case of anachronism: far less familiar but far more significant. This is anachronism that results from imaginative projection onto oneself. This latter sort of anachronism holds a secret: the secret of what my father is.

now I have to do whatever it takes to look after my son! My father felt like someone had given him a strange puppy, a puppy that would never grow up, and to whose needs he would spend the remainder of his days ministering. Give him time. He is new at this.

There are words that insist that I am real – insist they are more than merely words. There are words that insist I was born of a real mother and a real father, born in some actual place at some actual time. But they would be just words, and one can never know, just by looking at them, that they are anything more than words. But there are also words that, instead, tell of a thought that sometimes whispers to me in the quiet hours. The whispers tell me that I was born not of a mother's womb but of something else entirely. I was born of what a mythical someone said to a non-existent someone else in a time that never was.

In *The Birth of Tragedy*, the book that destroyed his name and later remade it for generations then unborn, Nietzsche tells his version of the myth of Midas' capture of Silenus, the donkey-riding demi-man, tutor to Dionysus the god of wine.[10] Though perpetually drunk, Silenus still managed to evade the hapless Midas for many months. When finally captured, Silenus was asked a question: 'What is the best and most

---

10 *The Birth of Tragedy out of the Spirit of Music* was Nietzsche's first book, published in 1872. At the time, Nietzsche, twenty-seven, was the youngest ever chair of Classical Philology at the University of Basel. It was a strange book, neither really philology nor philosophy, and its reception was 'disappointing'. Deteriorating health saw him live much of the rest of his life as, essentially, a disabled mendicant, living off his meagre retirement stipend from Basel and the kindness of friends and admirers. He went completely mad in 1890, and died ten years later. As we say today in the profession: thank God for tenure.

desirable of all things?' His answer: 'For humans, the best for them is not to be born at all.'

If Silenus' answer to Midas was correct – that the best for which humans can hope is never to be born – then the reaction of my father was, perhaps, sagacious. Could this possibly be? The intimations of dislocation experienced by my father, his vague sense of horror: are these the recognition that a monstrous wrong has just occurred?

The reasons for being born, or not being born, usually focus on the parents. It seems my parents wanted a child. Or, at least, they had no decisive objection to letting a happy accident that would change their lives forever run its course. Other prospective parents might not be ready, or might feel that the time is 'not right', and will take various measures to avoid conception or, if that is too late, to prevent birth. These sorts of reasons are all parent-centred reasons: reasons that focus on the parents – on what they want and how they see their lives proceeding. Parent-centred reasons can be both positive and negative – both for and against conceiving the child.

There can, in principle, be broader reasons than this. Sometimes a parent-to-be might enjoy the messianic delusion that the future child will do great things for humanity, achieve, invent or discover something that will improve the lot of every single human being – world peace or a cure for cancer, and things like that. If they were true, rather than delusions, these would be humanity-centred reasons for having the child. Strangely, few parents-to-be find themselves in the grip of the inverse-messianic conviction that their child will do terrible things for humanity – be a serial killer, or invent and release a new deadly plague, or start a world war – although the odds on this are surely no worse than those on the more optimistic delusions. If these inverse-messianic intuitions were, in fact, true they would provide humanity-centred reasons against having the child.

There can be even broader reasons: environment-centred reasons. My parents were not alone in their procreative endeavours – theirs were merely the early cannon soundings of a vast population explosion. During the first fifty years of my life, the human population of this planet more than doubled – from just over three billion to more than seven billion. In the same time, the number of species of non-humans on the planet more than halved. Each new human life puts an additional burden on an already creaking planet and this, therefore, provides an environment-centred reason against having their son – evidently a reason of which my parents were unaware or by which they were unmoved.

There is another category of reason, seldom considered, and this reason is, in effect, the focus of Silenus' response to Midas. The category is of me-centred reasons: Myshkin-centred reasons, or child-centred reasons more generally. These are reasons based not on the benefits or deficits for parents, humanity or the environment, but on the benefits or deficits for the child who is yet to be born.

Suppose – contrary to fact, this is a thought experiment – that, before I was conceived, my parents took the time to investigate their genetic compatibility. The results, to be quite frank, were not good. Because of an unfortunate combination of genetic circumstances, any child they had would, with a high degree of probability, suffer from an extraordinarily rare medical condition. As a result, he or she would be born into unbearable suffering – intense pain that would never abate, that could not be mitigated by narcotics or other medical interventions, and would continue right up to the end of his or her, thankfully short, life. My parents were largely reasonable people and would have accepted that, in these circumstances, it would be unconscionable to proceed with conception. I'm talking about conception, not birth. Some people think – I have absolutely no evidence that would number my parents among them – that once a child is conceived, matters should be allowed to take their natural course even though his or her future prospects are grim. Perhaps it is 'all part of God's plan', they might say, which raises a broad swathe of issues that I do not want to address (such as, for example, why God would employ a plan based on the suffering of an innocent child, and so on – Dostoyevsky is very good on that, by the way[11]). To point out that the current question – the question raised by Silenus – lies outside this swathe, let me be clear that I am talking about conception and not birth. If my parents had known with certainty, or even a high degree of probability, that the child they were planning to conceive would be born into unrelenting suffering, then they would not, I am confident, have proceeded with the conception. In this, they would have been swayed by a child-centred reason: a reason based on the interests of the child, specifically the interest the child has in not suffering.

In these imagined circumstances the child has not yet been conceived. So the suffering that would have swayed my parents is hardly actual suffering. But nor is it, really, future suffering: for if my parents did not proceed with conception, there would never be a future child who suffered. It is not

---

11 He is indeed. See, in particular, *The Brothers Karamazov.* Suppose, Ivan asks Alyosha, you could create a perfect world, but only by torturing to death 'one tiny creature'. If suffering is all part God's plan, then His plan, Ivan concludes, 'is not worth the tears of one tortured child'.

future suffering as such, but future suffering that might be. In other words, it is potential suffering. If we agree with my parents that it would have been unconscionable to conceive a child in these circumstances – those of unbearable and unrelieved suffering – then, it seems, we are committed to this principle: that the merely potential suffering of a child counts as a reason against conceiving it. Potential suffering is a relevant factor that we have to take into account when we decide whether or not to produce or permit another life. Potential suffering is, in other words, a child-centred reason against creating a child.

Some adopt an attitude of wilful naivety in the face of the possible: it's too abstract, hypothetical, even fanciful – let us deal only in concrete facts. This is a feigned stupidity, worthy only of the politician: we deal in the possible all the time. A woman goes into a doctor's office, and says, 'I want to get pregnant.' It sounds like the beginning of a questionable joke, but it's actually the beginning of a philosopher's thought experiment – and there is often a difference between the two.[12]

The doctor tells the woman to take folic acid supplements, to ensure the child is not born with spina bifida. Although she has the supplements sitting in her house, the woman decides she can't be bothered to take them, and nine months later her baby is indeed born with spina bifida. I think most would conclude that the woman has done something seriously wrong. All she had to do was take some pills. As the result of her failure, harm was done to the developing foetus,

12 The thought experiment was invented by Derek Parfit (although my father's example has some unimportant differences of detail), and can be found in his hugely influential book *Reasons and Persons* (Oxford University Press, 1984).

22

and this harm seriously detracts from the quality of life of the eventual person. Her child can, if he or she lives long enough, later legitimately complain: 'Look what you have done to me! How could you have been so thoughtless?'

Consider, now, a variation on this scenario. As before, the woman tells the doctor that she wants to get pregnant. This time the doctor tells her that she is exhibiting traces of a virus that can produce severe physical abnormalities in babies if it occurs during pregnancy. The doctor strongly advises her to wait three months, by which time the virus will have cleared her system and she can then safely conceive. The woman, however, declines to wait, and her baby is, sadly, born with abnormalities that significantly diminish its quality of life.

I think most would agree that the woman has, in this second scenario, also done something very wrong. All she had to do was wait three months and the baby she would have had would, in all likelihood, have been born healthy and happy and with far better prospects for future well-being. However, curiously, the child born to her cannot legitimately make the same sort of complaint as the baby born with spina bifida. The mother has an available reply. 'If I had waited three months, then a different egg would have been fertilized. And so the resulting baby would not have been you. The only way you could have existed would be if I had conceived at the time I did. The only way you could have existed would have been in your present form.'

The mother is, of course, correct. Different egg necessarily yields different person.[13] The asymmetry between the two cases is a result of the fact that in the first case harm is being

13 This is known as the principle of the *necessity of origin*. Virtually no one doubts it.

done to an already existing individual. This individual is not yet a person but a foetus. Nevertheless, it does exist and will develop into a person. There is a continuous track through space and time carved out by one and the same object: an object that is initially a foetus and later a person. When the woman neglects to take the folic acid supplements, harm is done to this already existing thing.

In the second scenario, there is no already existing thing. When the doctor advises her to abstain from conceiving for three months, he is protecting not any actual being but a possible being. Therefore, if you agree that the woman did something wrong in failing to delay her pregnancy, you are also committed to this claim: possible people count morally. When trying to work out what is the right thing to do in a given situation, you have to take into account not just actual people but also possible ones.

It seems, then, that the possible are in the moral club. They count, morally speaking. We have to take into account the impact of our actions on them too. From here, things quickly become very strange. Like all parents, mine really had no idea of what the future had in store for their yet to be conceived child. Not unreasonably, then, the only attitude they could really adopt was que sera, sera. Of course, it is overwhelmingly likely there will be a certain amount of suffering in my life. And we have already seen that this as yet potential suffering counts as a reason against my conception. But, they might have thought, unless I am monumentally unfortunate, or they turn out to be monumentally bad parents, surely my suffering will be outweighed by my happiness? Can't potential happiness be a reason in favour of conception, a reason that can outweigh the anti-conception bias of potential suffering?

Silenus

I don't know if my parents would have been realistic in making this assumption – had they made it. It is, I think, an open question whether the happiness in a person's life will outweigh the suffering. Maybe it's not even that. On their list of things to read, I would not expect to find any mention of the German idealists. But if they had read Schopenhauer they might well have come to a different conclusion. Schopenhauer argued that suffering would necessarily outweigh happiness in all lives. His arguments were, actually, quite good ones. But Schopenhauer's issue is not mine. In time, we will find out the relative measures of happiness and suffering in my life. But, at the moment, I am talking about what happens before this life begins. The suggestion is that my potential happiness – the potential happiness of one who is not yet a glint in his father's eye – provides a reason in favour of my conception. More than that, the suggestion is that it provides a reason substantial enough to outweigh the negative reason provided by my potential suffering. But here is the problem: the idea that potential happiness can provide any sort of reason in favour of conception is difficult to defend.

Suppose you discover (it doesn't matter how: God, time travel, take your pick) that the fertilized ovum you and your partner can, with a little bit of largely agreeable industry, easily produce this month – from a particular sperm and a particular egg whose constitutions are of unprecedented and never to be repeated quality – will develop into a child who will lead a life of unbounded happiness. Blessed with intelligence, athleticism, stunning beauty, emotional stability and extraordinary good luck, he or she would be a veritable golden child, beloved of the gods – if there were any. The only problem is that you have no plans to have children. You are not ready. The time is 'not right'. Perhaps it never will be 'right'. The extraordinary happiness of the extraordinary child is, at this point, only potential happiness. Are you committed to having the child so that this potential happiness can be actualized, even though you have no wish to do so? Common sense certainly says no. Opinions differ about whether, having conceived a child, you are morally obliged to continue with the pregnancy, and about the conditions under which a termination might be justified. But, as I mentioned, I am talking about conception, not birth. And the common-sense view is that you are never obliged to conceive a child if you don't want to – no matter how fantastic you suspect his or her life is going to be. If common sense can be trusted on this matter, it seems it commits us to another claim: merely potential happiness does not count in the way that merely potential suffering does. Once it reaches a certain level of intensity and probability, the potential suffering of the child is a decisive reason against conception. But the potential happiness of the child – no matter how great – is not a decisive reason for conception. Indeed, it is hardly a reason at all.[14]

Therefore, there seems to be a curious and, when you think about it, deeply disturbing asymmetry between potential suffering and potential happiness. The potential suffering of the future me is something that my parents should have taken

14 You have to suspect that this appeal to common sense is questionable, given the claim that possible people count. If you accept that possible people count morally as well as actual people then it may be that you are, in fact, obligated to conceive the golden child – and common sense be damned. Common sense, I suspect, was left in the dust, several pages back, as soon as we bought Parfit's argument about the pregnant woman. I buy the argument, actually. A utilitarian thinks that you are obligated to increase the overall amount of happiness in the world. If conceiving the golden child does that, then you are obligated to conceive. The appeal to common sense is, accordingly, unconvincing.

into account when they were deciding whether or not to conceive me. But the potential happiness of a future me – that is of no relevance at all. But, like all parents, the position in which they would have found themselves, when I was a mere possibility to be considered and nothing more, is one where they must compare potential suffering and potential happiness. How could it be otherwise? I am a mere *possibilium*. My potential suffering says they should not conceive me. My potential happiness says nothing at all. My potential suffering counts against conceiving me. But my potential happiness counts neither for nor against. So, there are always me-centred reasons against conceiving me, but never me-centred reasons in favour of conceiving me. So, it seems, I can only conclude I was a ghastly mistake. Not because I'm going to be a murderer, or start a world war – probably – but because there were good me-centred reasons for not having me, and no good me-centred reasons for having me. When they conceived me – my estimates place the deed sometime around the winter solstice of 1971 – my parents, it seems, simultaneously wronged me.[15]

This isn't an argument for suicide. As I remember it, Silenus might also have mentioned to Midas that the next-best thing after never being born is to die soon. But the argument I have just rehearsed doesn't support that claim. The argument turns

15 My father seems to be relying heavily on a version of an argument developed by David Benatar in his book *Better Never to Have Been: The Harm of Coming into Existence* (Oxford University Press, 2011). I suppose it is something of a relief that most people didn't buy Benatar's argument – even if they couldn't pinpoint exactly where it went wrong. On the other hand, if he had managed to convince a couple of billion baby-makers to give it a miss for a generation or two then the world might be in a rather better condition. Perhaps I wouldn't have to wade along Caroline Street to reach the house where my father once lived.

on the peculiar asymmetry between potential suffering and potential happiness. Once I am born, my suffering and/or happiness are no longer merely potential: they are now actual suffering and actual happiness. And so the argument no longer applies. The argument is not even necessarily an argument for abortion. It could be argued that once the relevant egg is fertilized, a new individual comes into existence – an individual that will one day be named 'Myshkin' – and the good or bad things that befall this individual are now actual good and bad things and not merely potential. So, the argument doesn't apply as cleanly or obviously to abortion. What it is, however, is an argument against conception. And, let's face it, if the argument is sound – and if you really believe it – the issues of abortion and suicide take care of themselves.

I am in good company. The argument applies not just to me but also to any possible child. Its potential suffering counts against conception. Its potential happiness counts for nothing at all. There are never child-centred reasons for conceiving a child, any child, and there are always child-centred reasons against. If this is right, it seems the ideal human population on planet earth would be zero. Even worse, the asymmetry between potential happiness and potential suffering would seem to be applicable to other creatures also. That is, you could run a parallel argument to show that, for example, any given animal – if sentient – should not be conceived. It would seem that the ideal population of sentient creatures on this planet (or, for that matter, any planet) is zero. After the better part of 14 billion years never venturing beyond the darkness of the unconscious, the universe, through blind processes of random mutation and natural selection, produced consciousness. This was a monumental point in the development of the universe. Now one little piece of the universe – a conscious creature of some sort – could become aware of other little pieces of the universe. In this sense, the universe, slowly but perhaps surely, started to become aware of itself. This is how some forms of Hinduism think of God. The universe is born when God shatters himself into an uncountable number of pieces, and then slowly reassembles. From the numberless voices of the Tower of Babel, consciousness slowly learns to speak in one voice, to read from one verse. Consciousness is God putting Himself back together again. And, as it turns out, He shouldn't have bothered.

This is not just Silenus: we've left him in the dust miles back. This is Silenus on steroids.[16]

16 Okay, but shouldn't the stunning implausibility of this conclusion – all sentient life is a mistake – give my father pause? It's all very well running with thoughts, but sooner or later it's going to be time for a reality check (and this coming from a philosopher!). So, I suspect he has gone wrong somewhere. Of course, deciding that an argument is fallacious is one thing. Working out exactly where the wrong turn is made is quite another. Here is where I think it happened. The idea that possible people count invites confusion. Let's accept that possible people count. Now, there is a clear temptation to infer another claim: potential suffering is bad. This does not follow, however. Potential suffering is not bad: it is only potentially bad. Suppose I am considering having a kid. I should take into consideration the potential suffering of my yet to be conceived child. Why? Because I have also been convinced by Parfit that possible people count. However, it does not follow that the potential suffering of this yet to be conceived child is a bad thing. How could it be? It is only potential suffering. We should take possible people into account, but it is still true that their suffering becomes a bad thing only when it becomes actual suffering. Similarly, the potential happiness of a yet to be conceived child becomes a good thing only when it becomes actual happiness. In other words, the inference from 'Possible people count' to 'Potential suffering is bad' is a non sequitur. Now, perhaps a solution begins to suggest itself. If a child is not conceived, its potential suffering never becomes actual and so never becomes a bad thing. So, its potential suffering is not, in fact, a reason against bringing a child into the world. Its actual suffering would be a reason against having brought it into the world, once you had actually done it. But the child's potential suffering is not a reason against doing so. Maybe that's it. I'm not sure. Maybe it doesn't help at all.

3

Animal

The fully enlightened earth radiates disaster triumphant.

Theodor Adorno and Max Horkheimer,
Dialectic of Enlightenment

My mother entered the room clad in the armour of her inability to understand exactly what was about to happen. I was her first child, and apparently unwilling to vacate my accommodations of the preceding forty-one weeks. My worldly introduction was, therefore, via induction – apparently a painful affair (for her, that is – I don't remember much). But she wasn't going to think about that. Get in – get the Funny Gas as soon as she could prise it from the grasping and unsympathetic hands of the NHS – and get home. Nitrous oxide: she might as well have been asking for the Hope Diamond. She was spared nothing. Nothing. Pain beyond description, pain that turned the body and mind inside out: strange warpings of the laws of experiential possibility. And the huge-headed misbegotten idiot who had done all this to her just stood there, useless, holding on to a leg more to steady himself than anything else. He actually had the temerity to look shaken. His eyes even went wide with fear at one point towards the end.

I think most people would conclude, correctly, that my father had received by far the better end of the deal. The divergence in their subsequent emotions is, therefore, interesting. To be sure, there were some choice moments immediately following the birth that they were able to share. The moments before my first roar were, of course, chillingly elongated. Then: further anxious seconds while my fingers and toes were counted and found to add up to the desired number. There followed an eternity of escalating terror while the rather bungling midwife shared her ruminations on the possibility of oxygen deprivation and brain damage. 'He doesn't look like a normal baby' – words every new parent is just longing to hear. The brain damage issue was eventually put to rest when the doctor – hastily summoned but whose arrival was indolent at best – pointed out that while my face was, indeed, a little bluish, the rest of me was decidedly pink. You see, I was inconsiderate enough to emerge OP – *occiput posterior* – facing up at the sky instead of down to the earth. My face, as a result, bore the brunt of the contractions. Battered and bruised – I came into this world looking as if I'd just gone twelve rounds with Manny Pacquiao.

It was at roughly this point that the emotional reactions of my parents began to diverge. My mother was still in what, up until about twelve or so hours ago, she would have described as intolerable pain. She was far beyond the point of anything she formerly knew as weariness. But when they placed me in her arms, and I, with gusto, began my first open-air meal, she was suffused with a sense of the rightness and reality of it all. Whatever else happens in life, she thought, whatever the future holds, this is the way it should be.

*

The first birth: that is when we see it. Subsequent ones are not so revealing. You're ready for it by then, your emotional response gently tutored by familiarity. The diverging reactions of two parents upon the birth of their first child are a symptom of duality that lies at the heart of the human being, a schism that lies coiled in the human soul like a worm at the core of an apple.

Aristotle, it is widely believed, defined human beings as rational animals. He didn't explicitly say this. What he actually said was that one element of the human soul has a 'rational principle', one that is often resisted by a competing irrational element. This irrational element of the soul derives from our desirous, appetitive animal nature.[17] For Aristotle, our rationality is what makes us unique: only humans have rational souls. He didn't mean by 'soul' what we have come to mean by it – an ethereal ghost in a machine. That was a later, Christian, conceit. When Aristotle talked of the soul, he had in mind what we might call a *nature*. Humans have a rational nature. This differentiates them from all other animals.

Nevertheless, humans remain animals. Our rational nature is coupled with its animal counterpart. Animals have 'locomotive souls'. By this, Aristotle meant that animals move, and not in the way that a plant moves, swaying in the breeze. The animal moves itself: it is self-moving. This locomotive nature is the essence of animals, and distinguishes them from plants, whose nature is merely 'nutritive'. However, in many animals, this locomotive nature brings other things too. Most importantly, it comes with an ability to feel. There is a close connection between movement and sentience. There is little

17 *Nicomachean Ethics*, Chapter I, 13.

reason for a plant to become sentient.[18] Being unable to move, it can do nothing to flee the sources of its discomfort. A conscious tree that could feel the woodman's axe would be a monstrously unfortunate creature. With movement, however, comes a rationale for feeling. And with feeling come other things: desires, appetites and something that Aristotle called 'passions', but which we now know as 'emotions'.[19] We are rational, but we are also animals, and so our nature involves both reason and emotion.

So much that has proved decisive in the history of human thought can be born of subtle nuances, barely discernible decisions of emphasis. The decisive movement in the conjuring trick, as Wittgenstein once put it, is the very one that we thought least worthy of notice.[20] Aristotle was, above all other things, a subtle thinker. For him, reason and emotion may be distinguishable, but in a healthy, well-functioning person – a virtuous person, as Aristotle put it – they are not separable. Your reason might allow us to recognize a case of injustice, for example, whether this injustice is directed

---

18 Any evolutionary development involves investment of resources: genetic resources to develop the relevant structure and energy resources to maintain it. Developing and maintaining whatever brain structures are responsible for consciousness – although we are still not sure what they are – would be a costly endeavour. Therefore, in the absence of any pay-off – for example, if the creature were unable to escape the source of its pain – this development would be evolutionarily inefficient, and there would be strong selection pressures against it. See Richard Dawkins, *The Extended Phenotype* (Oxford University Press, 1982) and Mark Rowlands, *The Body in Mind: Understanding Cognitive Processes* (Cambridge University Press, 1999), Chapter 4, for statements of this idea.

19 See, for example, Maxine Sheets-Johnstone's study of the relation between consciousness, cognition and movement in *The Primacy of Movement* (John Benjamins, 2011).

20 Ludwig Wittgenstein, *Philosophical Investigations* (Blackwell, 1953), trans. E. Anscombe, paragraph 308.

towards yourself or another. But part of what is involved in recognizing injustice is having an appropriately negative emotional response. A virtuous person will deplore injustice when she sees it, and so will feel an appropriate amount of anger or indignation. The details are not important. The vision is. In the virtuous person, reason and emotion are inextricably intertwined. Our rational nature and our animal nature complement rather than contradict each other.

Unfortunately, a brief perusal of the history of thought is enough to show that the subtlety of Aristotle is somewhat idiosyncratic. Aristotle's vision of reason and the emotions as woven together in the virtuous person had to contend with what proved to be a fundamental rule of human thought, in effect its First Commandment: where there is a distinction, thou shalt elevate it into a dichotomy. In fact, this dichotomizing tendency preceded Aristotle. His teacher, Plato, had already compared the emotions to an unruly steed, powerful, stubborn and licentious. Reason was the horse's rider, who must take a firm guiding hand. You would expect this sort of imagery from Plato, but not from Aristotle, a keen biologist who never lost sight of the fact that humans were also animals. Whatever Aristotle's intentions were, Plato's dichotomizing tendencies won.[21]

The following centuries saw an increasing divorce of reason and emotion, even during the medieval period – which was, without too much exaggeration, merely a series of footnotes to

---

21 This is actually rather unfair to Plato. There is no 'rider'. He used the analogy of a chariot. Reason was the charioteer, but there were two horses, one noble the other not. The noble horse corresponds to the rational emotions. Plato accepted that emotions could be rational – he merely claimed, plausibly, that not all of them were. On this matter, Plato was much closer to Aristotle than my father realizes. The dichotomization of reason and emotion came later.

Aristotle.[22] The divorce was finalized in the work of René – 'father of modern philosophy' – Descartes. Like Aristotle, he thought rationality was the defining feature of human beings. He also accepted that human beings were composite creatures. But he took a dim view of the non-rational part of us. Animals are essentially mechanical entities. The same is true of the animal part of us – our bodies. But the rational part of us, Descartes argued, can never be mechanized. No physical mechanisms could ever be rational. Rational transitions of thought – processes of reasoning, rational inference and deduction – could never be instantiated in a physical mechanism: neither the brain nor anything else. Therefore, Descartes concluded, there is a part of us that, being rational, will forever be non-physical.[23] In contrast with Aristotle's relaxed, non-committal use of the term, now we are dealing with a soul, of an uncompromising ghost-in-a-machine variety. Each one of us has an essence that is rational and, therefore, non-physical. The rest of us – our non-rational corporeal component – is unimportant. By the time I lie in my mother's arms, the divorce from our animal nature will be complete. Indeed, it will have been complete for more than three hundred years.

From the privileged perspective of the present, Descartes's claims turned out to be laughably off target. Not only have we been able to embody rational inferences in machines, these turned out to be the easiest sorts of mental process to mechanize, and machines turned out to be very good at them.

---

22 Compare Alfred North Whitehead: 'The safest general characterization of the European philosophical tradition is that it consists in a series of footnotes to Plato.'

23 Descartes, *Meditations on First Philosophy* (1641), particularly the second and sixth meditations.

Building a machine that can defeat the greatest chess grand-master: we've been there and done that. Building a machine that can perform mathematical calculations of a speed and enormity that eclipse human capacities: that's simply another day at the office. But building a machine that can feel, that can have emotions, has proved much harder. It may or may not be an intractable task, but at the moment we're not even close. And yet we persist with the fantastic conceit that it is our reason that elevates us above everything else.

There are two different ways of thinking about morality that follow closely the contours of the division between reason and emotion. Broadly speaking, one can think of morality as, fundamentally, a matter of calculation. Or, one can think of it as a matter of compassion. As one might expect, given the victory of Descartes in the matter of our essential natures, the conception of morality as calculation has dominated. Very different moral theories – even ones traditionally regarded as implacably opposed – are united by their conception of morality as a matter of calculation.

Utilitarianism, perhaps the most influential moral theory ever invented, tells us that morality is a matter of maximizing utility. In working out what we should do, we must calculate which course of action would produce the greatest good for the greatest number of people.[24] The idea of the good has

24 The expression 'the greatest good for the greatest number' is associated with Jeremy Bentham, the father of modern utilitarianism. Versions of this idea can, however, be found in earlier thinkers, such as Leibniz and Francis Hutcheson. As a way of stating the basic idea of utilitarianism, it is inaccurate. The goal is to produce the greatest good, but whether this is for the greatest number is not directly relevant to the utilitarian. Indeed, how to ensure a just distribution of the good is a problem for utilitarianism.

been understood in different ways by different versions of utilitarianism, but two conceptions are particularly prominent. Hedonistic utilitarianism claims that the good is happiness: we should always attempt to increase the overall amount of happiness in the world. Preference utilitarianism claims that the good is satisfied preferences, and so our aim should be to increase the overall number of satisfied preferences in the world. You might think: what's the difference between happiness and satisfied preferences? Not much, really. There are some subtle differences that show themselves in some contexts but not others. Sometimes a satisfied preference will not yield happiness – I might, for example, prefer that you die rather than I die but nevertheless cannot regard either prospect with any relish. Conversely, I may not be made specifically unhappy by my unforeseen painless demise that occurred during my sleep, but this nevertheless is incompatible with my preferences.

There is a feeling that often assails me in my encounters with utilitarian writers – one that I can never quite assuage. This feeling is that the person I am reading has – in a way that is difficult to pin down with any precision, but is nevertheless vaguely terrifying – slowly but decisively lost the plot. Consider Peter Singer, probably the most influential contemporary utilitarian.[25] A more than decent man, there is no doubt, someone who has done a lot of good in his life, but nevertheless, his appearance in my neonatal ward would, let us say, not exactly be reassuring. Singer advocates preference utilitarianism for those who have the relevant preferences, and hedonistic utilitarianism for those who do not. This puts

25 See, for example, his *Practical Ethics* (Cambridge University Press, 1980).

me, the neo-nascent me who lies feeding in my mother's arms, in a predicament. I have some preferences, of course. Enjoying my first extra-uterine meal, I would prefer if it were to continue, at least for the time being. As yet, however, I have no concept of death. As a result, Singer would infer – I think questionably – I can have no preference to go on living. If I do not understand that I might not live – and I cannot understand this without a concept of death – I can have no preference for the alternative. Therefore, Singer concludes, killing me – especially if this were done painlessly and before I had time to suspect that something injurious was afoot – would violate none of my preferences. Therefore, according to preference utilitarianism, there is nothing directly wrong with killing me.

I say 'directly' wrong. I would hope my parents have preferences for my continued survival. If so, killing me would violate their preferences, and so could be condemned on preference-utilitarian grounds. This, in the morality industry, is what is known as a side effect. But the appeal to side effects seems to miss the point. Is it really true that if I were killed, the only harm done would be to my parents and not to me? That does seem strange. What if, for example, my parents had no objection to my death? Perhaps they decided, all things considered, that it might be a good idea to play it safe. All this blueness – the doctor says it's just bruising, but can he really be sure? Perhaps it is oxygen deprivation after all? To be safe rather than sorry, let's get rid of this one and try again. In such circumstances, the preference utilitarian will have a tricky time scrambling around trying to find some reason why I should not be killed. Perhaps the doctor or nurses would object? But what if they side with my parents? That is the problem with appealing to side effects: you can always imagine situations in which they don't apply. And this reveals what would be for the neo-nascent me, if I were capable of understanding it, a hard truth: if preference utilitarianism is true, there is nothing directly wrong with killing me. If any harm is done by my death, that harm is done to someone else.

Perhaps I might find succour in the hedonistic form of utilitarianism? Unfortunately, this seems unlikely. Hedonistic utilitarianism has trouble accommodating death at the best of times, and the death of neonates lies far beyond its area of competence. If hedonistic utilitarianism is right, someone's death counts as a bad thing only if it decreases the overall amount of happiness in the world. But the person who dies is gone – they are neither happy nor unhappy. So, there are only two ways in which my death might be thought of as a bad thing. The first is, if it makes other people unhappy, my parents, grandparents and perhaps the general population would be made unhappy by the discovery that babies were routinely dying in their hospitals. But no matter how sophisticated we become, no matter how ingenious our conceptual manoeuvrings, this cannot alter the fact that we are still appealing to side effects. If we are hedonistic utilitarians, we have to conclude that there is nothing directly wrong with my death – indeed, nothing directly wrong with the death of anyone. This seems, to anyone not already in the grip of a hedonistic utilitarian outlook, far-fetched.

There is another way in which my untimely demise might detract from the overall amount of happiness in the world. For the utilitarian, it doesn't matter when someone is made happy, just as long as the overall amount of happiness increases: happiness over time is just as important as the happiness that exists now. My death would eliminate all my future happiness. It would eliminate all my future misery too. But if we assume – let's be subjunctive optimists – that in the life I would have lived there would have been a net surplus of happiness over misery, then we could argue that killing me is wrong because it decreases the overall amount of happiness over time.

Unfortunately, my possible happy future isn't going to save me. While the hedonistic utilitarian does not care when someone is made happy, neither does he or she care *who* is made happy. Consistent with hedonistic utilitarianism, my parents could decide to play it safe, have me killed quickly and painlessly – as long as they later have another baby who lives a life that is just as happy as the one I would have lived. If these conditions are met, then, as far as hedonistic utilitarianism is concerned, there is nothing wrong with killing me. I must hope that hedonistic utilitarianism is not true, because, if it is, I am utterly and entirely replaceable.

There it is. There we have it. This is where calculation leads us. It is as if we are watching a slow-motion philosophical train wreck. One moment, you are holding a newly born child in your arms, listening to its cries, its slurps, its gurgles and its giggles. In the very next moment, you are thinking: 'Oh yes, I could kill this one, as long as I replace it with another that will be just as happy.' Reason unrestrained by emotion, calculation untrammelled by compassion, breeds only monsters.

Compassion is as much a part of our natural history as are our bodies. Nevertheless, it has, historically, occupied a relatively marginal role in thinking about morality. Occupying these margins was the seventeenth-century Scottish philosopher David Hume, who argued that having emotional responses of an appropriate sort in appropriate circumstances is part of our natural history.[26] Imagine you encounter a baby – the neo-nascent me, for example – abandoned by his parents, exposed, *à la grecque*, to the elements and soon to die. It would be natural, biologically natural, to feel distress at my predicament and try to help me. This distress you feel is the form your compassion takes. The failure to feel this would be a sign that something has gone very wrong on a basic biological level. Those whose emotional response is aberrant – who don't feel emotion when they are supposed to – we now label psychopaths.

Compassion is part of what we are, a consequence of the processes that have brought us into existence. Hume's idea that morality has an emotional, rather than calculative, foundation is a theme later taken up by Darwin.[27] The 'social sentiments' as Darwin called them – roughly, feelings of concern for members of one's group – have a straightforward evolutionary explanation. These sentiments are the glue that holds mammalian social groups together. As such, these sentiments are truly animal.

However, to say that a feature is natural – a part of our biological inheritance – does not mean that it is immune to influence or distortion by cultural factors. Compassion may be in our genes, but the way our genes are expressed can be crucially dependent on cultural circumstance. Compassion – what we are compassionate about and the extent to which we are compassionate about it – varies dramatically from one historical father, attending the birth of his child, to another.

26 See Hume, *A Treatise of Human Nature*, Books 2 and 3 in particular.
27 Darwin defends this view in both *The Descent of Man, and Selection in Relation to Sex* (1871) and *The Expression of the Emotions in Man and Animals* (1872).

A Good Life

The ancient Greeks – practitioners of infanticide – would have had little compassion for the neo-nascent me – not enough to make a difference to my fate. More than that, even within a culture, the emotions we feel can be dramatically distorted by specifics of conditioning and reinforcement.[28] Compassion is easily warped, crucially shaped and driven by factors that often work in a subterranean fashion, beneath the level of our conscious scrutiny. When this happens, one of the only protections we have is our reason.

Reason is not enough: before you know it you'll be killing and replacing babies. Emotion is not enough: it is far too erratic and easily led. Therefore, some say, finding a balance

---

28 I don't think anyone seriously doubts this any more. The only question is the extent of the distortion. In the one corner, there are those who cling to the traditional idea of character – an idea that runs all the way back to ancient Greece. In the other, there is *situationism*: the view that one's moral sentiments are extremely sensitive to distortion by environmental factors. Indeed, to speak of distortion is not strictly accurate, for it presupposes that there is a human nature to be distorted. Situationism, at least in its stronger forms, denies there is such a thing. Situationism was born with the famous Stanford Prison Experiments, conducted by Philip Zimbardo and colleagues in the early 1970s. A group of student volunteers was divided randomly into 'prisoners' and 'guards', and assigned a number of conventional roles based on the category they were assigned to. In surprisingly little time, the 'guards' started behaving in unexpectedly brutal ways. The same phenomenon, Zimbardo argued, was responsible for more recent behaviour by real guards in the Abu Ghraib prison camp. Zimbardo's book *The Lucifer Effect* (Random House, 2008) provides a good general introduction. Nothing in the debate between situationists and traditionalists is uncontroversial. But without becoming embroiled in this, there is a more familiar point. Even when it is not warped in the relatively dramatic ways envisaged by the situationist, compassion is variable, partial and often chauvinistic. As Stalin put it: 'The death of one is a tragedy. The death of a million is a statistic.' If we base all on compassion, then there is a clear danger: we will focus on the one, on the tragic, at the expense of the faceless many.

between reason and emotion is the key. Brilliant – except this, of course, is not an answer but a problem.

It would be premature, on this day of my birth, to speculate about the relative measures of good and evil – of happiness and suffering – I shall occasion: the ratio with which these qualities will cluster around the little pathway I cut through space and time. But one thing seems absolutely certain: I am going to do some damage. Someone, at some time, is going to suffer because of me. And it may be that most of the damage I do will occur when reason and emotion are working together.

When reason and emotion coalesce in a human life, that is when the real fireworks start. When we think of human evil, we tend to think of spectacular atrocities embodied in wars, genocides, ethnic and religious cleansings. And we also tend to suppose that this evil comes from our animal natures: primitive hatreds disgorged from an animal soul that we should and would excise if only we could. This is naive. Reason, as Horkheimer and Adorno have argued, also has its dark side.[29] The mechanized killing fields of modern war are devised by human reason. Reason designed the gas chambers. More subtly, we always like, if at all possible, to rationalize our hatreds – for then we feel they can legitimately be given licence – and one should never underestimate the ingenuity of reason in providing justifications for our hatreds. Tribes, religions and political doctrines: all, to a greater or lesser degree, ex post facto reasons to hate. Hatred may be part of our animal nature, but justifications and exculpations for this hatred are the province of reason. Reason provides our hatreds with focus and direction. Reason makes our hatreds

---

29 Max Horkheimer and Theodor Adorno, *Dialectic of Enlightenment* (1944).

effective. The union of reason and emotion will manifest itself as ugly scars and defacements in the lives of each of us.

This problem we might think of as a fixed point in my moral space: a place to which I shall return over and over again during the course of my life, and by varying routes – some straight, others circuitous, some familiar, others unlikely. The problem is not just to be rational, and not just to feel emotion. It is not even to be rational and feel emotion together. The problem is to feel emotion rationally: to rationally emote. Aristotle understood the centrality of this to a moral life: 'So also getting angry ... is easy and everyone can do it; but doing it to the right person, in the right amount, at the right time, for the right end, and in the right way is no longer easy, nor can everyone do it. Hence, doing these things well is rare, praiseworthy, and fine.'[30] What Aristotle says about anger is also true of compassion and the emotions more generally. It is crucial to feel them towards the right person, in the right way, at the right time, in the right amount and for the right end. But just how does one learn to do that? On this matter, Aristotle – like the truly great philosopher he is – gives us no advice whatsoever. Or, more accurately, his advice is the sort given to someone who, in an old joke, asks, 'How do I get to Carnegie Hall?' Practice. Practice. Practice. The ability can only be acquired through habit. And habit requires a life, and perhaps a lifetime.

30 Aristotle, *Nicomachean Ethics*, 1109a27–30.

4

Lies

Le coeur a ses raisons que la raison ne connaît point.

Blaise Pascal, *Pensées*

'Shut up, Four Eyes!'

Troy is a game that relies crucially on the virtue of honesty. Swordplay, for a six-year-old in a largely stickless schoolyard, amounts to waving one's arm around in front of an opponent, who is reciprocating in kind, both of you making tcchh-tcchh-tcchh sounds to simulate, in your fledgling minds, the clash of steel on steel. At some point, you lunge forward and try to tag the opponent in the midriff with your knuckles, metacarpals or phalangeal knuckle (that extra centimetre or two can be crucial) without being similarly tagged yourself. If you are successful, the opponent is thereby rendered 'dead', and must sit out the rest of the game, which ends when the members of only one side are left 'alive'. There are multifarious opportunities for dissent. First, there is the rather thorny issue of who gets to be the cool characters: Achilles, Hector, Ajax, Odysseus or Diomedes – at a pinch, Paris, maybe. But no one wants to be sulky

Agamemnon, cuckolded Menelaus or the stinky guy
Philoctetes. Once the game begins, the odds are, of course,
unacceptably stacked in favour of boys with longer arms.
Boys with unassuming arms, such as myself, survive on
speed and the arts of manoeuvre and misdirection. The principal source of discord now revolves around the issue of
death and in what circumstances – precisely – one can legitimately claim that it has occurred. Direct strikes to the torso
are officially regarded as mortal, whereas strikes to the arm
can legitimately be regarded as merely maiming ('tis but a
scratch' – but one is, nevertheless, subsequently required to
hold one's arm in an awkward manner, as a badge of one's
mutilation). However, this is always a complex interpretative
transaction. Where the torso ends and the arms begin – the
penumbral, disputed region of the shoulder – is a continuing
source of friction. Worse, while direct blows to the torso are
officially regarded as fatal, glancing blows are not regarded as
such. Thus, one often sees the rather unseemly drama of one
boy shouting, 'You're dead!' while the other, clutching his
ribs, but still stabbing forward with his phalangeal knuckle,
responding, 'No, you just wounded me!' As you can imagine,
it isn't uncommon for our play fighting to escalate into real
fighting.

I assume it was some such interpretative disagreement
that was the cause of the numero-ocular slur in question.
The insulter was David B, and the insulted Andrew C, the
only boy in our class (girls didn't count) who possessed the
requisite number of eyes. I never liked David B. If there was
an interpretative disagreement going on, I was pretty sure
who was going to be on the wrong side of it. David B was a
liar and a cheat. He and I had come to blows over this on
more than one occasion. More than that, there was a

callousness, and a meanness of spirit, to him that I had begun to discern, even though I had, at that time, no clear idea of what these were. Still: Richard B laughed, Adrian W laughed, Mark M laughed, Vaughan T laughed. What could I do? Really? I could feel their eyes turning to me, on me. Are you with us? Or are you judging us? I didn't feel good about it. My mother had told me to be nice to people, and this seemed a long way from being nice to Andrew C. Anyone who could have seen into my heart would have known that my chuckle involved, at the very most, only half of this organ. But I chuckled. I did it.

And that is why, the following morning, I found myself a member of a line of boys standing in the office of the fearsome Mrs Beatrix Maywood: the headmistress of my primary school. First impressions can be deceiving. When I mentioned we were playing Troy, for example, perhaps this conjured in you an image of the little Myshkin and his fellows at Eton or Harrow, or some other Brideshead for six-year-olds, playfully dramatizing the fruits of our demanding classical curriculum. Not a bit of it. Fate had something else in store for me: Blaen-y-Cwrw primary school – or 'infant' school as they called them, bizarrely, back in those days. Blaen-y-Cwrw school, on Pond Road – that speaks volumes, doesn't it? In America, a mere suggestion of water is enough to get a road christened Lakeshore Drive, or something else suitably aspirational. Pond Road, that is as aspirational as it gets in Nant-y-Glo – 'The Brook of Coal' – clinging to the bleak, discoloured, forgotten end of the western valley in what was then Monmouthshire, and became Gwent. We weren't reading the *Iliad* at Blaen-y-Cwrw: *Troy* was on the telly the other night, mun.

Beatrix – Trixie to her friends – Maywood is another case in point. Her rather severe features, pinched and angular, and horn-rimmed spectacles strongly suggested – to continue with the classical theme – noxious harpy. That was, indeed, the consensus. But once she had been beautiful, educated and happy. Trixie lost her husband at a young age to TB. They had moved away together, but she quickly came to understand that her memories of her husband were so inextricably linked to the places they had lived, loved and laughed together when they were young that, from afar, she could no longer remember the man of her wedding day but only the walking corpse he would later become. She returned home to her memories, and took a teaching position in the local primary school. That was forty years ago. Two years from retirement now, alone and childless, she kept a bottle of sherry in her desk. She'd have a wee tipple when she arrived in the morning, and then just enough to keep her topped up through the day. The teachers knew, of course – her every breath was a confession.

'You know why you are here, I assume.'

'No, Mrs Maywood,' we intoned, largely in unison.

'The reason you are here is a letter I've received from Andrew C's mother. You were laughing at him because he wears glasses. Is this true? Tell me: what kind of vile creature would do that?'

She started to work the line. She glared at each of us in turn: her horn-rimmed stare alighted first on David B and worked its way, at roughly ten-second intervals, down the line. I stood at the end of the line, and as the suffocating pressure slowly built, crystallizing around me like a carapace, an idea started to form, a wonderful story that quickly pushed its way to my lips and out into the air that surrounded them.

Lies

'We weren't laughing at *him*, Mrs Maywood, we were laughing at a joke.'

'Really?' she intoned the word slowly, drawing it out. 'And what joke would that be?'

Yes, the acid test. A lie will always need another lie to give it sustenance. Lies must hang together in packs. Stand or fall together in packs. There followed perhaps the greatest cognitive achievement of my young life so far, an achievement delivered under the most hostile of circumstances. I felt my favourite joke elbowing its way up to my lips: 'There are two cows in a field and a bull. One of the cows says to the bull: "Don't charge me, don't charge me, I've only got 50p!"'

There: it was done. The lie had found itself a pack. A liar was born. And, you know what? It worked. I don't know why. I'd like to think Trixie Maywood recognized my lie to be a notable intellectual achievement for a six-year-old and wanted, at least unofficially, on the q.t. as it were, to acknowledge it. More likely, she simply saw an obvious lie and an even more obvious easy out – a way of not having to bother with the tawdry business any more. Whatever the reason, I learned a valuable lesson that day: lying works. It's not that difficult, and it really does work.

Lying, I suppose, is what our schoolyard games were all about. Some psychologists and anthropologists like to explain games, such as our game of Troy, as the way we learn hunting or fighting skills. I suspect this is because such psychologists are, without exception, adults, and have long forgotten just how good it feels to play, to pit your skill and cunning against an opponent and operate at the limits of your bodily abilities. I do not think we need to look outside the game to find its point or purpose. But if there were an external point, I suspect it would have much more to do with

49

social skills than hunting. These games are how we learn to lie. Not just to lie but, far more important, to lie well, to lie skilfully. We learn how to distinguish what we can get away with and what we cannot. You know you received a 'killing' blow. But no one else saw it, and you think you might be able to present it as less than mortal. Or, your opponent is weak, below you in the class pecking order, and you believe you can intimidate him into accepting the falsehood. The explicit lie, dreamed up in one's head, is always born from, and built upon, these games we play.

I felt good about the lie. If I denied it, I'd be lying. But I didn't feel good about Andrew C, and I made sure I was extra-nice to him for the next few days.

Lying is wrong. 'You should not lie' – says the Bible and my mother, among others – because lying is immoral and you should not be immoral. But what does 'should' mean here? Why should I not be immoral? After all, I have just demonstrated that being immoral can be very useful. Plato once recounted the mythical story of Gyges, a humble shepherd who stumbled upon a ring of invisibility secreted away inside a cave.[31] With the possibility of being caught – and the resulting sanction – being reduced to near zero, Gyges murdered and seduced his way to the top – the top, in this case, being the king of a long-forgotten country called Lydia. If you came into possession of the ring of Gyges, *would* you be moral? More pertinently: *should* you bother being moral?

The Abrahamic tradition, the religions of Abraham –

---

31 The story is found in Book 2 of the *Republic*. Plato didn't believe the mythology, of course. He was using this device as a way of making graphic this central question of morality: why be moral?

Christianity, Judaism and Islam – supplies one answer. Yes, you should, because God is watching: the ring of Gyges would not hide you from His eyes. This answer to why one should be moral explains the 'should' of morality in terms of the 'should' of prudence. One should be moral because it is prudent to be moral. If one is not, then God will undoubtedly smite one at some future, yet to be determined, point and/or send one to a less than desirable post-life neighbourhood. Was God watching me in Trixie Maywood's office that day? A considerable body of evidence suggests this is unlikely. But even if we completely ignore this and assume – as many do and many don't – that God exists, this does seem to be a flimsy reason for being moral. Most importantly, for those who believe in God, it doesn't seem to be a reason that would impress God very much at all.

Suppose you are a person with the darkest desires imaginable. Murder, torture, rape and other assorted brutalities: you name it – you want to do it. There is only one thing holding you back. You have a nagging suspicion, one that you can't quite shake – no matter how much you would like to – that there is a God who will send you to hell if you act on these desires. Eventually you arrive at the Pearly Gates, having led a life whose actions were as clean as your desires were dark. God awaits you and peruses your black heart. Is He going to conclude, 'Yes, you're exactly the sort we want in here'? I think we have to admit that this is rather unlikely.

The most obvious secular attempts to explain why one should be moral simply reiterate the main themes of the Abrahamic tradition. Morality reduces to prudence. So, you really would like to murder a few rivals – who doesn't feel like that from time to time? And while you're at it, why not steal their houses and possessions? The problem is that acting in this way is rather risky. If you do it to others, then you can be sure that there is a long list of assholes out there that will try to do it to you. Far more sensible – far more prudent – is to accept certain limitations on what you can do as long as other people accept the same limitations on what they can do. I'll scratch your back if you scratch mine. Or, at least, I'll refrain from sticking a knife in your back if you refrain from sticking one in mine.

This is the social-contract view of morality.[32] The social contract is a hypothetical agreement that restricts what each of us may, legitimately, do in the struggle for survival. It is not an actual agreement. It is not as if concrete historical people ever sat down together and thrashed out the terms of this contract. Imagine what a bloodbath that would be! Getting all these people together, none of whom had yet agreed on a contract concerning how they were to behave. You would, presumably, need a pre-contractual agreement to specify how everyone was to behave in the contractual situation. But how would you get that without sitting everybody down and ... then you would need a pre-pre-contractual agreement to specify how everyone was to behave in the pre-contractual situation. And so on and so forth – this is what philosophers call an infinite regress. The idea of the social contract as an actual, historical, agreement makes no sense. The agreement is merely hypothetical.

But how, one might wonder, can anyone be bound by a

32 Historically, social-contract models of morality are associated with the English political philosopher Thomas Hobbes (1588–1679), particularly in his book *Leviathan* (1651). The most influential modern defence of the social-contract model – very different in spirit and content from Hobbes's account – was developed by John Rawls in his *A Theory of Justice* (Belknap Press, 1971).

merely hypothetical contract? The answer is that we have all implicitly agreed to the contract. We have implicitly agreed to it because it is in our long-term rational self-interest to agree to it. By accepting the contract, we gain two things: protection from those who would hurt us, and aid from those who could help us. Life thereby becomes less risky, a significant step up from a state of nature 'red in tooth and claw', as Hobbes once put it.[33]

This social-contract answer, however, doesn't seem to avoid the problem of Gyges and his ring of invisibility. It is all very well to say that you'll refrain from sticking a knife in someone else's back, but if no one can see you do it, and if doing it would be very useful to you, then why not? This is a symptom of a more general problem. The authority of the contract is based on the possibility of being caught and punished if you breach its terms. The possibility of sanction is essential to the efficacy of the contract. As a consequence, suppose you can effectively dissemble: make others think you are obeying the terms of the contract while actually flouting them. If you could do this, you would garner all the benefits of the contract – mutual protection and mutual aid – while acquiring none of the costs. You wouldn't actually have to help anyone, and you wouldn't actually have to protect anyone – as long as you could make people think you were doing these things. The contract, in this way, rewards deception: it turns lying into a virtue. In the contract, image is everything. The contract does not actually answer the question of why I, Myshkin, should be moral. It answers only

33 Actually, my father is mistaken. It was Tennyson, not Hobbes. 'Who trusted God was love indeed/And love Creation's final law/Tho' nature, red in tooth and claw/With ravine, shriek'd against his creed.' (*In Memoriam*).

the question of why I should seem to be moral: why I should cultivate the skill of making people believe I am moral.

The Abrahamic and social-contract answers to the question of why you should be moral amount to this: someone is watching – whether God or society – and he, she or it will punish you if you are not moral. The 'should' of morality, therefore, reduces to the 'should' of prudence. One should be moral in the same sense, ultimately, that one should eat a diet low in saturated fats and triglycerides. There is, however, another sense of 'should', and Immanuel Kant – the eighteenth-century German philosopher – deployed this in developing his answer to why one should be moral.

If you believe that I told a lie to Trixie Maywood, you should – logically – believe that I told a lie to someone. It may not have occurred to you to formulate this rather uninteresting belief, but you can't very well deny it if someone were to say, for example, 'Oh, so Myshkin told a lie to someone.' If you have a belief, then you should, logically, believe whatever this belief entails. Kant argued that the 'should' of morality should be understood as this 'should' of logic. For example, consider what Kant would say of my performance in Trixie Maywood's office: 'What would happen if everyone did that?' In asking this question, Kant does not mean to draw attention to the baleful consequences of universal lying. That is the sort of thing a social-contract theorist would say. His point is subtler: not everyone *could* do that. Suppose everyone tried to adopt a policy of lying whenever it suited him or her. Soon, no statement could be trusted, and so no one would believe what anyone else said. But then the practice of stating things would become pointless – for the point of that practice is to instil belief in those who hear one's statements (or, at the very least, to get them to do things on the basis of their believing that what you say is true). But if making statements were a pointless activity, then people would stop doing it. Soon, no statements would be made. But if no statements were made, then no intentionally erroneous statements – aka lies – could be made either.

In this way, lying, as a general policy, cancels itself out. It is a self-undermining policy: not the sort of policy that could be consistently adopted – that is, adopted by everyone. Kant's answer to why we should be moral, then, is this: immoral practices are inconsistent practices. You should be moral in the same way that you should be consistent.

This is an ingenious idea whose only drawback seems to be that it doesn't work. It doesn't, that is, answer the question of why one should bother being moral.[34] The question 'Why should one be moral?' is actually ambiguous. It could mean 'Why should people in general be moral?' or it could mean 'Why should a particular person – me, for example – be moral?' At best, Kant's approach might be able to answer the first question. But it doesn't even address the second.[35] It might be true, for example, that if people in general were to lie all the time, then the practice of making statements would be abandoned, thus undermining the possibility of making intentionally erroneous statements. If so, the general policy of lying would be self-undermining or inconsistent. And this

34 It should also be pointed out that Kant's theory has some very implausible consequences. Lying is wrong, in Kant's view: end of story. It is always wrong to lie, even if, say, a mass murderer, evidently out on one of his killing sprees, asks you whether you happen to have a large axe handy (you do). This sort of implausibility stems from Kant's insistence that moral rules are categorical – right or wrong in a way that is logically divorced from their consequences.

35 Richard Taylor makes this point in his *Good and Evil* (Prometheus Books, 1970).

may be a reason why people in general should not lie whenever it suits them. But my policy of lying whenever it suits me – assuming I had such a policy, that is – would not be inconsistent or self-undermining.

I can best make this point by referring to myself in the third person, narcissistic though this may be. The policy of Myshkin lying whenever he feels like it doesn't cancel itself out. It can be an utterly universal policy, adopted by everyone. Thus, some random person might say:

'My policy is that Myshkin can lie whenever he finds it convenient.'

'Are you Myshkin?'

'No I'm not, that's Myshkin over there. My policy pertains to him, not to me.'

In principle, everyone could adopt this policy: the policy of letting Myshkin lie whenever he feels like it. This general, universally adopted, policy does not undermine itself.

The upshot is that while Kant might have provided a reason why people in general should be moral, he has not given a reason why any given individual person – such as I – should be moral.[36]

*

36 Maybe this is right. But a Kantian would deny that moral rules are allowed to mention specific individuals. They have to be completely general. On the other hand, the account of the form of a moral rule is not the same thing as an account of why we should be moral. Indeed, the argument that this is the form a moral rule must take is dependent on the idea that moral rules must be adoptable by everyone. So, the Kantian can't appeal to the form a moral rule must take in order to justify the idea that moral rules must be adoptable by everyone without begging the question. My father's discussion here is a vastly truncated version of a very complex debate. For more complexity, see Bernard Williams, *Ethics and the Limits of Philosophy* (Fontana, 1985). Williams would accept my father's conclusion, if not the manner in which he reaches it.

I am still searching for reasons why I should be moral. Prudence doesn't give me a reason. Logic doesn't give me a reason. And morality clearly can't give me a reason. I cannot explain why I should be moral by appealing to moral reasons – because why someone should bother with moral reasons is precisely the question at issue. I can't say, for example, that I should be moral because that's the right thing to do. Because the question is why I should concern myself with doing the right thing. The appeal to a moral reason in this context would beg the question.[37] Therefore, when I try to understand why I should be moral I cannot understand this 'should' in the prudential sense. I cannot understand it in the logical sense, as a 'should' of consistency. And I cannot understand it in the moral sense. I appear to have run out of 'shoulds'. I have to conclude that there is no reason I should be moral.

This is a striking drawback of the calculative conception of morality – the conception of morality as grounded in reason. If we think of morality in purely calculative terms – as, for example, a process of computing what course of action will produce the greatest good for the greatest number – then we are ultimately left with no reason for being moral. No moral calculation can ever provide us with a reason to perform the calculation or adhere to its results. I want a reason for being moral – something to convince me that I should be good rather than bad. But reason has told me there can be no such reason.

37 Philosophers lost the expression 'begging the question' sometime in the first quarter of the twenty-first century. Philosophically, 'begging the question' denotes a specific fallacy – the *petitio principii* fallacy of assuming the truth of what you are trying to prove. The general public used it in a much less specific way. For them, begging the question simply amounted to raising a question. Eventually, the common usage won, as it always does. My father is here using it in the stricter, philosophical, sense.

This looks unfortunate – until we remember that the demand for a reason is a demand *of* reason. The previous sentence is almost, but not quite, a tautology. It is the species of almost, but not quite, tautology that Pascal exploited when he wrote: 'The heart has its reasons of which reason knows nothing.'[38] There are demands of reason, but also other demands.

Modern thought has been dominated by demands for justification. The demand was there at the birth of the modern *Weltanschauung*, with Descartes's attempt to justify the common belief that there is an external world outside of us.[39] His justification wasn't very good – and Kant would later claim it was the 'scandal of philosophy' that no satisfactory proof of the external world has ever been provided.[40] The idea of providing a justification for morality is conceptually located within this modern, Cartesian, project.

Sometimes demands for justification are best not met head on. Sometimes you have to sidle up to these demands. Sometimes you have to sneak around the back and punch them in the kidneys. One way of doing this is to show that the demand for justification is illegitimate. All justifications, as Wittgenstein pointed out, must come to an end somewhere. I reach bedrock. My spade is turned.[41] If morality is bedrock, then our task is not to provide a justification for it, but to learn to be comfortable without justifications.

It may not be possible to justify being a good person. But,

38 Blaise Pascal, *Pensées* (1665), no. 423.
39 René Descartes, *Discourse on Method* (1637) and *Meditations on First Philosophy* (1641).
40 Immanuel Kant, *Critique of Pure Reason*, B Edition (1787), p. xl.
41 The idea is found in some posthumously edited notes of Wittgenstein's, published together as the book *On Certainty*, translated by Elizabeth Anscombe and edited by Anscombe and G.H. von Wright (Blackwell, 1969).

miraculously, some just turn out to be good anyway. For such people, being good is a part of their basic biological endowment. They naturally feel distress at the undeserved misfortune of others, and will do their best to mitigate it. Some people are just nice – which is not the same thing as being moral but, arguably, lies in the same general vicinity. Maybe I'll be one of those people. The potential is there. You can see it in my distaste for the baiting of Andrew C and in my resolution to be nice to him afterwards, even though I'd escaped any punitive consequences for my lie.

There is nothing in these observations that supplies a justification for morality – nothing here that provides a reason to be moral. It is simply an observation: some people all of the time and – probably – most people some of the time manage to do quite well as moral creatures. It is easy to see why we would like more than this. It is people like David B that make us want more. It is one thing dealing with people whom nature has filled with the milk of human kindness – the people who, naturally and effortlessly, feel sorry when others suffer and try to do something to remedy it. But the milk of human kindness is unevenly distributed. Some people have very little or none of it. 'Don't do that – it's wrong!' you might say to them. But the only response you will get is 'So what?' That is when and why we want a justification for being moral.

Much of the first half of the twenty-first century saw politico-terrorist-religious movements cutting huge swathes of misery across the Middle East, and sometimes elsewhere: routinely crucifying and/or beheading the men they encountered, and raping and/or enslaving the women and children. We want a justification for morality because we want to be able say to such people: you should not be doing this. We want to provide them with a reason that shows them their error. This is our fundamental mistake. Their failure is a failure of reason, but not an atypical one. Given the way a fanatic sees the world, his or her behaviour can be perfectly rational. The fanatic is driven by warped metaphysical views – and his acquisition of those views is certainly a failure of reason.

But warped metaphysical views are the province of many of us. In terms of their metaphysical credentials, the views of fanatics are no less rational than those of more mainstream believers: their views are simply more vicious. Their distinctive failure is, therefore, a failure not of reason but of emotion. The emotional life of the fanatic is so different, so alien, and it has become so biologically aberrant, that it undercuts the possibility of genuinely communicating with them. There is nothing we can say. We might think we want a reason why this person should not behave in the way that he or she is – a reason we can hold up in front of him or her and say: 'Look!' But this is not a person to be reasoned with anyway. You cannot reason with such a person. You cannot argue with him and, often, you cannot bargain with him. All you can do is stop him.[42]

---

42 My father's attitudes are situated in the geopolitical context of the first half of the twenty-first century, and his position is not unproblematic. After all, we may think that of 'him', but he or she almost certainly thinks the same of 'us'. Then, it would seem, it is simply a question of who is able to stop whom. This is about as far from morality as it is possible to get, assuming might is not the same thing as right. Philosophers will recognize a familiar problem. The emotional reactions we have to situations are a matter of the way the world is. One cannot, as Hume and others have pointed out, draw any legitimate inference from the way the world is to the way it ought to be. That an emotional response is natural, for example, does not mean that it is right. This is the famous 'is–ought gap', and it is seemingly unbridgeable. If there is no reason to be moral, we are simply left with the way the world is, with no resources left to advocate any view on how it ought to be. And the world is not pretty. That is just the way it is.

5

God

Nihilism stands at the door.
Whence comes this uncanniest of all guests?

Friedrich Nietzsche, *The Will to Power*

My teachers have been plugging the God line for nearly five years now, and it grows less convincing by the year. While daily discomfort might conceivably bring one closer to God, sitting crossed-legged on a cold, bare tiled floor for thirty minutes every day, five days a week, being coerced into singing maladroit songs or into closing one's eyes and muttering nonsensical strings of words, is not really selling it for me. And, I must admit, I'm occasionally a little confused. Our Father, who does art in heaven, gives us bread, and doesn't like us to trespass. But even when I think I understand the message, I'm not sure I like it. A ten-year-old boy likes his heroes to be of the action variety. Crucifixion does sound very unpleasant, and one would have to be absolutely barking to effectively volunteer for it. It would never have happened to, for example, the Hulk. If the Romans tried to detain Bruce Banner in the Garden of Gethsemane, the consequences would be entirely predictable. Don't make me angry. You won't like me when I'm angry. Could Jesus take the Hulk? Perhaps that's unfair – no one can take the Hulk. But Jesus gave us no reason to think he would triumph even over a non-super-powered hero like Batman. Occasionally, my hopes are temporarily raised. I like the bit where he assaults some guys in a temple – a dispute over money, I gather. So Jesus was a bit tasty after all, I think. However, he never backs this up on any consistent basis. Sometimes, he would talk the talk: I came not to bring peace but a sword. I like that. But where is this sword? You never hear about it again. He could have used that at Gethsemane, given his lack of, for example, titanium claws that would shoot out of his knuckles when he found himself in a spot of bother. Oh, shit! Here comes Mrs Watkins, glaring at me. Better get back to singing.

The subsequent years augmented my natural childlike distaste for religion. Sometimes I was told that without religion there could be no such thing as morality. One no more needs religion for morality than one needs to accept crucifixion just to get one's point across. Morally good actions are the ones commanded by God. Morally bad actions are the ones forbidden by God. And if there is something He neither commands nor forbids, then God presumably doesn't care about it too much. These claims are ambiguous. Is a good action good because God commands it? Or does God command it because it is good? The first option is known as 'divine-command theory'. It is the fact that God commands something that makes it good. It is the fact that He forbids it that makes it bad. God's decrees make things good or bad. In the second option, God's decrees do not make something good or bad. Rather, they reflect what is already good or bad, independently of those decrees. The second interpretation allows that good and bad, right and wrong, exist independently of God. It is just that God knows – in His usual infallible way – which is which. Therefore, His decrees are utterly reliable indicators of what is right and what is wrong.

Divine-command theory is an implausible and worrying doctrine. It is implausible because it makes good and bad, right and wrong, totally dependent on the arbitrary decrees and decisions of God. And that's why it's worrying too. Suppose God wakes up tomorrow and decides: 'Right, time for a change!' All the things he has hitherto decreed are good will now be bad, and all the things he has hitherto decreed are bad will now be good. So, murder, torture, rape and other assorted forms of nastiness instantly become the right or good thing to do. Kindness, compassion – all the stuff preached by His son (aka Himself) in fact – now instantly become morally pernicious. Worse, what if, in fact, He made this change some time ago, but just never got around to informing any of us. There's a fat chance of getting into heaven now, what with ignorance of the law being no excuse.

There may seem to be an obvious answer to this problem. God wouldn't do this because He is good. God wouldn't suddenly decree that murder, torture and rape are all morally unobjectionable because He is a good God, and a good God would never do that. But that is exactly what you can't say if you believe the divine-command theory. This response presupposes that there is a standard of good (and bad) that is independent of God. If God's decrees or commands actually make things good and bad then there is no way one can externally evaluate God's decrees and commands. They are, by definition, correct, morally speaking – for there is no other independent standard of good and bad by which these decrees or commands could be judged incorrect – and so one has no basis for saying that a good God wouldn't do this.

The alternative – and, I have to say, from where I'm standing it looks a good one, at least if you want to believe that morality is grounded in God – is to abandon the divine-command theory in favour of the second option. God's commands do not make something right or wrong. But they do, in an utterly reliable way, reflect what is good and bad. God's commands and prohibitions track right and wrong – right and wrong that exist independently of those commands and prohibitions.

This view presupposes that moral good and bad exist independently of God – if not, there would be nothing for God's commands and prohibitions to reflect. But, if so, then the possibility of morality does not require God. The key to being a morally good person is to make sure your own actions reflect these independent standards of right and wrong, just as, we are supposing, God's decrees reflect them. But if there can be morality without God, then God begins to look a little like an unnecessary middleman. Why not just work out what's right and what's wrong on our own, and make sure our actions fall into line?

There is, of course, one possible remaining role for God. He may not create good and bad, but He can certainly tell us what they are. In effect, we have a choice. We can try to work it out on our own: to identify what is right and what is wrong, using our own flimsy and fallible intellectual capacities. Or, we can let God work it out for us, and then just go with what He (or, more accurately, one of his assorted and self-appointed earthly representatives) tells us.

The problem is: there isn't really a choice at all. Whether

we strike out alone or place our trust in God, ultimately we are still going to have to work it out on our own. Suppose we decide to place our trust in God. The first question: which God? If there is more than one, we have to work out in which one we are going to place our trust. That is something we are going to have to do ourselves – employing the aforementioned flimsy and fallible intellectual capacities.

There's only one God, some say. Different religions are simply different manifestations and interpretations of this one God. It is not clear what evidence there is for this claim, but let's accept it for the sake of argument. Where, then, are we going to find the results of this one true God's ruminations on right and wrong? In some or other religious text, presumably – these are purportedly the words of God. But religious texts abound, and more than a few of them are patently incompatible. So, even if the different religious texts are merely interpretations of the one God, we still have the problem of working out which book to trust and which to disregard. We can't appeal to the word of God to do this, of course: we are trying to work out precisely which is the (genuine) word of God. So, we are going to have to do this on our own.

Even if we could narrow down our search to one religious text, our problems would just be beginning. Religious texts are notoriously open to interpretation, combining what seems like sensible advice with gross contradictions and outright stupidity. Among the things forbidden by the Christian Bible are sex before marriage (Deuteronomy 22: 20–21), getting tattoos (Leviticus 19:28), haircuts of a certain sort (Leviticus 19:27), entering the House of the Lord if you have had the misfortune of having your penis cut off or otherwise injured (Deuteronomy 23:1), having your palm read (Leviticus 19:31), gossiping (Leviticus, 19:16), speaking in church if you are a woman (Corinthians 14:34–5) and divorce (Mark 10:11–12). If your kid gives you a bit of backchat, you are required to put him to death (Exodus 21:17). Working on the Sabbath is also punishable by death (Exodus 31:14–15). And if your wife should jump in and help you during an altercation with another man, you are required to cut off her hand (Deuteronomy 25:11-12).

I assume these are rules that few today will want to endorse. We reject them because they fail to cohere with strongly held moral intuitions. If you believe in God, you might ask yourself: does God really want me to kill my son, just because he said, 'F**k you, Dad!' If you decide that He doesn't – and, intuitively, killing does seem a little harsh – then you have two choices. The first, and most obvious, is to accept that the Bible was written by fallible – indeed, often stupid and vicious – human beings. The word of God may be in there somewhere, or at least in the vicinity, but you have to sort the wheat from the chaff to identify what it is. The other choice is to develop the theme that the Bible couldn't have really meant that, and then develop an alternative interpretation, for example: 'When men strive together one with another, and the wife of the one draweth near for to deliver her husband out of the hand of him that smiteth him, and putteth forth her hand, and taketh him by the secrets, then thou shalt cut off her hand, thine eye shall not pity her.'

I wish you the best of luck with the alternative interpretation. The important point is that these two strategies amount to the same thing. We have to second-guess the Bible, or other preferred religious text – either what it says or what it seems to say. And the only way we can do this is by using our fallible and flawed intellect. In doing this, we may well work, as the philosopher John Rawls once put it, from both ends: assessing texts and their interpretations in the light of how well they cohere with our existing moral intuitions but, when necessary, not being afraid to adjust or replace these intuitions in the light of the text we have come to regard as superior. In the end, if all goes well, we arrive at a position of what Rawls called 'reflective equilibrium' – where interpretation and intuitions have been maximally satisfied and mutually aligned.[43]

The great irony of the appeal to God as a guide to morality is that these are precisely the sorts of things we would have to do anyway if we struck out on our own. They are precisely the sorts of reasoning processes we would have to follow when we try to work out what is right and wrong, good or bad, without supernatural guidance. On the one hand, there are moral claims and the principles that underlie them. On the other, there are our moral intuitions. When there is a divergence between the two, we must reject the moral claim or the moral intuition, or both. Or we might find ways of modifying each so that the divergence is eliminated. Appealing to God as a guide to moral right and wrong, therefore, does not eliminate ethical reasoning: it simply reiterates it – in a marginally mutated form. We can believe in God all we want. It is not going to get us out of doing ethics.

1.

At this point, I feel obliged to make my first lengthy intercession. If there is one thing on which most philosophers are preternaturally smug it is the topic of just how much we don't need God any more. We have left all that medieval nonsense

43 Rawls, *A Theory of Justice.*

behind. I'm not so sure we really have. My father's arguments are clear, compelling – and, arguably, hopelessly off target. His point, taken in itself, is a good one: the appeal to God will not allow us to identify right and wrong. If we want to know which actions are right and which actions are wrong, then, unfortunately, we are still going to have to do work of our own. Moreover, this work – the balancing of principles and intuitions – will be of the sort we would have to do anyway, even if there is no God. This is a claim about our knowledge of right and wrong: of how we can know which actions are right and which ones are wrong. It is what philosophers call an epistemic claim: a claim about knowledge in some or other domain. There is, however, a more basic question: what makes something right or wrong? This is not an issue of how we know what is right and what is wrong. It is an issue of what it is for something to be right or wrong. It is, as philosophers say, an ontic, rather than epistemic, issue. The real worry that morality may not be possible in the absence of God is an ontic one.

2.

The concepts of right and wrong are inextricably entwined with another concept: duty, or obligation. If an action is wrong, then one has a duty not to perform it. If a situation is good or right, then one has an obligation not to undermine or hijack it. If there are such things as right and wrong, then there must also be such things as duty and obligation. But where do these come from?

The most obvious way a duty or obligation can exist is as concomitant with a law. A legal obligation, for example, can exist only if there is a corresponding statute. The statute grounds the obligation – brings the obligation into existence.

God

Moral obligations are, of course, not the same as legal obligations. Many things that are immoral – lying, cheating and breaking promises – are not, or need not be, illegal. And many things that are legal can be monstrously immoral. Nevertheless, we cannot understand how a legal obligation could arise in the absence of the requisite law. It is, similarly, difficult to see how a moral obligation could arise in the absence of a corresponding moral law.

There are two obvious ways in which there can be moral laws. The first is that God exists and He is the lawgiver. If this were the case, then we would have a clear understanding of the idea of moral duty or obligation. God's laws create moral obligations in essentially the same way that the state's laws create legal obligations. If God doesn't exist, however, then we cannot explain moral obligations in this way.

The alternative is that the relevant moral laws are human rather than divine. Clearly, any society is going to require rules to regulate the interactions of its members. Some of these will be rules of etiquette. It is rude to pick one's nose in public. Some of these will be moral but not legal. Lying, and cheating on one's spouse, are generally regarded as immoral but not illegal. Some rules are legal but not moral. On which side of the road one should drive is a matter of legality but not morality – although failing to observe the law can, of course, have moral implications. And some rules – the particularly serious ones – are both moral and legal. Murder is, in general, both illegal and immoral.

No society can function without an array of legal rules, moral rules and, arguably, rules of etiquette too. Each of these rules can generate their own kinds of obligation. I have a legal obligation to refrain from committing murder and to drive on the correct side of the road. I have a moral obligation *to refrain from committing murder, and also not to lie and cheat. I have a duty of civility or decency to refrain from picking my nose in public.*

There is, therefore, a familiar way of making sense of the idea of moral obligation in the absence of God. We can understand this obligation as engendered by a society's moral rules. Rather than having a divine origin, moral rules are conventional: they are simply a matter of which moral customs a society happens to adopt. This has the advantage of making the idea of moral obligation clear: a moral obligation is as understandable as the idea of a moral convention. But it also has a distinct disadvantage. It robs the idea of moral obligation of any deep legitimacy. This is because a mere moral convention, ungrounded in anything else, lacks any deep legitimacy.

3.

If society is the maker of moral laws, moral laws will vary from one society to another. Therefore one's moral obligations will similarly vary. This fact of ethical variation between cultures – cultural relativism – has been noted since different societies first began encountering each other. The ancient Greeks noted that while they buried their dead, the Callatians ate them. Even within a single country or region, morality can vary from one society to another. The morality of Athens was different from that of Sparta. Those who forced the introduction of Sharia law on many pockets of Europe in the third decade of this century had a very different moral code from those who unsuccessfully resisted it.

Cultural relativism is a simple fact: obvious and undeniable. If there is nothing more to morality than cultural norms, then it follows that morality is relative: right and wrong vary from society to society in the same way that legal statutes vary from society to society. But this relativism is just an illustration of the point, and not the point itself. The variation of moral norms from one culture to another is a contingent fact about the world. Suppose things were different. Suppose all cultures agreed on right and wrong. Or suppose there were just one monolithic culture. In such circumstances, we could point to some universally accepted moral rules and argue that it is these that provide substance to the idea of moral obligation. These universally accepted rules are the moral laws, and therefore everyone is morally obligated, or has a moral duty, to abide by them. Their widespread, even universal, acceptance matters not one bit. They are still just conventions, with nothing deeper underlying them that could legitimize them or guarantee their truth.

The deeply conventional nature of morality had, I think, implicitly been conceded in the way moral philosophers went about their business in those days – and, indeed, still do. The idea of reflective equilibrium is, of course, a clear admission that there is nothing more to morality than convention. We start with various rules or principles that 'we' just happen to accept. And then we compare these with various intuitions that 'we' just happen to have. If principles and intuitions do not cohere, we adjust them – working from one end or both. Perhaps a principle will have to be sacrificed, or perhaps an intuition. More satisfying: perhaps we can, with suitable modifications to each, make the two fit. At the outset of this process, the legitimacy of the principles and the intuitions is assumed. Reflective equilibrium may eventually dictate that we abandon one or both. But that they are legitimate starting points – suitable grist to be fed into the mill of reflective equilibrium – is not doubted. If these *principles and intuitions are what we accept and have, then this, by itself, is sufficient to guarantee at least their initial legitimacy. There is no basis or standpoint from which these might be judged and found lacking. Considerations of reflective equilibrium might yield a result. But, if they do, it is only on the basis of an uncritically accepted input.*

Reflective equilibrium is just one example. More generally, the procedure of practical moral philosophy is one of working out the implications of principles we already, uncritically, accept. You believe A. Then – look – you are logically committed to also believing B. And given one further assumption, C, you are also committed to believing D. You want X to be true – you want a world where X is, in fact, the case. But you will get this only if Y and Z are also true. Therefore, if you want X, you must also want Y and Z. Moral philosophy, in the last century and this one, became very good at that sort of investigation: charting the logical connections between moral claims. But the question of whether you should believe A, or whether you should want X: it is nowhere near as good at such questions. These foundational questions are, typically, left aside, at least when the subject is practical moral philosophy. This is a reflection – a resigned acceptance – of one simple fact: they have no foundation or, at least, none that we know of. Morality is conventional, through and through. Any legitimate sense of moral obligation or duty must derive from moral conventions.

After all, from where else would this foundation come if not from human convention? It cannot come from God's law, since we are supposing He does not exist. If it comes from neither God nor human convention, there would have to be some other law – neither divine nor human – that grounded the idea of moral obligation. What this law is, where it comes from and how it could possibly exist have never been made clear – and that is putting it mildly.

4.

The term 'ethics' comes from the Greek ethos. Originally, ethos simply meant 'habit' or 'custom'. Ethos shares a common root with ethnos, the Greek word that denoted 'people like us'. Ethos, accordingly, was usually understood to denote the customs or habits of people like us. That is how ethics was originally conceived. In the absence of God, this is how it still must be conceived. The idea that it could be something more than this is a product of religion, and its idea of a God-made law superior to the laws of man. An atheist who believes that ethics could ever be anything more than custom or convention is in the unenviable position, as Sartre once put it, of believing in the God-made law but not in the God who made it. As the child of human convention, the idea of moral obligation is perfectly legitimate. But a child of a law that is neither human nor divine is a child conceived in sin, the illicit issue of a law without a maker.

If there is no God, then moral obligation can come only from human convention. And if there is no God, there is also no standard by which we can evaluate or rank these conventions. We cannot judge one to be better than or worse than another, because there is no extra-conventional standard on which to base this judgement. This is the real challenge to morality posed by the non-existence of God. Nietzsche thought that the consequences of this would be world-shattering: nihilism – the abandonment of moral values – was an almost inevitable consequence. But it hasn't happened that way. Large swathes of the world, of course, never abandoned the belief in God. But even in the secular world, *the rejection of God was not accompanied by the rejection of values. On the contrary, the secular world championed its 'values' just as stridently as its non-secular counterparts. It fought, and continues to fight, wars over those values. Nihilism was, in effect, kept at bay by an illusion: the illusion of a law without a maker. Nietzsche was wrong – but perhaps only about the timing. Illusions do not work forever. Illusions always crumble – but sometimes do so only gradually. Less and less the wars fought were about values, and more and more they became about 'interests' – the non-moral counter-part of values. Nihilism was not a sudden insight, but a slow realization that gradually seeped out into the world and into those – like my father – who inhabited it.*

6

Symmetry

If you arrived in heaven by train, it would look like shit. Everywhere always does. But if luck is with you – smiling beatifically down on you that day – you might just get to see an angel.

One afternoon in the autumn of my seventeenth year I was summoned to the office of Mr Sumner, Headmaster. I was, I think it is fair to say, not entirely unconcerned by this turn of events. Mr Sumner was a rather elegant, silver-haired old gentleman, with a friendly smile – and an astonishingly foul temper. He always wore a navy blazer and a bow tie, and you could invariably see your face in his shoes – which is where anyone with any sense would be looking if he happened to talk to them. Mr Sumner was not a man for pleasantries – neither with pupils nor, rumour had it, with his teachers. If he talked to you at all, there was a 99 per cent probability that you were in trouble. On the way to the office, I made a mental checklist of all the things that might have occasioned this summons. Unfortunately, the one I kept coming back to was my far from occasional disappearances from classes these past few months. After arriving at school in the morning, and getting that crucial tick in the register, I would sneak off with my girlfriend Sandra – ironically, it was often during biology lessons – to do the sorts of things seventeen-year-old boys and girls did. Her parents both worked, and her house was conveniently empty: all day. I was pretty sure that discovery and eventual censure were just around the corner. But I just couldn't help myself, seventeen-year-old hormones being what they are.

'Myshkin, good, sit down. The time has come for us to discuss something – a rather important matter.'

Jesus, I thought, and in one of life's great ironies, I wasn't entirely off the mark.

'Do you know where I went to university, Myshkin?'

'I heard it was Oxford, sir.'

'Indeed it was: Ruskin College, Oxford. More years ago than I care to remember. And do you know why I came here, to this school?'

'No sir.'

'There were no government scholarships in those days. I had been accepted by Ruskin College, but there was no money to send me. The money came from the workers' cooperative – the 'Kwop', as you've probably heard it called – and it was given to me on condition that on obtaining my degree I should return here to advance the state of local education. And so that is what I did. Do you know how many people this school has sent to Oxford, or even Cambridge, as a result of my efforts?'

'I've not heard of anyone, sir.'

'That's because there isn't anyone, Myshkin. Not one –

zero. We had a few who were close, but they fell short for one reason or another – "not Oxford material" the reports would say. The stench of failure: that is the legacy I shall leave behind me. What a waste of a life.'

'Yes, sir . . . I mean—'

'You, however, Myshkin, are my last roll of the dice. This is my way of saying your O-level grades are good enough for them to take you seriously, and I'm assuming you can repeat that sort of performance at A level. Your athletic talents will also stand you in good stead. So, to cut a long story short, you are applying to Oxford.'

'I am, sir?'

'Yes, you are. I would advise Jesus College – I have a contact there. Don't get your hopes up. You probably won't get in. They'll find some or other reason to decide you're "not Oxford material".'

'Yes, sir.'

'The next thing you need to think about is what subject you are going to take. Any thoughts on that, Myshkin?'

'No sir.'

'Well, you'd better get your thinking cap on.'

Now, almost a year to the day, a devastatingly intimidating admissions interview, an impossible exam and some fortuitous A level results later, I stood on platform two of Oxford railway station trying, largely unsuccessfully, not to stare at the most beautiful woman I had ever seen. Where I grew up, the brutal industrial disaster of a town I called home, the girls could be undeniably pretty. I had few complaints, actually. But never in my life had I seen anyone like this vision surrounded by suitcases. In fact, if you replaced the suitcases with a large clamshell, and relocated Oxford to the coast, I might have been looking at Venus, new-born from the sea. (I'm talking about the Botticelli Venus, not the Titian Venus.)

It would be attributing far too much competence to my conscious mind to say that the word 'exotic' instantly registered in it. My conscious mind was never the most reliable part of me: prone to tantrums, lapses of concentration and unconscionable, unannounced leaves of absence, it was, at this precise moment, too shocked to do much registering of anything. But I've always had a healthy unconscious – not in the nineteenth-century steam-engine Freudian sense but in the shiny twenty-first-century information-processing sense. And that part of my mind, the more important and efficient part that went on assimilating information when the conscious tip went walkabout, knew immediately that this – exotic – is what she was. My reliable and efficient unconscious saw chestnut-brown hair cascading down over an olive-skinned, perfectly symmetrical face. After a few moments, that face looked in my direction and broke into a blindingly white, and once again perfectly symmetrical, smile. Poor Sandra – freckled, auburn-haired Sandra – the prettiest girl in my class. Only a few hours ago we had exchanged tearful goodbyes and promises of undying love. She never stood a chance. The moment that smile trained itself on me was the precise moment I began to forget Sandra. Don't think too badly of me. Life had equipped me poorly for this. I was doomed.

'Excuse me,' said the olive-skinned, perfectly symmetrical vision, 'but can you tell me how to get to Jesus College?'

7

Personality

*An abortion must be induced before the onset of
sensation and life. For what is holy will be distinguished
from what is not by means of sensation and life.*

Aristotle, *Politics*

Aglaya Silveira's name was a reflection of nature: of her
Russian mother and Brazilian father. Her familiar name –
Olga – was a reflection of nurture: the people of South
Florida, where she was born and had lived for the first eighteen years of her life, found 'Olga' much more convenient to
say than 'Aglaya'. If you live in a place where the ambient
temperature oscillates between hot and hellish, one unnecessary syllable can make all the difference. It will be quickly
dispensed with, following a well-beaten path into oblivion,
hot on the heels of other unnecessary items: long pants, long-
sleeved tops and real shoes. Even two syllables are pushing
it. Some of the stoners in her school – her expensive, private
Coconut Grove school – couldn't rouse themselves to anything longer than 'Ol'.

When she was younger, Olga's father, whom she loved

more than anyone else in the world, had given her two pieces of advice. The first: 'Don't worry about an old crock like me. I've had my time. Go off and live your life.' The second piece of advice was a response to her mother, whom Olga loved dearly but could never quite persuade herself to like. Her mother's plan had always been for Olga to be a doctor or, failing that, a lawyer. Her father's attitude towards this plan was one of gentle subversion. 'Why would you do something that lots of people can do? Find something that no one can do, or very few can do, and then go and do it.' He had a heart attack and died shortly afterwards, thus rendering his first piece of advice both hauntingly prophetic and, for precisely that reason, touchingly redundant. The second piece of advice stuck. Olga lived by it. And this piece of advice was decisively shaping our present conversation.

Olga had arrived in Oxford as a Rhodes Scholar from Columbia University. We had met at the station, taken a taxi together to the College, and eaten dinner together that evening. We kissed for the first time a few days later, alone, late at night, in the Junior Common Room, watching an old black and white film, *The Lost Weekend*. The kissing had continued largely unabated ever since – eight months and counting.

I'm not really sure what she saw in me. Her history did reveal a leaning towards jocks, and I fitted the bill in that respect, even if she found our strange sports mystifying. I wasn't unduly harsh on the eye either, but it's highly relative, of course. By the standards set by British university students I was up there, a contender. By the standards set by the beautiful people that populated the photographs in her room, I was an inbred stumpy troll. People of the New World have certain advantages that I lack, most obviously a vast genetic pool from which to pick and choose the finest combinations of heritable traits. Look at Olga: Brazilian, that's already a melange, and Russian. Compare that to my lot, who almost certainly arrived here at some point before the Romans and couldn't be bothered to go anywhere since.

In a sense, genetics was the topic of our current conversation: specifically, whether my Bronze Age pond genes were going to be allowed to swim in her vast genetic oceans. At some point in our often-more-than-once-a-day sexual entanglements, a condom apparently hadn't done the job it was supposed to do. I don't remember any obvious signs of mechanical failure, although I have to admit that the post-coital debriefing of condoms is not a forte.[44] Whatever went wrong, Olga was pregnant: about seven weeks, her GP – cue her remonstrations about not even being able to get an ob-gyn in this backward country – had informed her.

At the time, I was going through a living-for-today-and-letting-tomorrow-take-care-of-itself phase. There is a certain sense of invincibility that accompanies being in love, especially when it is for the first time. My counsel: 'Let's just go for it, Olga. We'll survive.' My offer wasn't entirely motivated by largesse. In fact, it wasn't at all motivated by largesse. A baby was an undiscovered country for me – and, in general, undiscovered countries tended to make me very nervous. But on the other hand, from the moment I woke up each morning, the thought of Olga returning to the US – which she was scheduled to do in a few weeks' time – would start gnawing

44 Oh lovely! That's an image I am going to have to carry with me to my grave.

at me: nibbling away at my present happiness as it nibbled away at our future together. Dropping out of Oxford, taking a menial job, negotiating a screaming baby with a full nappy: I could do that. And I really think I would have done that (although one can never really know until push turns to shove).

I regaled her with stories. There was, for example, the story of Mark B, my best friend in school. The woman that Mark called his 'sister' was in fact his mother. His 'mother' and 'father' were really his grandparents, and the men he called his 'brothers' were really his uncles. Everyone knew this, and I assume Mark did too. But it wasn't really something you would want to talk to him about, so I never did. When he was fifteen, Mark impregnated his girlfriend Alison, and, maybe not wanting the cycle to begin all over again, he got a job, dropped out of school and looked after his kid. The moral I extracted from this story was simple: if Mark B can do it, so can I.

The lesson extracted by Olga was rather different: 'And just what is Mark doing now, Myshkin?' She would then regale me with counter stories. She was the nominal subject of these stories, but it was a new Olga, subtly different from the one I loved. This new Olga was portrayed as acquisitive and extraordinarily high-maintenance, and as one had no intention of raising a minimum-wage baby. But most of all, the stories returned to, and revolved around, the same point. I, Olga, do not want to do things everyone does. I want to do things no one does. I wasn't happy, but I understood that I had absolutely no chance of getting Olga to do anything she didn't want to do. In the end, reluctant acquiescence was my only choice.

*

Personality

Some say life begins at conception. In one sense, this is trivially true. Of course, conception isn't a momentary thing: it's not like sticking a pin in a balloon and – bang – there is a new life. Conception is a process that takes around twenty-four hours – culminating in syngamy, the point where the genetic materials from the sperm and egg have completely fused. At this point, however, it seems pretty clear that a new single-celled entity exists. This zygote is clearly alive and, if all goes well, will eventually become a normal adult human being. Therefore, it doesn't seem unreasonable to suppose that life begins at syngamy.

On the other hand, it is difficult to know what to make of this. In 'The Curious Case of Benjamin Button' – a short story by F. Scott Fitzgerald – the eponymous central character ages backwards. He is born as a seventy-year-old man, and eventually becomes a baby. Suppose this process were to continue on, back into the womb. He becomes a foetus, then an embryo (that is, the intermediate stage of development that occurs roughly between day six – when the zygote is implanted in the womb – and day sixty) and finally a zygote. If I were a Benjamin-Button-like figure, would I still be around by this time? On the contrary, I suspect I would be long gone.[45] If this intuition is sound, there is no reason to suppose that I am around when the zygote first appears. The zygote is alive and human but it is not yet me. We might refer to it – a kind of Prince inversion – as the zygote subsequently known as 'Myshkin'. More accurately, it is the zygote that will subsequently *be* Myshkin.

---

45 This thought experiment was employed by Jeff McMahan in his book *The Ethics of Killing: Problems at the Margins of Life* (Oxford University Press, 2002).

A Good Life

The same is true of later stages of the entity that will be me. Consider the embryo of seven weeks, the age at which Olga's suspicions coalesced into the definitive discovery that she was pregnant. A seven-week-old embryo is roughly the length of the nail on one's little finger. It has a heartbeat, and its face is beginning to form, as are its hands and feet. There is some disorganized neural activity, though not enough to support thought or conscious experience. If I were reverse-ageing in a Benjamin-Button-like manner, would I still be around by the time I had reached this stage? Again, I think this is unlikely. My demise would have occurred at some point before then. By parity of reasoning, when we flip the ageing processes back around the right way, I think I should have to conclude that the embryo that will subsequently be known as Myshkin is not yet I.

This, of course, raises the question of what I am: of what I must be if this living human individual that will become me is not yet me. My intuitions of non-existence as zygote, embryo or foetus presuppose something like John Locke's definition of the person. One tends to think that the term 'person' and the expression 'human being' mean the same thing. On Locke's view, this is not so. A person, according to Locke, is 'a thinking, intelligent being that has reason and reflection and can consider itself as itself, the same thinking thing, in different times and places'.[46] If you are a person, you must be able not only to think, but to have thoughts of a certain sort: thoughts about yourself. You must be able to 'consider yourself as yourself'. As a result, you will be able to have thoughts about your past and about how you would

46 See Locke, *An Essay Concerning Human Understanding*, Book 2, Chapter 27.

like your future to be. Most humans are persons in this sense, but not all. An anencephalic infant, for example, would not qualify as a person in Locke's sense. Nor, perhaps, would some humans with severe brain damage. If Locke's conception of the person is correct, my intuitions of non-existence in zygotic, embryonic and foetal form are, it seems, justified. None of these things is a person. I am a person. Therefore, I am none of these things.[47]

Epicurus once argued that death was not a bad thing. More precisely, he argued that death could not harm us. While we are around, death has not happened, and so can't have harmed us yet. And when it happens, we are no longer around to be harmed. So, either way, death cannot harm us.[48] Most have not been persuaded by Epicurus' argument, and for those who want to resist his conclusion Locke's account of the person provides a promising means. Death harms us, on this view, precisely because we have desires about the future: desires to go on living, desires to achieve something at some future time – desires that our death would clearly stymie. It doesn't matter that when we die we will no longer have these desires. We have them now. Death thwarts them. That is why death harms us.

This account of the harm of death works only for persons. You cannot have desires about your future unless you can

47 The inference is questionable, and depends on whether 'person' denotes a substance sortal or a phase sortal. That is, is the category of a person like that of a human? 'Human' denotes a substance sortal. If you are human, then you are human as long as you exist. Or is it more like that of being a father – a phase sortal – something that you can be at certain times you exist and not be at other times? My father assumes the former. I'll let this objection slide as I suspect his argument can be reformulated in phase-sortal terms.
48 Epicurus, 'Letter to Menoeceus'.

think of yourself in that future. And you cannot have thoughts about yourself in some possible future unless you can have thoughts about yourself. Therefore, Locke's account of the person not only provides a way of making sense of my intuitions about when I would and would not exist, they also have a clear moral implication. Death is a bad thing only for persons, since only persons can have desires about the future. If the zygote, embryo or foetus is not a person, there is nothing directly wrong with killing it.[49]

There is that word 'directly' again: it's not insignificant. Remember side effects? Just because something is not a person does not mean that we have no moral obligations towards it. It just means that we have no moral obligation to not kill it, or to save it from being killed. If something can suffer, on the other hand, then we might very well have an obligation to not inflict unnecessary suffering on it. Suppose we abort a foetus, and suppose this is a painful process. Then, we might be doing nothing wrong in killing the foetus, but still be doing something wrong in causing it to suffer. Abortion would be morally permissible, but only if it were painless. Not so long ago, late abortions (the ones where the foetus is most likely to be able to feel pain) were performed by injecting a salt solution into the amniotic sac – a method that causes the foetus to go into convulsions and where death

---

49 I am struck by the divergence between my father's views on the ethics of infanticide and those on the ethics of abortion. He excoriated Peter Singer's views in developing the former, but in this chapter he sounds very much like Singer. Surely this has nothing to do with the fact that in the former case he was the potential subject of harm and in the latter this subject is someone else? Who? I wonder. Anyway, my father's account will soon be subjected to my mother's scary, laser-like scrutiny.

would take up to three hours. If the foetus can feel pain, and if we assume that convulsions are going to involve a lot of it, this method is morally abhorrent.

While this method is an extreme case and is no longer generally employed, it is not clear that other methods (e.g. vacuum aspiration, surgical dilation and evacuation and so on) will be painless. However, if it could be shown that in certain stages of development the foetus is incapable of feeling, this would remove the current worry. There is no evidence that a zygote can feel pain. In fact, given what we know about the neural basis of pain – the structures, mechanisms and processes that underwrite it in humans and other animals – we can effectively dismiss this possibility. But we have very good evidence for the claim that a near-term foetus can feel pain. Indeed, if babies can feel pain – and no one seriously doubts this – then it is certain that near-term foetuses feel it also. The ability to suffer appears somewhere along the foetus's developmental trajectory.

Pinning down a precise point where this happens is not possible, given our current state of knowledge. The best we can do is make educated guesses, and then allow some leeway for the possibility that we have made a mistake. If you're not sure whether something can suffer, then as a general rule of thumb it is probably best to give it the benefit of the doubt. Some think that the development of the cerebral cortex is a necessary condition of suffering. If correct, this would mean that the ability to suffer does not arise in the foetus much before thirty weeks. I suspect this is too stringent a requirement. The role of the cortex seems to involve locating and classifying pain – not feeling it as such. Before pain messages reach the cortex, they pass through the thalamus, and this has led many to look to thalamic development as the decisive indictor of when a foetus can suffer. Of course, the development of the thalamus is itself a process rather than an event, and the issue of when there is sufficient thalamic development to make suffering possible is a difficult theoretical matter. But even on the most radical accounts of thalamic development, we are probably looking at eighteen weeks at the earliest before there is any semblance of an ability to suffer. If you want to be really safe, add a few weeks. Death does not harm the foetus because it is not a person. And, before fifteen weeks or so, suffering does not harm the foetus because it cannot suffer.

Some think that to determine the morality of abortion by looking at the actual features of a foetus is misguided. Crucial to the foetus, and its moral status, is not what it is but what it is becoming. The foetus may not be a person, but it certainly has the potential to become one – and barring interference or misfortune will realize this potential. The moral status of the foetus – and the reason why abortion is wrong – is a matter of the potential of the foetus: of what it will be and not what it is.

I doubt this will work. The idea that your potential properties can give you an actual moral status is dubious. Being born in the USA, Olga has the potential to become US president: a goal that accords nicely with her father's second piece of parting advice. So, Olga, we might say, has the property of potentially being US president. However, this doesn't mean that she now, at this time, has the actual rights of the US president. Potential properties can give you only potential rights, not actual ones. The potential of the foetus to be a person can no more give it the moral status of a person than

Personality

Olga's potential to be president gives her the status of president.

This, you might think, is an unfair analogy. Being the president is an exceptional property few attain. But, in the absence of outside interference, almost all foetuses will become persons. You might insist there is a difference between what we might think of as normal and exceptional potential. Becoming a person is part of the normal potential of a foetus. Being president is not part of the normal potential of anyone. Therefore, perhaps, we can rephrase the argument against abortion in terms of the idea of normal potential? Abortion is wrong because it is part of the normal potential of a foetus to become a living human being.

I shall reformulate. At the time Olga and I faced these deliberations, I had the potential to be an old man. That was part of my normal potential – nothing exceptional about it. There is an attitude that many have towards the old – sometimes tacit, often explicit: they deserve, putting it roughly, to be cut a little slack. Their views are not quite 'on message' – a little racist perhaps, a little sexist probably, if they are men. 'Women shouldn't drink pints,' an old man once told us, at The Lamb and Flag in Oxford. Cut him some slack, I told the rapidly purpling Olga – he's old. My implicit attitude seems to be this: the old have the right to be given a little leeway on things like this – a right to a certain sort of toleration not accorded their younger counterparts. Suppose this were true. It would not follow that the I who said this to Olga, the I who was still a young man, had this right – just because I had the potential to grow old. A merely potential property does not give one actual rights, no matter how normal or likely it is that one will eventually have this property.

*

Olga will return to the States in a little over three weeks. There, she will have her pregnancy terminated. Any tears I shed will not be for the embryo-soon-to-be-a-foetus that lives within her. I'm far too self-absorbed for that, I assure you. It is the loss of our future together – more accurately, my future with her – that assaults me, not the loss of this something that is yet no one. Poor, woebegone me. And if any trace of sentiment were to work its way into some corner of my heart or intellect, it would find stony ground. I've tidied these arguments up a bit: glossed over the hesitations, and excised the dead ends and blind alleys down which my reasoning would often stumble. But, broadly speaking, these are the arguments around which my conclusions – and then my convictions – eventually crystallized. Killing a foetus is not directly wrong because it is not a person, and it is only a person that death can harm. Killing a foetus can be indirectly wrong to the extent it involves suffering. This muddying factor is removed as long as the foetus is killed before it becomes capable of suffering. Fifteen weeks is playing it safe. And Olga will be several weeks to the good side of that.

Wittgenstein once wrote: 'The real discovery in philosophy is the one that enables me to stop doing philosophy when I want to. The one that gives philosophy peace, so that it is no longer tormented by questions that bring itself into question.'[50] I suspect I neither sought nor needed peace, but if I had, these are the arguments that would have delivered it.

50 Ludwig Wittgenstein, *Philosophical Investigations*, paragraph 133.

8

Nice

I feel I should say something at this point. Fear not: I won't make a habit of these interjections. And, being nowhere near as loquacious as Myshkin, I expect I'll be brief. But I do feel obliged to say a little because, after all, it is me – my life and my decisions – we are discussing. So, let me see: yes, I am, apparently, the acquisitive, superficial and high-maintenance baby-killer. Myshkin didn't even seem to consider the possibility that my decision was based on what was best for him as much as for me. He was bewitched by a romantic notion of him working some minimum-wage job, assuming he could get one, and coming home to his family in our tiny council flat on some, possibly dangerous, estate and whiling away his spare hours playing soccer with junior in the park. His mind still inhabited the country of his childhood. I know where he was coming from. I actually met his parents, you know – they were very nice – and I saw where he grew up. Poor but far from terrible – and he thought it was going to be like that.

But the world changed, and it wasn't going to be like that at all. Let's put me to the side for just a minute. Do you know how long he would have been happy with this arrangement? No time: no time at all. If I'd said yes, I would have consigned him to a life he hated. And I couldn't do that to him. Someone, in this relationship, had to be the grown-up. Realism and responsibility were not among Myshkin's strengths at this time in his life.

There is more to it than the impact the baby would have on our lives. Have you noticed anything about Myshkin's arguments so far – anything that they might be missing? Some little thing they might have overlooked? I'll tell you what it is. Me! I do not feature in these arguments at all. For Myshkin, there is a foetus. His focus is on the foetus, and the features it has or lacks that would give it a right to a continued existence. For me, however, there is not a foetus but something quite different: there is a foetus-that-is-growing-inside-of-me.

Before we get to what I think, let's dispose of Myshkin's arguments. First of all – a purely rhetorical point – they are not really his. They are canonical arguments of the contemporary moral philosophy of that time. Myshkin read them, rehearsed them and ultimately swallowed them hook, line and sinker because he needed to. His total reliance on Locke's idea of the person – this cult of personality that had infected him at Oxford – was a similarly bovine concession to fashion. Second, there is my more important, logical, point. The implications of this Lockean idea were staring him in the face all the time. He couldn't see them because he absolutely needed to not see them. If being a person is crucial, then there is no moral objection to infanticide any more than there is to abortion: as long as it is painless and no one else has an objection. As an example of a human that was not a person, he cited the anencephalic infant. But it doesn't matter whether it is healthy or severely disabled: no infant is a person in Locke's sense of being able to 'consider itself as itself, the same thinking thing, in different times and places'. That ability – the ability to think thoughts about oneself – doesn't emerge, on some standard ways of estimating this ability, until around four years of age.[51] Whichever way you look at it, and however you try to finesse this point, if you rely on Locke to defend abortion you are going to have a big – baby-shaped – bullet to bite.

Suppose there is a person who has a strange medical condition, such that he can survive only if he is plugged into someone else. It doesn't matter what this condition is, or

51 I believe that my mother is referring to the false-belief test. Some children are watching a puppet show. One puppet puts an object in a box, and then leaves the stage. The other puppet then takes the object and moves it to another box. The first puppet then returns. The children are asked to point to the box in which they think the puppet will look for the object. To understand that the puppet will look in the first box requires understanding the concept of belief – because it requires understanding that the puppet will believe that the object is in the first box because that is where she left it. Until they are around four years of age, children will usually indicate the second box – the box to which the object was moved. Some take this to indicate that until then children lack the concept of belief. This is not uncontroversial. My mother also requires the additional assumption that you cannot think thoughts about your own mental states unless you can think them about others'. But while my mother may be guilty of a little hyperbole here – she was like that when she was on a roll – her central point is surely sound. Babies are not persons in Locke's sense. Any argument to the effect that abortion is permissible (simply) because foetuses are not persons seems to entail that infanticide is permissible too. Some have been willing to bite the bullet to which my mother refers. See, for example, Michael Tooley, 'Abortion and infanticide', *Philosophy and Public Affairs*, Vol. 2, No. 1 (1972), pp. 37–65.

what form the 'plugging in' takes: the basic idea is that he needs access to the life processes of another in order to stay alive. His method of securing access to these processes is to furtively enter the abodes of unaccompanied females, and hook himself up to them. But, here's the rub. Once he has done this, he must remain hooked up for a period of nine months. If he is allowed to do so he will, at the end of this period, be on his merry way with thanks and heartfelt gratitude for the woman's help. But if he is unhooked prematurely he will die. Suppose, finally, that I am this woman.[52]

Am I obligated to allow the man to remain hooked up to me for the nine months? I have not invited the man into my house with the promise of my aid. On the contrary, I knew he was running around the doing this sort of thing, and I took what I thought were reasonable precautions to keep him out. I made sure there were locks on all the windows – it was just unfortunate that one of those locks turned out to be broken. Now that he has hooked himself up to me, against my knowledge or consent, am I morally obliged to allow him to stay there for the next nine months?

It would, of course, be a very nice thing for me to do. But no one is morally obliged to do something simply because it's nice. It would be a very nice thing if I were to take a bullet for someone else, or throw myself on the proverbial grenade. But this doesn't mean that I am obligated to do these things should the situation arise. These sorts of actions go above and beyond the call of duty. And duty is, by definition, where one's moral obligations end. Of course, things would be dif-

52 This is a very well-known argument – as canonical as any of those employed by my father – first devised by Judith Jarvis Thomson, 'A defense of abortion', *Philosophy and Public Affairs*, Vol. 1, No. 1 (1971), pp. 47–66.

ferent if I had invited the man into my house and told him to make use of my body. The invitation is essentially a promise, and in making a promise I incur the obligation to not break it, or to do my best not to break it. And when you consider how serious are the consequences for the man, you can appreciate that this is a very serious promise. But I made no such invitation, and I took reasonable steps to ensure that I should not find myself in this predicament. Therefore, allowing the man to remain hooked up to me is strictly optional, morally speaking. I have no obligation to do this.

Myshkin is so male – and I don't mean that in a good way. He focused on the status of the foetus – is it a person, or is it not? Does it have the right of a person or does it not? From my perspective, this is utterly irrelevant. The man who hooks himself up to my body is clearly a person and so has the rights of a person. But it doesn't matter. I am still not obligated to allow him to use my body for the next nine months.

1.

I have to admit, when I first encountered this argument – many, many years ago – I thought it was utterly decisive. Its originator was not, in fact, my mother, but a philosopher called Judith Jarvis Thomson. Thomson's argument is based on the distinction between acts that are obligatory and those that are 'supererogatory'. An action is obligatory if it is morally required: it is a good thing to do and a bad thing not to do. But an action is supererogatory if it is a good thing to do but not a bad thing not to do. You can be morally praised for doing something that is supererogatory but not blamed for failing to do it. I still think Thomson's argument is interesting, but I am less convinced than I used to be. Two factors have slowly nibbled away at my conviction. At the root of both is the suspicion that the notion of the supererogatory is little more than a stealthy invention – designed to mute morality's unceasing demands. After all, from the standpoint of which moral theory would the idea of supererogation even make sense? If throwing myself on the proverbial grenade would increase the overall amount of happiness in the world, or augment the number of satisfied preferences, then the utilitarian tells me that is what I should do. I may not do it, but I should. And from the lofty perspective of Kant, it is not possible to make sense of the idea of a moral failing that is not a failure of obligation. If the moral law, in fact, dictates that I should throw myself on the grenade – I am not saying that it does, but if it did – then that is what I should do. A failure to do so would be a failure of obligation, not a failure of supererogation.

2.

From where did this idea of supererogation come? The origins of the idea can be traced to the New Testament. When asked what one can do to gain eternal life, Jesus responded: 'If thou wilt enter into life, keep the commandments ... but if thou wilt be perfect, go sell what thou hast and give to the poor, and thou shalt have treasure in heaven' (Matthew 19:16–24). It was then developed by the Catholic Christian tradition, receiving its most detailed expression in Aquinas's Summa Theologica. A more interesting question concerns not its historical but its psychological origins. What psychological need compelled people to put these words into the mouth of the redeemer – as his recipe for redemption, no less? The answer is not difficult: morality is just too hard. It is undesired, and may even be undesirable.

Put yourself in the position of the Church Fathers. They

say: taking a wife is no sin but a life of monastic devotion is better. For most, the monastic life is undesired. And if everyone were to adopt its vows of celibacy, soon there would be no one left to live this life – and therefore no one to worship at the altar of the Christian God. Thus, a monastic life for all is both undesired and undesirable. This crack in the fabric of morality – this is what the idea of supererogation was meant to disguise. It is an ad hoc solution to a fundamental problem with morality itself: its demandingness. Morality is too stringent and too needy. Either we reject morality or we add something to it – something to draw a little of its sting. The problem is that, from the perspective of morality itself, this added element makes no sense.

3.

Even if we could make sense of the notion of supererogation, there are further questions that may be raised about my mother's argument. Much of her argument dwelt on the fact that she had not invited the stranger to hook himself up to her. If she had promised him the use of her bodily organs, then this, she accepts, would have transformed her behaviour from the merely supererogatory to the obligatory. But she did not do this. The guiding principle seems to be this: because she did not voluntarily assume responsibility for the stranger, anything she does for him can only be supererogatory rather than obligatory. The voluntary assumption of responsibility for someone is a necessary condition of having obligations towards him or her.

If this is the principle on which her argument is based, then her position is untenable. I see a small child, drowning in a shallow ornamental pond. This is a situation not of my making. I have not voluntarily assumed responsibility for the *child – indeed, I have never seen her before. However, there is no one else around to help. Is it really plausible to claim that I have no moral obligation to save her? If I choose to save her, would this simply be a morally optional act – an act of kindness or charity – rather than something that morality mandates? Should I really not be blamed if I were to walk away? This is implausible. I wouldn't exactly have murdered the child, but in the pantheon of things that are very, very wrong, my failure to help is not too far removed. But if, more plausibly, we accept that I do have an obligation to help the child, then we must reject the principle that we have obligations towards a person only if we have voluntarily assumed responsibility for her.*

I know: pregnancy is not like this. The drowning child I could save at minimal inconvenience to myself. But a pregnancy – like the stranger who hooks himself up to unknowing women – is going to take around forty weeks and, even ignoring the potential health risks and other complications, that is an awful lot of trouble to go to. Maybe it's too much trouble. I think for a lot of people it will be. Try telling the frightened teenager with the religious-zealot parents, or the woman who has been raped, that it's no trouble. But whether it would be too much trouble for everyone, I really don't know. I would not support any restrictions on a woman's right to choose, because I think this would lead to so many problems that it simply is not worth it. But if something is really a choice, then we must always allow for the possibility that it is a bad one. And it is good to keep sight of the potential fragility of judgements about what is and what is not 'too much trouble'. People vary enormously in what they perceive to be too much trouble. For some peculiarly selfless and agreeable people, 'nothing is too much trouble'. Such people, on the current suggestion, will actually have more moral obligations than the selfish person who thinks only of himself and for whom any other-benefiting action is always 'too much trouble'. The idea that the amenable have more moral obligations than the acrimonious is silly.

4.

There is another point my mother makes, however, and I found this far more convincing. This is what she said:

I am really not sure where this leaves the issue of abortion. But I do know that it leaves morality looking far richer, more sophisticated, complicated, vibrant and confusing than Myshkin ever dreamed. He loves his categories. For him, things are still just black or white. Abortion is either right or wrong, and these are the conditions under which it would be right, and these are the conditions under which it would be wrong. This is a very Anglo-Saxon way of looking at things. But we Latinas are much more subtle. There is black and there is white and there are non-denumerable monochromatic shades of in between. We traverse a world that is always a little bit wrong and a little bit right and how much of each depends on countless, and often unknowable, features of circumstance.

Myshkin, like Locke, was compromised by the illusion that you are either a person or you are not. Being a person is like switching on a light: it is either on or it is off and there is no in between. But suppose there were a dimmer-switch? Suppose being a person were more like being tall. Being tall is something that you eventually become, and there is no precise point in this process at which one is transformed from the category of the not tall to that of the tall. Nevertheless, despite the absence of a clear dividing line, some people are tall and some people are not. Becoming a person is a process that is protracted and often hard, and there is no fixed point at which one steps over the border and becomes a person. The longer you are along this road, perhaps, the worse abortion becomes, from a moral standpoint. But this doesn't mean it's not always a little bit wrong and a little bit right.

I believe this is exactly the right way to think about abortion. But I am hardly impartial, and I have to acknowledge that my judgement may be significantly clouded: not just because I am a man, either. My mother had a plan, a plan that my father did not know about.

9

Subfusc

Toleration and the Right to Believe[53]

A Dissertation Submitted in Partial Fulfilment
of the Requirement of the Degree of Bachelor of Arts,
Faculty of Literae Humaniores, University of Oxford

L. N. Myshkin

---

53 Among my father's notes was his old typewritten undergraduate dissertation from Oxford. This is something that one writes towards the end of one's final year. Like most undergraduate dissertations, it was a long and unwieldy affair, much of it taken up with historical exposition and analysis, in particular of the debate between William James and W.K. Clifford on the ethics of belief. He had clearly been making efforts to abridge this dissertation for inclusion in his manuscript, but this process was incomplete. I decided to complete the abridgement, and believe these resulting pages are faithful to his intentions. It is a weird blend, stylistically, of undergraduate formality and old-age rambunctiousness, which suggests he revisited and fiddled with it more than once.

A Good Life

1. Introduction: Mill on Freedom

Any view on toleration and the freedom of thought and expression – their scope and justification – must define itself in relation to the view defended by John Stuart Mill in <u>On Liberty</u> (1859). Mill presented four arguments against what he called 'the suppression of opinion'. They apply most obviously to the issue of what we would call 'free speech' or 'freedom of expression', but also to the thought or opinion that lies behind this expression.

First, the danger of suppressing an opinion is that the opinion suppressed may turn out to be true. The opinion may not seem intuitively plausible, but to assume that it must be false is to assume that one is infallible. Therefore, all silencing of discussion or opinion involves an assumption of infallibility.

Second, even if the opinion suppressed turns out to be false, unless we are allowed to challenge popular opinions they will turn into what Mill called 'dead dogma'. There's a difference between believing something that happens to be true and understanding <u>why</u> it is true. Considering challenges to your belief forces you to defend it, and this can allow you to understand it better; in particular, it can allow you to understand what makes it true. Suppose you believe that a certain practice – abortion, for example – is wrong. Others will disagree with you. If you want to respond to those who disagree with you, you can no longer simply assert your belief that abortion is wrong. You now have to defend it. Whatever form the defence takes, the very act of defending a belief allows you to understand it better – to understand <u>why</u> it is true, and not merely <u>that</u> it is true.

Third, Mill argues, if a true opinion is not debated, the

meaning of that opinion may be lost. So, whereas his second argument was concerned with the <u>justification</u> of a belief, his third argument is about the <u>meaning</u> of a belief. Unless we continually debate ideas, we may forget what they really mean. Mill uses the example of religious claims or beliefs that were once living but now have solidified into dogma: 'I am the resurrection and the life' provides a useful example. Believers might intone this claim during a church service, for example, without really understanding what it means.

Fourth, often it is not simply that one opinion – the popular one – is true and the unpopular alternative is false. Often there is a grain of truth, or more than that, in the alternative. If so, the real truth might involve a combination of elements of both opinions. Which elements of an opinion should be preserved and which should be rejected can often only emerge through a process of free debate.

In this dissertation I shall take up where, I believe, Mill prematurely stopped. That is, while I do not contest the arguments of <u>On Liberty</u>, I shall argue that they are incomplete. Mill's view is about the obligations a government has to its citizens: in this case, the obligation to permit, except in the most extreme of circumstances, freedom of thought, discussion and expression. The focus of this dissertation is different. Here, the focus is on the obligation a citizen has to himself or herself. It is one thing to say that a government should not suppress ridiculous beliefs. I agree. But, it is still true that you have an obligation to yourself (and perhaps others) to try not to hold ridiculous beliefs. While ridiculous beliefs should not be suppressed, having a ridiculous belief is, nevertheless, a symptom of failure – a failure on the part of the person who has it. The same is true of expressing ridiculous beliefs, but my focus will be on the having or holding of ridiculous beliefs, whether or not they are ever expressed. This does not mean that the view I defend has no political ramifications. It clearly does, and I shall explore some of these towards the end of this dissertation. But my primary focus will be on the individual, not the state.

2. The Curious Case of the Moral Right to Believe

Consider the following case. This is an actual case, although I shall embellish it a little. A young philosophy professor in America is trying to teach his students philosophy of religion – the usual arguments for and against the existence of God that form the core of most philosophy of religion classes. One of the students complains on the grounds that his most cherished beliefs are being attacked. 'I have a right to my beliefs,' the student says. Apparently the university's administration agreed with him: philosophy of religion was dropped from the curriculum.

The student asserts that he has a right to his beliefs. But it is, I think, genuinely unclear what sort of right this could be. Sometimes you have what we might call an <u>evidential</u> right to your belief. That is, you have a right to believe something when you have enough evidence in its favour. Thus, one has no evidential right to the belief that the moon is made of green cheese, for example. If there is no evidence, or not enough evidence or compelling evidence against, there is no evidential right. But this sort of right cannot be what the student was asserting. The various arguments for and against the existence of God are precisely the sorts of things that might provide evidence one way or another. In objecting to these, the student was objecting to the process of acquiring the sort of evidence that might establish, or undermine, an evidential right to his belief. Instead, the student seems to be asserting a <u>moral</u> right to believe. The student thinks he is morally entitled to a belief even if he has no supporting evidence for it.

The idea of a specifically moral right to believe something is a curious one – especially when there is little or no evidence in support of the belief; but it is still curious even when there is. To see why, consider Joel Feinberg's influential analysis of the concept of a right. According to Feinberg (1970), to have a moral right to something is to have a <u>valid claim</u> to it. So, you have a right to, say, education if you have a valid claim to it. You don't need to be able to make the claim yourself – others can do that for you. Thus a young child, for example, can have this right even though he or she doesn't understand it and so cannot claim it in person, so to speak. A claim is valid if it is grounded in, or entailed by, a correct moral theory or principle. But a claim is always both a claim <u>to</u> something – in this case, an education – and <u>against</u> someone. So, if a child has a right to an education this also means that he or she has a valid claim against other people – that they do not prevent his or her access to this education. This is a minimal account of rights. Some people build more into the idea of a right than this – many think, for example, that if a child has a right to an education, other people have a positive duty to promote his or her access to it, and not merely the negative duty of not preventing access. However, in this dissertation I shall assume only Feinberg's minimal account because it is as uncontroversial as you can get.

On Feinberg's analysis, if you have a moral right to something – a given commodity, freedom or treatment – then others have the duty to not wilfully deprive you of that something. Therefore, if you have a moral right to a belief, it follows that others have a duty to not wilfully deprive you of that belief — even if that belief is false or entirely lacking in evidence. The most obvious way of wilfully depriving someone of a belief is by effectively criticizing it: by providing conclusive or compelling evidence against it. Therefore, it seems, if you have a moral right to a belief, others have the duty not to criticize your belief.

It is clear that this entails, among other things, a blanket ban on freedom of expression. Not only could one not criticize the beliefs of others, in many circumstances it is doubtful one could even defend one's own beliefs. Let's suppose that you hold one belief, and I hold another. But our beliefs are incompatible: if mine is true, yours is false, and vice versa. Thus, in defending my belief — putting forward reasons or arguments in its favour — I am, in effect, simultaneously attacking yours. Therefore, if we assume that any belief held by one person will always be incompatible with certain beliefs held by others, it seems that no one has a right to defend his or her beliefs.

Things would become even more ridiculous if we were to adopt accounts of moral rights that are less minimalist than Feinberg's. According to these views, I would not only have the duty to not wilfully deprive someone of their beliefs, I would also have the positive duty of promoting their access to their beliefs. So, if my belief were incompatible with yours, it would seem that I have the duty to criticize my own belief in order to bolster yours. This is, in effect, a reductio ad absurdum of the view that there is a moral right to believe if we combine this with non-minimal analysis of the concept of a right. But even if we assume only Feinberg's minimal account, the blanket ban on freedom of expression is, surely, too great a price to pay.

Other ways of explaining the idea of a moral right to believe are equally unpromising. The possession of a right is often conceptually linked to the idea of <u>respect</u>. If you have a right to something, then I have the duty to respect this. But the idea of respect seems wholly inappropriate when we are talking about the right to believe. If you hold a stupid or abhorrent belief, then surely I have no duty to respect it. If you are a Nazi, for example, then I certainly have no duty to respect your beliefs. I can regard your beliefs with contempt, even if you never act on them. Nor, for the same reason, do I have any duty to be interested in your beliefs or help you promote them. Therefore, we cannot explain the idea of a right to believe in these sorts of familiar ways. The idea of a moral right to believe is, therefore, curious – perhaps even mysterious.

3. The Moral Right to Believe: An Analysis

There are, it seems, two possibilities. The first is that the idea of a moral right to belief is misguided: there is no such right. The second is that there is another account of this right that we have not yet considered. In the remainder of this dissertation, I am going to defend the second option. There is a coherent way of understanding the idea that we have a right to our beliefs. This way, however, is unlikely to be of comfort to the student who objected to being taught philosophy of religion. The right to believe, I shall argue, is a specific form of another, more familiar, right: the right to autonomy.

Imagine someone who holds a strange belief. Let's call her Olga. Olga believes the creator of the universe and all that dwell therein is a flying spaghetti monster: Pastafari (praise his noodly appendage!).[54] While strange, this belief is otherwise harmless. Olga does not try to convert unbelievers (still less slaughter them). She does not try to force schools to teach the

Pastafarian version of Creation. In fact, she tends to keep her belief pretty much to herself. She won't lie about it, but neither does she broadcast it.

Suppose, as a friend of Olga, you are worried about this strange belief, and would prefer that she didn't have it. There are various methods you have at your disposal to get her to not have it any more, ranging from gentle persuasion all the way up to lobotomy. It is pretty clear that Olga has the right to not be disabused of her belief by way of a forced lobotomy. To do that to her would violate her right to autonomy. The same is true of more subtle options such as brainwashing or even hypnosis.

Wilfred Sellars (1956) drew a useful distinction between what he called the 'space of causes' and the 'space of reasons'. What makes these forms of belief-change violations of Olga's autonomy is that they are merely causes of this change and not reasons for it. Causes, in this sense – 'mere' causes, we might call them – are things that happen to you or are done to you: lobotomies, brainwashing and hypnosis all fall into this category. But, belief-change can also be brought about by reasons. Reasons are things you have, not things that happen to you. The difference is like that between running for the sake of your health and running because someone has tied you to a car. Changing Olga's belief by way of reasons is quite different from changing it by way of causes. You would do this by persuading her that her belief is

54 Pastafari – the flying spaghetti monster that created heaven and earth – first appeared in 2005, in an open letter of protest to the decision of the Kansas State Board of Education to permit the teaching of intelligent design in its classrooms. Obviously, then, its appearance here is an anachronism. I include it because, while it does not appear in my father's dissertation itself, it does appear in his attempted abridgement of it.

contrary to widespread evidence. So, you point out facts pertaining to the fossil record, the Burgess Shale, the alternative Darwinian account of evolution and so on. You might not be successful in changing Olga's beliefs (she might think that the Burgess Shale is Pastafari's way of testing her, for example). But, if you succeed, you will have changed her beliefs by giving her reasons. Basically, you will have said to Olga: These are my reasons for not believing in Pastafari, and this is why I think they should be your reasons too.

Stripping Olga of a belief by applying causes violates her autonomy. That is why it is wrong. Stripping her of a belief by offering reasons does not violate her autonomy. That is why it is morally legitimate. With regard to the morality of taking away someone's beliefs, it's not so much what you do as the way you do it.

This idea can be used to explain, in part, what it means to have a moral right to a belief. You have a moral right to a belief in the sense that you have the right to not be denuded of your belief by methods that belong to the space of causes but only by ones that belong to the space of reasons. This is true no matter how silly or morally abhorrent the belief. We may, justifiably, prevent people acting on abhorrent beliefs (at least if their actions are likely to harm others), but we may not prevent them having these beliefs – if such prevention employs methods belonging to the space of causes.

This, however, is only half the story. It corresponds to Feinberg's idea that to have a moral right to something – a commodity, freedom or treatment, for example – is to have a claim against people that they do not prevent your access to that thing. However, as Feinberg's analysis makes clear, to have a moral right also involves a valid claim to something. This other element of Feinberg's view must be captured if we are to have the full story of the sense in which Olga has a moral right to her belief. The best way to understand this, I think, is as the mirror image of her claim against others.

Olga has a claim to her belief in this sense. She can defend it – but only in a certain way. She has the right to defend her belief, but not by slaughtering infidels, lobotomizing them or even hypnotizing them. She has the right to defend her belief using methods that belong to the space of reasons – methods of rational persuasion – rather than the space of causes. In other words, she is allowed to defend her beliefs only by using the same methods of rational persuasion that others are permitted to use against her when they try to get her to reject the belief.

Putting these two ideas together, we finally arrive at what it means to have a moral right to believe:

(1) Other people have a duty not to deprive you of your beliefs using methods that fall outside the space of reasons.

Other people can use persuasion but they have a duty not to use force.

(2) You have the right to defend your belief, in the public arena, using methods that belong to the space of reasons.

That is, you can defend your belief through rational persuasion but not force. The idea of a moral right to believe is the conjunction of these two claims.

One might wonder, not unreasonably, why any of this is important. I shall conclude this dissertation with some remarks on this issue of significance.

4. Conclusion: Why This Matters

At stake, ultimately, is the sort of society we live in and the sort of people that are going to populate this society. Our society is becoming increasingly diverse: in many ways, but most importantly for this discussion, ideologically. Ideological diversity is the direction in which all societies are heading, bar the fanatically repressive ones. The question most societies must, therefore, face is how to deal with ideological diversity – with the existence of different and often mutually incompatible belief systems within an overarching society.

Many people think that to criticize a person's beliefs is to show that person a lack of respect. I think that, in fact, the opposite is true. To fail to criticize the beliefs of another, when you think those beliefs are false and you can show why, is to show them a lack of respect. It is a failure to respect them as rational creatures, capable of amending their beliefs on the basis of new evidence – creatures sensitive to, creatures that inhabit, the space of reasons.

There is a tendency, slowly becoming endemic in our society, to confuse racism and what we might call creedism. This is a gross confusion. Racism is the belief that a person's race is a determinant of their moral worth. Lacking in any supporting evidence, and having pernicious social consequences, racism is a stupid and abhorrent ideology. Creedism, on the other hand, is the criticism of a person's beliefs and not, at least not directly, of the person who believes. That someone whose beliefs one criticizes may have a skin of a different colour is merely an accidental feature of this criticism. One is criticizing not their skin colour – that would be racist – but their beliefs. And one is not criticizing their beliefs because of their skin colour – that too would be racist. One is criticizing

111

their beliefs because of their <u>content</u>, and only their content: not the colour of the skin or any other irrelevant feature of the believer. Any diverse society must install creedism as one of its core governing values.

Criticism and toleration are not opposed. Once we think that they are, we are dealing with a kind of bigotry.[55] Some suppose that to criticize someone's beliefs evinces a lack of respect for that person. I have argued that the opposite is true. To suppose that criticism of beliefs should not be tolerated in an ideologically diverse society is to suppose that the people of that society are less than they are: that they are incapable of defending their beliefs by rational means. It is to assume, in effect, that they do not inhabit the space of reasons. Criticism, argument, disagreement and dissent: these must be the core values of the multicultural, multi-ideological society.

References

Feinberg, J. (1970) 'The Nature and Value of rights', in J. Narveson ed., <u>Rights, Justice, and the Bounds of Liberty: Essays in Social Philosophy</u> (Princeton, NJ: Princeton University Press).

Mill, J. S. (1859) <u>On Liberty</u> (London: Longman, Roberts & Green).

---

55 The word 'bigotry' does not appear in my father's dissertation and, with its echo of the expression 'soft bigotry of low expectations' associated with a certain G. W. Bush, one has to suspect that it, too, is an anachronism. When Bush used that expression, his concern was with the economically or socially disadvantaged rather than the ideologically different. Being a bed-wetting academic, of a reasonably stereotypical sort, I hate to sully my father through this sort of association. Nevertheless, it is clearly the sort of thing he had in mind.

Subfusc

Sellars, W. (1956) 'Empiricism and the Philosophy of Mind', in H. Feigl and M. Scriven eds., <u>Minnesota Studies in the Philosophy of Science</u>, Vol. I (Minneapolis: University of Minnesota Press).

1.

β+?+☺ Just kidding. But it is an astonishing thing to see one's father in the grip of this sort of childlike optimism. What a lovely world he describes, or presupposes. It was in the air, I suppose. Around this time Francis Fukuyama was declaring the end of history in the final, perfect form of government: Western liberal democracy. The Cold War had ended, the Berlin Wall had crumbled: who could blame either of them for the baseless optimism? How could my father know that time would be so unkind to his little tract?

2.

But perhaps he should have been more careful. Why would anyone think of humans as rational, autonomous individuals, capable of listening to, understanding and acting on reasons – when all the available evidence seems to point the other way? Certainly, he had no evidential right to this belief. A healthier respect for this evidence might have allowed him to see that criticism, argument, disagreement and dissent would be consigned to the dustbin of history, replaced by their contemporary successors: civility, decorum, conciliation and compliance. In my world, gross moral turpitude is one thing. But bad manners are something else entirely: far graver, far more unforgivable. The idea that criticism could be a way of showing respect – for a person if not his beliefs – has long been interred. Now we must, above all else, make sure we do not say or think anything too interesting. My father really didn't see this coming? He didn't anticipate our growing infantilization? That the truth of today would become just another product, whose purchase was an entirely personal decision? We don't care about logic, evidence or argument. We don't even have beliefs any more, not really. We no longer believe things; we merely 'like' them. We sift through this world of spurious information until we find someone who says something we like – perhaps because we think it already, usually for entirely non-rational reasons. And then we visit only places that say the same thing. But he knew this, of course. It's been this way for fifty years.

3.

But it was there, in these words he wrote: the thread from which everything ultimately unravels. My mother's Latin half informs me that, where humans are concerned, there are no exclusive categories, but just various shades of in-between. Rational autonomy is not something we have, but a limit we might, on our good days, approach or approximate. But there are so many more bad days. How much of a difference is there between a lobotomy and brainwashing? How much difference is there between brainwashing and a lifetime spent in front of a TV or computer screen: newspapers, magazines, blogs, chat forums, advertisements all trying to sell the truth – all trying to provide us with the critical 'nudge'. I'm not saying there is no difference between a rational, autonomous subject and a brainwashed automaton: the absence of a firm distinction is not the absence of a distinction. But it does all shade by degrees into the other. The consistently rational, autonomous subject was merely a dream of the Enlightenment, and we must all eventually wake from the dream.

114

Subfusc

The truth is that the world my father describes is just too harsh for our now delicate sensibilities. That one's beliefs may be constantly under scrutiny or attack, that one must always be prepared to refine and reformulate one's beliefs, that one must always be ready to respond to and, where necessary, refute the conceptually or evidentially hostile approaches of others, the knowledge that if one drops one whit below the best of one's abilities then one's cherished beliefs become vulnerable: it is an exacting life described here. There is little stomach for it any more. The life of contentment – ushered in by the vast material successes of liberal democracy – has scant tolerance for discomfort, whether bodily or intellectual. The result has been what Nietzsche called 'Russian fatalism': 'That fatalism without revolt which is exemplified by a Russian soldier who, finding a campaign too strenuous, finally lies down in the snow. No longer to accept anything at all, no longer to take anything, no longer to absorb, to cease reacting altogether.' As a result of this sickness, respect has been replaced, supplanted, by its anaemic descendant: civility.

When Hegel had put the last full stop to the last sentence of his rather large book *The Phenomenology of Spirit*, he believed that this moment marked the end of history – for history was simply the process of the universe becoming aware of itself through the human spirit, a process that, Hegel modestly believed, culminated in his writing of this book. As I put the final full stop to my own modest treatise, I could, of course, hardly harbour such lofty ambitions. I tried – believe me – but wasn't quite able to pull it off. But even if I had, any satisfying sense of Hegelian closure would be denied me by the little matter of final exams: exams that, my little bedside clock tells me, begin tomorrow, in around five hours' time.

A Good Life

I made sure my ensemble was within easy reach. A slate-grey suit with black shoes and socks, a white shirt and matching bow tie, a little black cloak that hung down as far as my arse and, last but not least, there was a black mortarboard. This is Oxford for you. This *regalium* is known as *subfusc*, and is required livery for Oxford undergraduate students when they are engaged in official university business, such as exams. I had been dressed like this when they first admitted me to the university, three years ago – via a ceremony conducted in Latin, it goes without saying. And I duly dusted it off every June for final exams. This would be the last time, one way or another.

A knock at my door: 'Yo. Myshkin. Dude. Phone call, bro.' That was Dave. He was from Cornwall, but somewhere along the way had obviously mistaken this for southern California. When I arrive at the house's communal phone, I am greeted by a familiar voice.

'Myshkin! Hey, it's Olga. How are you?'

'Olga, I was just thinking about you, sort of.'

'Oh, really, well I'm very flattered, sort of. Anyway, I figure you'll be finishing up at Oxford any day now. I'm going to India. Want to come with?'

10

Lotophagus

Live your life as a work of art.

Friedrich Nietzsche, *The Will to Power*

'You have any hashish? No? Do you want to buy some?'

The words were unremarkable. A not insignificant portion of the economy of the borderlands between Jammu-Kashmir and Himachal Pradesh was based on selling hashish to foreign travellers. Slightly more remarkable was the fact that the mouth from which these words emerged belonged to the superintendent of a rural police station – one to which Olga and I had recently been invited.

We had been on a bus to Srinagar, intending to rent a houseboat for a couple of weeks on Dal Lake. But at the border of the Jammu-Kashmir, the bus had been stopped. A pair of local policemen had been tasked with removing foreigners from the bus and, as it turned out, we were the only foreigners. Sitting on our backpacks in the rear of a Mahindra, we were driven to a whitewashed country station a few miles down the road. Shepherded into the station through a block containing four small cells – in one of them, a prisoner sat on the floor and smiled ruefully up at us as we shuffled past – we were taken to a smallish room, in the middle of which was a table and on the other side of which sat the superintendent. Somewhere in his forties, he was a jovial, slightly portly man, with Brylcreemed hair and a pencil-thin moustache. After some entirely expected questions, pleasantly delivered and, to any impartial observer, lacking in perceivable threat – 'Where are you from?' 'Where are you going?' – came the entirely unexpected follow-up. He smiled, and gestured for us to follow him. The station was larger than I originally thought – built around a square courtyard, like a Roman villa. This courtyard had been entirely given over to the growing of marijuana plants.

My overall disposition during this encounter with the superintendent was a function of several factors – all of them pulling in the same general direction. I had been smoking hash almost daily since our arrival in India a month ago.[56] Hash makes me paranoid and jittery. Being removed from a bus and escorted to a police station in a far-flung land will hardly act as an emollient. Finally, and decisively: sitting at the bottom of my backpack was a brick of hashish not much smaller than my fist. Not too long ago it was somewhat larger than my fist, but Olga and I had been dutifully working our way through it for the past month.

I was, therefore, perhaps not as stable as I might have been. 'They can see right through me! They can see right through me!' Thus I was informed by a little voice that had been chirruping away inside my head, a more or less constant refrain, on the ride to the station. And when I saw the cells I

56 The hypocritical old bastard!

went into an unadulterated no ifs, ands or buts *Midnight Express* mode: picturing myself as an old man in one of those four cells, smiling ruefully up at tourists as they walked past, unaware, towards the same fate as me. And that was the good scenario – being entirely devoid of brutal guards or sizeable sodomitic cellmates.

My relief upon hearing the superintendent's words was, therefore, palpable. But only for a moment – Mr Paranoia won't give up that easily. A trap, possibly? 'You're nicked, mate: attempting to buy narcotics from a senior police officer – stupid.' Perhaps they have one of these laws about possession being okay but purchase not? Some places do, I think. Maybe that was the sole purpose of the marijuana courtyard? But suppose I declined? The enraged officer, whose livelihood depended on supplementing his meagre salary as a servant of the state with lucrative sales of hashish to Westerners, would search my bag. I'd be banged up for possession, and forced to resume my post in the dark interior of *Midnight Express* territory.

It was, it goes without saying, a no-brainer. The contents of my backpack being what they were, there was only one real option. Say yes. Buy. And hope. But Mr Paranoia, perched on your shoulder, allowing you to see with his eyes, will always tempt you to ditch the politic in favour of some twisted alternative. Happily, there was a part of me that paranoia couldn't quite reach – somewhere in the vicinity of the navel, I believe – and after several vicious seconds of indecision, I graciously accepted the superintendent's offer. To the man's great credit, he neither incarcerated me nor did he even stiff me on the deal. I bought another brick at what I had come to recognize as a fair market price. As it turned out, the superintendent was merely a nice guy. That's all.

My backpack was a little heavier and my soul a little lighter. The two policemen that had picked us up now dropped us off at a nearby village where, they informed us, a bus would be passing through in the evening.

When Olga had telephoned me and asked me if I wanted to go to India, I had come into possession of what was, for me, an unusual amount of money. A little slice of luck – for me but not for my dear old Auntie Anwen, who had to die to make this happen. I suspect, from my vague childhood memories of Auntie Anwen, that she might have preferred that I do something more 'improving' with the £500 she was kind enough to bequeath me – something that didn't involve travelling to India and smoking my body weight in hash. She might have been right. There were many questionable facets of the way I spent my inheritance – not least its utter banality. The going-to-India-to-smoke-hash-and-find-yourself thing was pretty much par for the course for middle-class kids – into whose financial ranks I had been temporarily propelled by the death of this mostly unremembered aunt – in those days. In defence of my younger self: I was there for the sex, and for a girl I had never really stopped loving for my last two years at Oxford. Drugs I have always been able to take or leave. I had no objection to doing them, and sometimes quite enjoyed them, but I never missed them when I didn't do them. Hash, in particular, did little for me. I wasn't averse to the effects – if the quality was good enough, which was a pretty hit-or-miss matter most of the time – but I did think that Olga, and the stoners I knew, tended to overestimate their quality and importance.

The issue of its banality aside, are there any other reasons for condemning my choice of inheritance disposal? Some think that drugs are an evil to be avoided under all circumstances. Perhaps Auntie Anwen was one of them. I am told that when she was young, she 'signed the pledge' to never let alcohol pass her lips – although she apparently relented (in impressive fashion!) in her later years. Typically, people who think drugs are evil have a specific conception of 'drugs' in mind. Their claim is informed, as Wittgenstein once put it, by a one-sided diet of examples. Unless they belong to some non-standard religious sect – Christian Science, for example – they probably don't have in mind legal drugs used for medical purposes. Typically, they don't even mean legal drugs used for non-medical, recreational purposes – alcohol, Viagra and so on. Their sights are trained on illegal drugs used entirely for recreational purposes. I'll just call them 'drugs' – but you can take me as referring to the illegal and recreational variety.

Being recreational is not enough to make something morally wrong – unless one is convinced by the most antediluvian form of Protestantism that regards everything that distracts from work as wrong. But nor is being illegal, in itself, enough to make something morally wrong. The connection between morality and legality is often tenuous and sometimes positively uneasy. Many things that are immoral are perfectly legal – the law relegates many aspects of morality to the private sphere. Conversely, many societies can have laws that are positively immoral. Therefore, issues of criminality and morality need to be assessed separately.

A statute that is not enforced is a worthless statute. The most obvious method of enforcement of drug laws is criminal prosecution. If there is any substance to the idea that drugs should be illegal, this means that the use of these drugs – or, rather, their possession, since use would be difficult to establish unless caught in flagrante delicto – *must* be punishable by criminal prosecution.

The default assumption in the drugs debate is that since they are, currently, criminalized, the burden of proof is incurred by those who would like them decriminalized. They have to make the case, and those in favour of keeping drugs criminalized need only respond to this. In some ways this makes sense: any debate has to start somewhere, and where you currently find yourself doesn't seem like an unreasonable place. From another perspective, however, this placement of burden of proof seems perverse. In general, the criminalization of something should always be a last resort, and so the burden of proof should always be with the proponents of criminalization. The reason for this lies in a basic precept of any free society. As John Stuart Mill once put it, 'The only purpose for which power can be rightfully exercised over any member of a civilized community, against his will, is to prevent harm to others.'[57]

Drug users often harm themselves. The extent of this harm depends on their drug of choice, and so it is difficult to speak in general terms. But there is no doubt that some illegal and recreational drugs will permanently fuck you up – organ damage, death and other inconveniences. If Mill is correct, however, this is no argument for criminalization. It is a good argument for providing the addict with help, perhaps, but not for criminalizing his or her predilection. For criminalization to be a legitimate option, the harm must be to others and not merely to oneself. And this harm must be more than possible harm – more than the shadow of harm imagined. Almost any

57 John Stuart Mill, *On Liberty* (1859).

activity can possibly harm someone else. In no other case does the merely possible harm that an activity might cause provide a justification for criminalizing that activity. The harm must be, if not certain, at least likely.

There is, of course, an impressive amount of sheer human misery caused by the illegal drug industry – the murders and turf wars, the racketeering, the beatings, the collateral damage on bystanders and so on. Almost all of this, however, is the result of the industry being illegal. Take that away – have drugs produced by pharmaceutical companies and regulated by governmental bodies – and most of the associated violence will disappear. There may still be illegal operators producing and selling on the cheap. But these would become a mostly marginal irrelevance – like the makers of moonshine. Obviously, one cannot cite the violence and misery that accompany the illegality of drugs in support of an argument against their legalization. That would be question-begging.[58]

A more promising line of argument focuses on the financial costs of treating drug addicts – costs that are borne largely by those who do not use. We might also expand the notion of cost to include the emotional cost to a user's family members and friends. Decriminalization, it could be argued, would encourage large numbers of people to engage in behaviour that inflicts a cost – whether financial or emotional – on other people. Therefore, the condition of likely harm to others is met. Decriminalization would likely cause harm to other people as well as to the user.

This argument might work if criminalizing drugs were an effective deterrent. But the available evidence does not

58 See footnote 37 for the relevant technical sense of question-begging.

support this. In the United States, nearly 100 million people have used illegal drugs at some point in their lives, and roughly 15 million have used them in the past twelve months. That is 100 million people that criminalization has failed to deter. The vast majority of these people do not, of course, become addicts – just like the vast majority of people who drink alcohol do not become drunks. Nevertheless, one might argue, decriminalization might encourage the other 200 or so million of the population to experiment. But it is difficult to find any evidence for this claim. In Europe, where being caught in possession is far less likely to result in criminal proceedings, drug use is actually lower than in the US. Moreover, survey after survey reveals the same thing. When a person starts using drugs, the possibility of their being caught and prosecuted plays little or no role in their deliberations. And when they stop using, this also has little to do with the fear of criminal prosecution and everything to do with acquiring some new responsibility – usually a new job or a new member of the family.

Nevertheless, one might argue, while the criminalization of drugs does not directly deter drug users, it does deter them indirectly – by inflating the price of drugs. Cartels have to buy planes, submarines; they must bribe officials and so on. This cost is then passed on to the consumer. This argument is unconvincing. If legally produced via pharmaceutical companies – who, by the way, first marketed heroin and invented LSD – then drugs would be subject to government taxation, and the level of taxation could be set at whatever level is deemed to be appropriately discouraging.

Criminalization of an activity is a last resort, and should be adopted only if the activity is likely to significantly harm those who do not engage in it. This condition is not met in the case of illegal recreational drugs. The primary harm done is to the user himself, and there is no evidence that criminalization will reduce harm to others. The case for decriminalization is, therefore, a strong one.[59]

The legality of drug use is one thing, its morality quite another. The claim that one ought not to use drugs is ambiguous: it can be understood morally or prudentially. Understood in the prudential sense, there is an obvious reason why one should not use at least some drugs: as hitherto mentioned, drugs can seriously mess you up. Prudentially speaking, I'm actually pretty anti-drugs. Many claim that marijuana is perfectly safe, but I know enough long-term users to be sceptical of this claim. But the prudential case against using drugs is then tied to deficiencies of drug design. Suppose a new drug is invented – one entirely lacking in the usual malign side effects. It is not addictive. It has no deleterious health consequences. It doesn't interfere

---

59 The arguments of this section appear to be heavily indebted to Douglas Husak, *Legalize This!* (Verso, 2002). It's both quaint and ironic to see my father so worried about marijuana use, given the vast spate of legalizations and decriminalizations that occurred worldwide in the first quarter of the twentieth century. With regard to marijuana, the legalizers routed their opponents. Ironically, it was the old who led the way. Turns out: when someone has been smoking hash for most of his or her life, they are not going to suddenly start disapproving of it just because their membership of the American Association of Retired Persons has arrived in the mail. Even more interesting, however, is that my father nowhere acknowledges that this has happened. For all one can tell, he seems completely unaware of it. This is one symptom of a tendency that is becoming increasingly prevalent in his writing. Since he is writing about a given time in his life, he can draw only on arguments and evidence available at that time. But an argument against or for criminalization is not restricted in this way. My father is clearly having problems with temporal perspective. The time at which he is writing is repeatedly collapsing into the time *about* which he writing.

with your ability to hold down a decent job. It doesn't even give you a hangover. What it does do is fill you with feelings of intense pleasure, and that is all. In this circumstance, the prudential case against drug use would collapse.

Nevertheless, there might still be a moral case. If you took this drug, would you be doing anything morally wrong? According to hedonism – which claims that the highest good attainable by humans is happiness – you would not. On the contrary, you would be doing something very, very right. It is easy to understand the rationale for hedonism. You might want money because you think it will buy you happiness. You might want health because it is truly difficult to be happy without it. But you don't want happiness for any other reason. You want to be happy just to be happy. Happiness is where the chain of reasons – the wanting one thing only for the sake of something else – stops. Therefore, most have thought, happiness is intrinsically or inherently valuable: valuable for what it is in itself and not for other things it might get you. As such, it is the most important thing for which humans can strive.

What is happiness? Here, things quickly become murky. Hedonism originated in various Greek schools of philosophy, Epicureanism in particular. But the ancient conception of happiness was quite different from the modern. The Greek word for happiness was *eudaimonia*, which literally means 'possessed by a good demon'. *Eudaimonia* had little to do with feeling good, and far more to do with attaining certain sorts of excellence – moral, intellectual, aesthetic and athletic. This is so different from the way we think of happiness today; we should admit that the ancients – the inventors of hedonism – weren't even talking about the same thing. Today, we think of happiness as a feeling of some sort akin to pleasure, but perhaps, in some way that is difficult to pin down, more 'deep and meaningful'. This is the modern conception of happiness – the *hedonic* conception – and it came to prominence a mere three hundred or so years ago.

It is difficult to pinpoint any clear and convincing difference between happiness, in this hedonic sense, and pleasure. Delightful spasms of pleasure – Olga and I certainly had our share of those during our months in India[60] – are not generally elevated to the rank of happiness. Whether this is justified is unclear. If it were simply ephemerality that demotes a feeling to the enlisted ranks of pleasure rather than to the officer class of happiness, then we could simply imagine an orgasm that went on long enough, or a new and wonderful drug where one hit produces feelings of pleasure that last a lifetime. On the other hand, if another tack is desired, someone who insists that happiness is pleasure can always be stubborn: happiness only comes in moments. Happiness is always a delightful spasm, or a transient eruption.

When the hedonic conception of happiness was born in the utilitarian movement of the eighteenth century, the general consensus was that happiness is a form of pleasure. Its advocates quickly had a choice to make. Does any sort of pleasure qualify? Jeremy Bentham, the father of utilitarianism, answered 'yes'. Pleasure is pleasure: it doesn't matter what sort of pleasure it is or what produces it. His follower John Stuart Mill disagreed. There are different forms pleasure can take, Mill argued, and only some of these qualify as happiness. 'It is better to be a human being dissatisfied than a pig satisfied; better to be Socrates dissatisfied than a fool

---

60 Another image that I would happily pour bleach on my brain just to forget.

satisfied. And if the fool, or the pig, are of a different opinion, it is because they know only their side of the question.'[61] This, of course, raises several issues. Most notably: why does Mill assume he knows what it is like to be a pig? Or, for that matter: why does Mill assume he knows what it is like to be Socrates?

For Olga and me, the stakes were high. And yes, I suppose the clumsy pun was more or less intended. If Bentham is right and pleasure is happiness, irrespective of its quality, then we were both undeniably happy during these months spent travelling. If happiness is the highest good, then, in our transient spasms of pleasure we attained the highest good in life – the meaning of life in any reasonable sense of that expression – and all at the tender ages of twenty-one and twenty-two.

Unfortunately for us, Mill would have taken a rather dim view of our hedonistic sorties. Better to be Socrates dissatisfied than a strung-out hippie satisfied – or a temporarily satisfied testosterone-monkey, for that matter. And if the hippie or monkey is of a different opinion, well, we know how that goes. Pleasure comes in various forms, some higher than others. The pleasure that goes with listening to a Chopin nocturne, or reading one of Sophocles' tragedies, is higher. The pleasure that goes with sex or hash is lower. Broadly speaking, it is the intellectual pleasures that are higher and the base bodily pleasures that are lower. It is easy to see what Mill has in mind, and why he might have this in mind. We wouldn't want to say that someone who, for example, spends many of his or her waking hours masturbating has attained the highest good in life.

61 John Stuart Mill, *Utilitarianism* (1863), Chapter 4.

Nevertheless, Mill's view is, I think, disingenuous: in effect, he tacitly abandons the idea that happiness is the ultimate good. I can explain via a perusal of my travel reading: Martin Heidegger's *Being and Time*, Jean-Paul Sartre's *Being and Nothingness* and Edmund Husserl's *Ideas Pertaining to a Pure Phenomenology and to a Phenomenological Philosophy* (Volume 1) – precisely the sort of Continental nonsense they would never let me read at Oxford. I carried those books all over India, and believe me those are heavy-ass books, especially *Ideas* 1. I didn't really understand them very well: the language they employed was unfamiliar and their mode of argumentation would not even be acknowledged as such in the institution that had given me my degree. But I assumed I got the gist, and during my frequent bong sessions with Olga I would often discourse, at immoderate length, on the ideas they contained. From this, I have to admit, I obtained great pleasure. Olga? That is a different matter. Let's just say she raised no objections.

Getting high is not like masturbating. It may not actually be a highly intellectual undertaking, but it can certainly seem that way to the person getting high. This is the key to the dilemma facing Mill. Hindsight informs me that I didn't really understand those books at all. My hash-fuelled speculations were pleasurable but intellectually inept: they were not intellectual pleasures because they failed to meet, let us call them, appropriate standards of competence. Not all things that seem like intellectual activities really are intellectual activities. Anyone who has ever got high knows this – at least, they do in the cold light of day. Therefore, not all things that seem like higher pleasures really are higher.

I was, in effect, the satisfied fool – but a fool who thought he was Socrates. Bentham wouldn't have cared: pleasure is pleasure, whether higher or lower, whether you're high or actually understand *Being and Time*. But Mill, on the other hand, did care. And that is why he can't consistently claim that pleasure – even in its higher form – can be the highest good. To see why, compare this fool who thought he was Socrates with the real Socrates – or at least a version of the real Socrates. This version is a peculiarly dispassionate Socrates, who engages in immaculate reasoning about abstruse matters of truth, justice, knowledge and reality: reasoning that is largely flawless and certainly meets any realistic standards of competence. This Socrates, however, obtains no pleasure from this. Instead, since he understands only too well the limits of his knowledge, his musings engender more a sense of dissatisfaction than pleasure. Which is it better to be? Socrates dissatisfied, or the satisfied fool? Mill, as he makes clear, sides with the dissatisfied Socrates.

Once he does this, however, he must abandon the idea that pleasure – even of the higher variety – is the greatest good. For Mill, it is the standards of competence that are doing all the work. This is the dog in Mill's version of utilitarianism; pleasure is merely the tail. When he says it is better to be Socrates dissatisfied than a fool satisfied, Mill makes it clear that he will always side with the standards of competence that make a pleasure higher than the agreeable feelings that make it pleasure. The agreeable feelings themselves can never be the highest good. That accolade belongs to the standards of competence to which these feelings must conform.

The result is that Mill's view is not really hedonism – not in the modern sense, at least. It is something else masquerading as hedonism. Mill's distinction between higher and lower pleasures was an unnecessary distraction. If you are a hedonist you must believe that happiness is pleasure. And you must also believe that pleasure is simply pleasure.

Once we have removed Mill's distraction, it is easy to see just how implausible is Bentham's idea that any pleasure will do as an account of the highest good in human life. One would have to be a wilful curmudgeon to resent Olga and me these snatched moments of pleasure. But there is a difference between a pleasure briefly taken and a pleasure that comes to dominate. Suppose this were to go on for the rest of our lives. We never come back from India. We spend our lives in the Himalayas, and continue having sex and smoking hash for the rest of our days.

In Greek mythology, the Lotus Eaters – the *Lotophagi* – were a tribe of people living on an island off the north coast of Africa. Their diet consisted almost entirely of the fruit of the lotus tree – a powerful narcotic – and the Lotus Eaters spent much of their lives in a state of blissful semiconsciousness. If hedonism were true and happiness were simply pleasure, the Lotus Eaters would exemplify the highest and most desirable form of human existence. Perhaps some people think this is true. Odysseus did not: he drove his crew off the island of the Lotus Eaters demonstrating, very clearly, that he would not have agreed with Bentham on the question of the human good.

I am going to have to side with Odysseus. Imagine a creature that is capable of only two things: experiencing pain and pleasure. That is all it can do: it can't move, it can't see and it can't think. If you wanted to promote the welfare of this creature, then all you could do would be to place it in a situation where it experienced as much pleasure and as little pain as possible. This best possible of all lives for our

131

imagined creature would be a sad waste of a life for a child. The reason is that the child has far more capabilities than the creature: the ability to walk and run, to think and reason, to talk, to write, to argue, to empathize and sympathize, to play, to paint, to love, and many more.[62] If we focus just on the relative measures of pain and pleasure in the child's life, then we leave undeveloped all the other capacities and abilities, actual and potential, the child possesses. The life that resulted would be a travesty.

If we had become Lotus Eaters, Olga and I, the same would have been true of our lives. The hash would eventually have taken its toll – it always does. But even if it hadn't – even if hash were completely and utterly harmless – a life lived in this way is a long way away from the best life a human can live. Tucked away in my backpack, beneath *Being and Time*, beneath *Being and Nothingness*, beneath *Ideas 1* – beneath, even, the fist-sized brick of hashish – is another, much smaller, book: Friedrich Nietzsche's *The Birth of Tragedy out of the Spirit of Music*. I didn't understand this either. 'It is only as an aesthetic phenomenon,' Nietzsche wrote, 'that existence and the world are eternally justified.' I didn't understand this because I had not yet lived. To see life as a whole, that is the most difficult of necessities. To have experienced what life has to offer and to understand as visceral certainty, rather than intellectual possibility, what it has in store. To have been elevated, by life, to heights undreamed of, and then beaten down again to depths unplumbed. There is a scribbled note of Nietzsche's, never published in his lifetime: 'Live your

62 This argument seems to owe much to the ideas of Martha Nussbaum. See, for example, her *Frontiers of Justice: Disability, Nationality, Species Membership* (Belknap Press, 2006).

life as a work of art.' The essence of any great work of art is restraint rather than licence; balance rather than abandon. A beautiful life is moving, inspiring, dramatic and colourful. It has suspense, conflict, crisis, courage and, perhaps, resolution. It will contain triumph and disaster, victory and defeat. The very best lives are unforgettable. An ugly life is clumsy, uninspired and eminently forgettable. The tragedy of the life of the Lotus Eater is that it is, fundamentally, an ugly life.

11

Rich

Ill fares the land, to hastening ills a prey,
Where wealth accumulates, and men decay.

Oliver Goldsmith, *The Deserted Village*

I deal in magic. I agree to buy a commodity, C, at a certain future date for a certain specified price. You agree to supply this commodity on that date for that price. However, no commodity will ever change hands, at least not between us. Or, at least, if it does, one or both of us has seriously miscalculated. I never wanted the commodity in the first place. Neither did you when you bought it. I wanted the future in order to sell it to someone else – before I have paid for all of it, and at a profit of course. They don't want it either – they will do exactly the same thing. And so on. Nothing ever gets sold. Nothing ever gets bought. And everyone makes money.

It's early evening, and I am in Blacks – my club. I love saying that, because, in my head, it still sounds weird. ('Why don't you join me at my club?' I've been dying to utter those words but the opportunity has, sadly, not yet arisen.) Everyone should have a club these days, or so I was told on my arrival in London. And a few days of standing ten deep at West End bars convinced me of the truth of it. If you like gently decaying elegance – shabby chic, with a discernible leaning towards shabby – you could do a lot worse than Blacks. If you are a media type or left-leaning journo, then Blacks is definitely the place for you. But it is a rather idiosyncratic choice for a junior derivatives trader. I could have opted for the surprisingly reasonable rates of the Oxford and Cambridge Club, but – to be honest – it is a little too suggestive of God's Waiting Room. The City of London Club – pricey, but I declined largely on existential rather than financial grounds. If you took the greatest writers and poets the world has ever seen, locked them in a room together and told them not to even think of coming out until they had produced the goods, the product of their collective pen would still not even begin to capture just how much I hate my job.

I get up at 5.00 a.m. There is a gym in my building, and I like to get in a quick workout most mornings. I arrive at my office around 7.00 a.m., when I will switch on my five screens and log into more than ten different programs. I arrange for each data feed to automatically update me on any news pertaining to the names I trade and on any pertinent broader market developments. I check to make sure my connections to all relevant exchanges are functioning properly. I calculate hedge limits and enter them into the order book. All this must be done by 8.45 a.m. The market opens at 9.00 a.m. and many of the day's juicier trades will be going down around 9.01. The rest of the day will comprise me clicking on a mouse and updating code. Lunch – there isn't any. There is no break – I might come back and find myself a hundred million in the hole. Instead, lunch is entirely a right-hemisphere affair: a cup of soup in my left hand, a mouse in my right. I usually finish around 7.00 p.m. Stressful? For some it isn't, for others it is. Unfortunately, I am one of the others. Some of my colleagues breeze through their days as if they haven't a care in the world. If this is an act, I am as yet a poor actor. And if it is an acquired skill, I have yet to acquire it. The known variables I can handle: there are straightforward algorithms to deal with them. I condense the underlying instrument's price, calculate the strike, the contract duration, prevailing interest rates, stock borrowing rates and dividend expectations. It's the volatility that kills me. But that is what I'm here for. We are known as 'vol' traders. The reductionist algorithmic stuff: a suitably trained monkey could do that. The volatility is where all the action is. You want to get as big a spread as possible, but if you quote too wide no one will trade with you because your prices are uncompetitive, and if you quote too narrow you will get picked off by a pronounced unidirectional market swing. This is where the judgement is required – in maximizing risk/reward ratios. At least, they *call* this judgement. I tend to think of it more as a monstrous and unjustifiable risk. The stress is killing me: I'm twenty-two and I swear I have an ulcer.

This is a strictly short-term deal, I tell myself (over and over again). Two years: two years, tops. Get in, get the money, get out. I like to think of my life on the model of a wrongful conviction. I go to jail for a couple of years, suffer considerably, but then am released with a massive compensation payment. Blacks – that is my hour in the exercise yard: something that will have to do until my time is served. After a day of this, I'm hardly going to go to the City of London Club and relive it all over again. Good for my career, without a doubt – I know my colleagues take my lack of socializing as a sign that I'm not going to cut it. But, as I say, I don't see this as a career. Blacks: my anti-globalization protest to the City of London Club's G8. That's my first reason for choosing it. The second reason is that those bastards at the Soho Club wouldn't take me. They hate City boys.

A further, unanticipated, bonus: at Blacks people have no idea of who I am or what I do. And so I get to eavesdrop on delightful conversations: passionate expressions of abhorrence for my profession and, by extension I suppose, for me. Those irresponsible bankers taking all those risks. There should be laws. They should be locked up. Yeah, yeah, maybe we should. You've had your Black Monday and your Black Wednesday: but believe me, boy, you haven't seen anything yet. But, I ask you, why would anyone live like this? Why would anyone put himself through it? Why would anyone do this without some compensating factor: such as, off the top of my head, the possibility of amassing a truly offensive amount of wealth?

I deal in magic. For money is what magic became when no one believed in magic any more. Magic doesn't go away that easily. Like magic, money does not need to obey the laws of the known universe. At least, we practitioners of money – we versed in the dark arts of wealth – can see no obvious reason why it should. On my way to Blacks, I passed a man carrying a placard: 'Jesus has returned!' When I got to work I did a quick calculation of how much Jesus would be worth on his return if he had invested wisely – or if someone had done it for him. Suppose that Judas, overcome with guilt, decided to put aside his thirty shekels of silver for Jesus on his return. If we assume a compound interest rate of 5 per cent and an initial exchange rate of 1 shekel = £40, then after two thousand years the sum owed to Jesus would be just over one octillion

Great British Pounds – that is, 1 with 44 zeros after it. If, during this time, the human race had managed to colonize the entire universe, there still wouldn't be enough wealth – on current ways of estimating it – to pay Jesus what he was owed. If you paid him out in £1 notes the volume of this pile of money would be around the same as that of the solar system. So, he would, at the very least, need a rather large bank to stash his earnings.

Money does not obey the laws of the natural universe. Everything else – everything that is not money – obeys the laws of thermodynamics: any closed system tends to the maximum disorder and energy can be neither created nor destroyed, merely converted from one form into another. Together these two laws have one clear and inevitable consequence. Things get worse. Things break down. They get smaller. As far as the rest of the universe goes: you can't win and, in the long run, you can't break even.[63] But money doesn't obey these laws. Things that do not obey the laws of the known universe are not real. Money is not real. It is magic. That is why it is so powerful.

I'm eavesdropping on a discussion. The topic is foreign aid, and the speaker is, predictably enough – we are in Blacks – bemoaning the fact that the developed world gives so little of it. I am transported back some years, to an argument I first encountered in Oxford.[64]

Suppose you are walking to work one day, and you come across a small child drowning in a shallow ornamental

---

63 The expression is due to Andrew Simms, *Cancel the Apocalypse* (Little, Brown, 2013).
64 Peter Singer, 'Famine, affluence and morality', *Philosophy and Public Affairs,* Vol. 1, No. 1 (1972), pp. 229–43.

pond.[65] No one else is around to help. You can easily save the child at small cost to yourself. The pond is too shallow to provide any conceivable threat to you. All that it will cost you is some wet clothes and possibly a late arrival at work. Should you – do you have a moral obligation to – save the child? It's a no-brainer. Think of the moral monster you would be if you declined to help. The underlying moral principle seems to be this: if you can prevent something really bad happening without sacrificing anything of comparable importance, then you should do so.

Some people live in conditions of absolute poverty. This is not the sort of poverty we often have to deal with in this country. I grew up in a comparatively deprived part of the country – in a town that some might call a shithole. The house of my childhood was a two-up, two-down worker's cottage, with a small extension built on the back for the bathroom and toilet. A pretty basic affair, you might think. I know some of my colleagues might conclude that I had an impoverished upbringing. Perhaps that's true, although it never really felt that way. But if it is, the sort of poverty in question is relative, rather than absolute, poverty. The house didn't fall down when the wind blew, or get washed away when the rain fell. We had enough food to eat: I can never remember going to bed hungry – a little peckish sometimes, but never really hungry. The taps were a reliable source of clean drinking water. Unlike my grandfather, I didn't have to join my father at the pit to provide enough money for the family to get by. When I got ill, I could visit a doctor. And if I got even sicker, there was a hospital not too far away in Abergavenny.

65 As you might remember, I also used this scenario in questioning one of my mother's defences of abortion. Singer was the inventor of this scenario in the article cited on p. 138.

A Good Life

People who live in absolute poverty have been handed a much shittier end of the stick than this. The houses they live in are shanties, and may have to be rebuilt every time there is a serious storm. They will probably be short of food for part or all of the year – sometimes having to choose between feeding themselves and feeding their children. They will never be able to save any money – and when things go wrong, as they often will, a moneylender is their only option. They won't be able to send their kids to school – even if there is a school nearby – because they need them to work. And there are no taps yielding clean, potable water. They will have to walk a considerable distance to find that – maybe miles. Their prospects of receiving effective health care when they need it are slim. The average life expectancy of people living in such conditions is around fifty – compared to around seventy-eight for the likes of me and other citizens of the developed world.

My poverty was relative – and that is usually the way it is in the developed world. But much poverty in the developing world is absolute. The World Bank estimates that around 1.4 billion people worldwide are living in conditions of absolute poverty.[66] And these people don't seem to be a million miles away – morally speaking – from the child drowning in an ornamental pond. The argument for helping these people parallels the argument for helping the child.

66 It is actually significantly higher than that now – closer to two and a half billion of the planet's nine billion human population. Nor is this sort of poverty any longer restricted to developing nations. Its creep into ever growing pockets of the developed world has been pronounced. The figures my father cites, and the overall picture underlying it, would have been true in the early part of this century, up until around 2015, when the population was a mere 7 billion or so. It is possible my father started work on this chapter as long ago as this.

First, there is the underlying principle: if you can prevent something bad without sacrificing anything of comparable importance, you ought to do it. Second, there is a moral claim that seems difficult to deny: absolute poverty is bad. Third, there is a factual claim: there is some absolute poverty we can prevent without sacrificing anything of comparable importance. Together, these lead to an obvious conclusion: we ought to prevent this absolute poverty.

'Ought' can sometimes sound a little bloodless. How much of a moral difference is there between killing someone and failing to save them? Would I be any more culpable if, instead of letting the child drown, I waded out into the water to finish him off myself? We often think there is a vast moral gulf between acts and omissions – between what we do and what we fail to do. According to the 'acts and omissions doctrine', there is an intrinsic moral difference between acting and failing to act. It would be very convenient if the acts-and-omissions doctrine were true. If it is not, then the scope of our moral obligations suddenly becomes much bigger. We are now not only responsible for what we do but also for what we fail to do. And it is possible to not do so very many things. At any given time I can do only one or two things – probably one, actually, since I am a man. But, at that same time, I can be not doing an indefinite number of things. Most of our lives are spent not doing things. It would be very convenient if the acts-and-omissions doctrine were true. Unfortunately, it is not.

There is often a significant moral difference between murdering someone and failing to save them. This difference is not in consequences – the person is dead, either way – but in intentions. Murdering someone requires malicious intent.

But the failure to save a murder victim might be the result of a variety of things. You might have no idea that a murder was being committed. Or, if you saw the murder occurring, you might have been too scared or panicked to act. Or you decided, after cool reflection, that the risks involved in the attempt to save the person were just too high. Not all of your reasons are necessarily edifying ones. But they are not as bad as the deliberate attempt to end someone's life. So, in this sort of case, there does seem to be a moral difference between acting and failing to act.

These considerations, however, do not support the acts-and-omissions doctrine. The doctrine does not simply say there is a moral difference between acts and failures to act. Everyone knows that. Rather, it makes a much stronger claim. There is an intrinsic moral difference between acts and omissions. The key is the word 'intrinsic'. What this means is that there is a moral difference between acts and failures to act that cannot be traced to differences in intentions or consequences (where these latter sorts of difference are merely 'extrinsic'). Whether you murder someone or fail to save him, the consequences are obviously the same: the victim is dead. But, usually, the intentions are different. Therefore, there are extrinsic differences between the act and the failure to act. To properly evaluate the acts-and-omissions doctrine we need to imagine a scenario where both the intentions and the consequences are the same. The consequences of the act and the failure to act are the same. And the intentions of the person who either acts or fails to act are also the same.

We can imagine this by putting a little more meat on the bones of the child-drowning-in-the-pond scenario. Suppose the child drowning in the pond is my nephew: a nephew I have decided to kill because he stands between me and a

considerable inheritance. Knowing his predilection for playing at an isolated pond, I resolve to follow him there and
drown him. This thought experiment now branches into two
possible scenarios. The first unfolds as planned. I arrive at
the pond, find my nephew there, and duly drown him. In the
second scenario, as I arrive I see my nephew slip, hit his
head on a rock and lie, unconscious, face down in the water.
If I pull him out, he will no doubt survive. But I leave him to
drown.[67]

Is my behaviour any better in the second scenario? Am I
any less culpable? I suspect not. In the above example, the
consequences of my act and failure to act are the same in
both cases: my nephew is dead. But also the same in both
scenarios are my intentions: I go to the pool with the intention of seeing my nephew dead. When consequences and
intentions are the same for both act and failure to act, the
implication is clear: both the act and the omission have the
same moral status. If I didn't exactly murder my nephew in
the second scenario, I did something just as bad. We might
even say that I murdered my nephew in both cases: once by
acting, and once by failing to act. And if we want to quibble
about the precise use of the term 'murder', we should remember that it would make little difference to my nephew.

We are not murdering those living in absolute poverty. We
are 'saved' by our intentions. There is no malicious intent in
our failure to act. These people that die on our TV and computer screens each day – it is not as if we want them dead, or
are taking active steps to ensure that they die. Rather, we

---

67 This classic thought experiment was originally devised by James
  Rachels, 'Active and passive euthanasia', *New England Journal of
  Medicine*, Vol. 292, No. 2 (1975), pp. 78–80.

simply cannot be bothered or, more charitably, do not feel empowered or able, to save them. We are like someone who stands and watches the child drown simply because it seems like too much trouble to do anything about it, or we don't feel able to do anything about it. We can't cite ignorance as an excuse. These people die in front of our telepresent eyes. All we have to fall back on is our callous indifference or our staggering incompetence. We may not be murderers, but we are not that far off. And what we are, precisely, makes little difference to those who live in deprivation and die prematurely because of it.

It is a truism that morality is about doing good things. And however you measure good – whether it's via happiness, pleasure, satisfied preferences or their converse, the absence of misery and so on – the basic truth seems unavoidable: my money can do a lot more good for them – the absolute poor – than it can for me. The most effective aid organizations can save a life for between £400 and £800. A life. Around £160 will provide life-transforming surgery for a child born with a cleft palate. You imagine the difference this would make to that child. For me: £160 – I could piss that away in a West End bar in a couple of hours, and I wouldn't even notice it had gone. Or, consider my membership of the club in which I now ponder these issues. At £1,835 per annum it is relatively modest by local standards. But imagine the good this money could do if I were to send it to someone who lived in extreme poverty. I could save four and a half lives with that, and fix eleven and a half cleft palates. I'd lose a moderately agreeable place to unwind after work. But what is that against the lives I would save or transform?

It doesn't stop there, of course. I can afford to part with a lot more than £1,835. If I were to give away half of my salary, I could still live very comfortably. Everything is relative, of course. My small but fashionable apartment in trendy new Canada Water would have to go, but I could more than eke out a living in some less fashionable London suburb.[68] Even Croydon would be a step up from a Third World shanty town. If I gave away the bulk of my salary, I'd still be a sizeable step up from absolute poverty.

The conclusion seems clear and compelling: I should give and give until I reach the Rubicon of marginal utility, the point where the drawbacks that accrue to me from more giving are less than the benefits garnered by any of those who receive. Some point will be reached – it is not entirely clear where it is, but there must be such a point – where the misery caused to me by the loss of more money will outweigh the happiness engendered in any recipient of this money. But even if I stop well short of this point, the moral seems clear. I should be giving away a lot more of my money than I actually do.

*

68 This tendency has been building for a while. Canada Water hasn't been new since the early 1990s – this is the time about which my father is writing. But the World Bank figures that he cites a few pages ago would have been true for the first ten or fifteen years of the twenty-first century – perhaps, then, true of the time at which he was writing. I mentioned earlier (footnote 59) that my father seemed to be having trouble with temporal perspective. Now these problems have seemingly become more pronounced. His tendency, as I mentioned, is to slide between the perspective *at* which he is writing and the time *about* which he is writing. Worse: there is no clear time *at* which he is writing. On the contrary, there is good reason to suspect that this book may have been written over the course of many years. He is writing *through* time rather than *at* a time. It is possible that this slippage of temporal perspectives is a device intentionally adopted by my father. But I think it more likely that he is becoming lost in time. My father is slowly being cut adrift from his temporal moorings. I shall have to address and assess this tendency – its significance and impact – soon.

The argument is logically compelling. Unfortunately – or, perhaps, fortunately, depending on how you look at it – this argument has to work in a world that runs not on logic but on magic, and pitch-black magic at that. Money will always firmly resist our best and sincere attempts to use it for good. Let us suppose I earn £100,000. Suppose also that, from a little research about the relative standards of living in my country and others, I judge that I can safely give £90,000 to the absolute poor without reaching the point of marginal utility. It doesn't matter whether this specific figure is the right one: it is the principle that is important. If I gave this money away, the quality of my life might decline con-siderably, but the quality of the lives of those my money touches would improve enormously – to a degree that out-weighs the diminution in quality of my life. £90,000 can make a huge difference to many lives in the developing world if it is distributed judiciously. However, I can donate £90,000 only because I earn £100,000 – I live and work in a society that pays me this much for what I do. My future, unfortunately, is not always in my hands. I might be fired. Or some global economic catastrophe caused by halfwits like me who pretend they know what they're doing might result in widespread job loss and drastic wage reduction.[69] Bad news again for the absolute poor, who would have received £90,000 from me – and from others similarly

---

69 It did, of course, in the global financial meltdown of 2008. That my father does not mention this is, I think, symptomatic of the problems I mention in footnotes 59 and 68. In this case, because he is writing about his life in, by my calculations, the mid-1990s (certainly post-1992, since he mentions Black Wednesday earlier in this chapter), he feels unable to comment on subsequent events, even though the per-spective he adopts in developing his arguments is not restricted to this time, and his arguments are, accordingly, tenseless.

endowed and inclined – but now have to make do with, say, £40,000.

The same effect can be achieved by means less dramatic than global financial meltdown. My £1,835 club membership, for example, goes to help pay the wages of Frank the doorman and Harry the barman. If they don't have wages, they can't buy things. And if their wages are reduced, they can buy fewer things. But then, the livelihoods of other people – livelihoods that depend on Frank and Harry buying things – also diminish. And so, if any of those people were inclined to give to overseas aid, the amount they could contribute would thereby decline.

There is a general principle at work in these examples. Suppose there are two societies: let us call them Rich and Poor. Rich is a developed society where the majority of people live in a state of absolute affluence. Poor is a developing one where most live in a state of absolute poverty. The more money migrates from Rich to Poor, the less money remains in Rich. Then, however, the buying power of people in Rich reduces, and wages will drop. But if this happens, less money is available in future to be transferred from Rich to Poor. Of course, it may also be true that the cost of food and other aid Rich might send to Poor is also reduced – when wages are systematically reduced, the cost of living sometimes comes down too (although, unfortunately, rarely as much as the reduction in wages). But that isn't going to help much. At best, we would have arrived at a situation of stalemate. The policy of donating a portion of one's income to Poor would have achieved nothing. The policy is, in effect, a self-undermining one. If everyone does it, then soon no one will be able to do it. The more Rich gives to Poor, the less Rich will be able to give to Poor.

A qualification: this worry is genuine only if the problems Poor faces are chronic rather than acute. If a problem is acute – and so is the sort of thing that can be solved, definitively, by throwing money at it – then I'm all for throwing money at it. This is a minor qualification only. The problems faced by Poor will rarely be acute. A child is born with a cleft palate. An acute problem, you might think: £160 will end it – transforming a child's life forever. But another child will already have been born with a cleft palate, and my prior act of redistribution will affect my ability to help him or her. Most acute problems are merely manifestations of chronic ones. As such, Rich's efforts to deal with these must be subject to this one unforgiving principle: the more Rich gives the less Rich will be able to give.[70]

The principle of marginal utility is going to be one of the first casualties of this principle.

The policy of Rich giving to Poor until the benefits for Poor are outweighed by the deficits for Rich is unworkable – not because Rich would never agree to it (although that is very likely too) but because it undermines itself. A more realistic principle would be this: Rich should give today only up to the point where it will be able to give at least as much tomorrow.

Even the 'I' of yesterday – the 'I' of these thoughts' devising, the 'I' who was a morally dissolute derivatives trader – can't fail to be struck by just how offensive this conclusion

---

70 This seems to be a form of free-market, trickle-down economics, popular in the 1980s and 1990s. I do not know if my father is describing something he believes now or something he believed then. Indeed, my own grip on 'now' and 'then' is becoming increasingly unsure.

is.[71] My calculations have led me to what is, in effect, a game-management strategy for the world's poor – more accurately, the inverse of a game-management strategy. The core of game-management strategies is the concept of maximum sustainable yield. If you like hunting deer, for example, you do not want to annihilate all the deer in your area, because next year there won't be any. You have to leave some around, so they will breed, replenish their numbers – and then you can blast away at them next year too. Kill only as many deer as will allow you to kill the same number next year. That way, in the long run, you will be able to kill the maximum number of deer.

For the world's poor, it seems I have arrived at a game-management strategy in reverse. The goal is now to save as many of the world's poor as we can in the long run. And we can do that if we give today only as much as will allow us to give at least as much tomorrow. Give too much today, and you sacrifice those in need tomorrow. Give too little today, and you sacrifice those in need now. There are exceptions. If a problem were genuinely acute, so that a donation today would obviate the need for one tomorrow, then it would be rational to donate. However, if the problems that our aid seeks to address are continuing or permanent – and most of them are – then it seems our efforts must conform to the principle of maximum sustainable donation. Dark magic has its logic. This logic is impeccable. And this is where it leads.

---

71 You see how he has now jumped temporal perspectives – something that his failure to mention the economic collapse of 2008 suggested he felt unable to do?

A Good Life

1.

It is time I do something to stem the recent flurry of footnotes. It is not important to point out that I don't buy my father's argument: that money-is-magic meme. My father paints a picture of money as akin to a pernicious, omnipotent force that thwarts us at every turn. I'm unconvinced. If we wanted to do something about the world's poor, I'm pretty sure we could. The importance of the argument lies not in what it says, nor in the conclusion to which it leads. It is what the argument shows, rather than says, that is crucial.

2.

The argument clearly draws on ideas that were popular at the time my father was working in London. It involves elements of trickle-down economics – although perhaps not in the crude form endorsed by people like Arthur Laffer and Milton Friedman. We need to keep wealth high in Rich in order that it might trickle down to Poor in the most effective and sustainable way. One might also detect the tacit influence of John Rawls, who argued that inequalities of wealth are justifiable to the extent that they benefit the least well off. We can tolerate the disparity in wealth between Rich and Poor, as long as this is to the perdurable advantage of Poor. So, as a neocapitalist defence of hanging on to your money, the argument is populated with the usual conceptual manoeuvres and suspects. As I said, I don't buy it. What is important, however, is not that I don't buy it: it is that, as far as I know, my dad didn't buy it either. The man I knew gave absolutely no indication that he thought this way – quite the contrary, in fact. This, then, is the puzzle: why does he appear to endorse this argument?

It is, of course, possible that he believed the argument and always did – and simply never expressed the views around me. More likely, I suspect, is that this argument is the most forthright, unintended expression yet of a phenomenon that has already crept into his writing on several occasions: anachronism. These ideas were popular at the time my father was working in the City. It is not beyond the bounds of possibility that he believed, or came to believe, those arguments then. But his manuscript is not written as a record of his beliefs at any particular time. It is written from the time-less perspective of someone who has picked up a thing or two over the years and is trying to explain what these are before it is too late. So, why would ideas that were indexed to a particular time in his life make their way into an analysis that presents itself as timeless? That the argument is here at all is anachronism of a peculiar sort: a point in the writing where the concrete and temporal insert themselves into the timeless – to disconcerting effect.

3.

My father was having his own issues with time. It may just be that this insertion is the result of confusion on his part. But the specific intentions of my father are not relevant. I am beginning to think that anachronism is the key to everything. I've taken a liberty. There is something I think you should read next. In my father's manuscript it appears towards the end – a section in the penultimate chapter. I think it is so central to what my father was trying to say – whether he knew what he was trying to say or not – that it is best read now. My father did not intend these remarks as a chapter of their own, and so I shall not present them as such.

*

My first memory is of Muhammad Ali and a nosebleed. The nosebleed was mine, but Ali played no role in producing it – assuming we are willing to rule out empathic action-at-a-distance. It was the night of Ali's fight with the fearsome George Foreman, and so I would have been around two years old. I don't know what I was doing up, sitting on the settee, during what must have been the early hours of the morning of 30 October 1974. I am told that I wasn't a great sleeper in those days. More likely is that my father just wanted someone to watch the fight with him. My mother would have had no interest, and my brother wouldn't be around for a few years yet. My father loved Ali with a fervour that, in hindsight, I find surprising. I remember an interview, a couple of years later, that Ali gave with David Frost. Ali playfully ridiculed the attempts of Frost – the man who had just helped bring down Nixon – to outwit him: 'You're just not fast enough, you're just not smart enough ...' I was too young to understand the backstory – of Watergate, of Frost's extraordinary interviews with Nixon – but my father understood. I remember him sitting in the armchair, watching the interview and cackling away like a loon.

I digress. After a dancing start, Ali lay on the ropes for the next seven rounds, taking a monumental beating. My father was not happy, and continually hurled unsolicited advice – 'Get off the ropes!' – at the TV. At some point during the eighth round, my nose started to bleed – you have to suspect some empathic neurological mechanism had a hand in this. My father ran off to grab a tissue, and completely against the run of the fight Ali promptly knocked Foreman out. My father hurriedly returned, tissue in hand. I remember the look of incomprehension – eyes flickering between the screen and me, as if I had played some duplicitous role in the affair, as if I were somehow playing a trick on him. His face slowly transformed from incomprehension to disbelief, and from disbelief to horror (*he had missed it!*), from horror to resignation and from resignation, finally, to delight.

This is one of the clearest memories I have and, no matter how many others are lost, this one never fades. And yet it cannot be. When Ali knocked out Foreman, my father would have been barely more than thirty years old. And yet the face I remember, flickering back and forth between the TV screen and me – is the face of an old man, the face of a man in his final years.

It is sometimes said that we are children of time. Heidegger thought that humans were the only creatures who really lived in time. But the truth is that our relationship with time has always been a troubled one. The possibility of anachronism haunts our every memory. What does this reveal about us? Many philosophers agree that our memories make us who we are. One does not need to be a philosopher to appreciate the plausibility of this claim. As Tennessee Williams noted in The Milk Train Doesn't Stop Here Anymore*: 'Has it ever struck you that life is all memory, except for the one present moment that goes by you so quick you hardly catch it going?' If it is true that our memories make us who we are, what does it say about us that the possibility of anachronism haunts our every memory? In his poem, 'The Rubaiyat of Omar Khayyam', FitzGerald writes:*

The Moving Finger writes; and, having writ,
Moves on: nor all thy Piety nor Wit
Shall lure it back to cancel half a Line,
Nor all thy Tears wash out a Word of it.

A Good Life

That the possibility of anachronism haunts our every memory means that FitzGerald's claim is simply false. If memories are the words written in us by time, the possibility of anachronism means that nothing is ever merely written. Memories are not fixed, immutable inscriptions of the past. There is nothing written that cannot be rewritten, revised, redrafted, re-crafted, recast: remade.

He did not realize it, but in the possibility of anachronism, I think, my father found the possibility also of goodness. Forget and forgive his amateurish speculations on the obligations of the rich. My father is soon to be remade.

12

Poor

When I was travelling with Myshkin in India, we saw some horrifying things. The leprosy was the worst. Those swarming hands held out to me, in front of my face: missing fingers or their stubby remnants. If you placed money in these shattered relics, they would just become more numerous and insistent. There was a girl, a tiny leprous girl – I say 'girl', but I found it impossible to identify her age, she could have been anywhere between ten and forty – who had a doll: a plastic doll with a big domed forehead, and swaddled like a baby. We encountered her in Jammu, and she haunted Myshkin's dreams from that day on. We returned to Jammu some months later, and he insisted that we find her: his dreams demanded this of him. She was still there, in the same square – where else would she be? – with the same doll and the same shattered fingers. We had given her coins the last time, but this time Myshkin gave her a note. I can't recall exactly which note, but I seem to remember it would have been around the equivalent of around £20. She could have lived for a year on that, at least. Her eyes flickered, momentarily, in disbelief, and then she shot out of that square like a scalded cat. I never saw her again. But, perhaps, Myshkin still meets her in dreams.

I said I wouldn't make a habit of these interjections. And I meant it. But I feel a little sorry for Myshkin and the man he is becoming. I rarely saw him during these years, but I can't imagine falling in love with the leathery trader who toyed with the idea of a game-management strategy for the poor. The Myshkin I knew, and fell in love with, was a man haunted by a leprous girl – a girl who carried a doll with her through the streets of Jammu and on, from there, into his dreams. And yet they are the same man.

Some would say – perhaps the man he would later become would say this – that Myshkin's motivation in returning to the square and seeking out the little girl was a selfish one. His sleep was being disturbed by the nightly intercessions of the girl's visitant, and he was simply – and selfishly – seeking relief from his distress. There is an old platitude according to which everyone is ultimately selfish – even when they appear to be behaving in the most altruistic of ways. If a person wants to give away all his money to the poor, or sacrifice himself to save the life of another, then he is merely doing what he wants to do – or what he prefers more than any available alternative. In the end everyone, always, does what he or she most wants to do. But always doing what one wants to do is the definition of selfishness. And this means that everyone is selfish.

This idea is banal, relying on a simple confusion. Why did Myshkin's memory of the girl distress him so much?

Poor

Would she have haunted the dreams of the later Myshkin? I would like to think so, but I really can't be sure. Whether a person is selfish is not a matter of whether he always does what he wants to do. Let us accept: a person always does what he wants to do most. It matters not one bit. It is what he wants to do that is crucial. It is what he wants – not whether he does what he wants – that decides whether he is selfish. If Myshkin were selfish, then the plight of the leprous girl wouldn't have affected him. If he were callous, she could not have scarred his dreams. His nocturnal distress was a mark of just how unselfish he was in those days. The truest memory I have of Myshkin from those days, a memory frozen in time, is a picture not of his face but of hers: a memory of her face as she looked at the money Myshkin had given her.

I suppose it was entirely natural that, at this time in his life, Myshkin would be drawn towards a capitalist defence of radical wealth inequality. Even so, it is easy to see the hesitancies and qualifications in his argument. He makes one qualification twice: the problems Poor faces must be chronic rather than acute. If they are acute then one is temporarily licensed to diverge from the principle of maximum sustainable donation. But isn't that the very issue? He asserts that the problems Poor faces will, in general, be chronic rather than acute and so sees this as only a minor qualification. But is there any evidence for this pessimistic assumption? Could one not argue that the purpose of wealth redistribution is precisely to transform the chronic problems of Poor into merely acute problems – problems of the sort Rich deals with every day? Pessimism is a core element of much scepticism about helping the absolute poor. Can we be sure that our contributions will not be siphoned off by corrupt Third World governments? Or perhaps they will be intercepted by criminals or terrorists? And isn't the requirement that we give away so much of our hard-earned money just too unrealistically demanding? Some of these worries are legitimate, some less so. But we should never forget that, whether it is employed intentionally or not, pessimism almost always comes down on the side of the status quo.

I don't want to dwell on these issues because I am far more interested in something else. One of the striking things about Myshkin's moral calculations is how utterly ineffective they are. Whether you calculate that morality requires you to give to the point of marginal utility, or whether you lean towards his idea of maximum sustainable donation, the end result is the same: nothing. What is the maximum sustainable donation Rich can make to Poor? No one really knows. Its calculation will be an incredibly complex and sensitive matter, involving not just the giver but also the effect of her giving on the society that creates the level of wage she receives. These calculations are beyond anyone, and all we can do is guess – with honesty and in good faith. And if I had to guess, if my life depended on coming up with a realistic estimate, I'd wager that it would be considerably higher than the 0.7 per cent of gross national income recommended by the United Nations General Assembly. It would be considerably higher than the 0.19 per cent of GNI actually donated by the United States and Japan, the 0.32 donated by Australia and Canada or the 0.38–0.43 per cent donated by most Western European countries. That would be my guess, anyway.

The greatest drawback of moral calculation is its utter inertia. Moral calculation is a bearded old man, hunched over a book of equations. His judgements may be correct. His determinations and appraisals may be faultless, and they may be widely acknowledged as such. But still, no one will listen to him. What he forgot to include in his calculations was any reason why people should care what he says.

The Myshkin who gave money to a little leprous girl was animated by Los, and not by Urizen. Cost-benefit calculations were the furthest thing from his mind. He was motivated by sentiment: a perturbing and poorly understood mixture of shock, guilt, horror and more than a smidgen of self-interest. But binding all these elements together – turning them into a combustible, dream-altering compound – was the defining ingredient: compassion.

The perils of compassion cannot be overestimated. There are perils to the compassionate person herself, and also perils to the recipients of her compassion. A life dominated by compassion is a hard one. Once you have seen little leprous fingers raised beseechingly towards your face, then you quickly come to understand that this world is a world of wounds.[72] Wounds become scars, and scars become hard: sometimes as hard as leather. The leathery trader that Myshkin has become will, perhaps, not let compassion back into his life for some time.

The consequences for the recipients of compassion can be even more dangerous, sometimes deadly. It goes without saying that compassion is a poor basis for designing strategies of wealth redistribution or policy decisions more generally.

72 Compare Aldo Leopold: 'One of the penalties of an ecological education is that one lives alone in a world of wounds.' *A Sand County Almanac* (Oxford University Press, 1949).

As Mother Teresa put it: 'If I look at the mass I will never act. If I look at the one, I will.'[73] It is difficult to be compassionate towards faceless masses. Compassion is always directed towards a face – or, at least, towards a manageable number of them. By directing one's compassion towards those whose faces one can see, one inevitably overlooks those whose faces are hidden – even though they are equally – or more – worthy of your help.

However, even if we focus on the one rather than on the many, the face rather than the faceless, the consequences of random acts of kindness – undisciplined compassion – may still be disastrous. The face of the tiny leprous girl was there for both of us to see, and so she became a recipient of our compassion. But that sort of money could get you killed in the slums of Jammu in those days. This thought assaulted me only years later, and I hope it decided to leave Myshkin alone. But that was just sloppy – intellectually sloppy – on my part and his. I hope no one saw what we did. I hope she secreted away our gift, and found a way of using it without drawing the wrong sort of attention. I hope, but I shall never know. It could be that girl died because of our compassion.

It is important to pin down precisely why Myshkin's conclusions are disconcerting. The idea of giving to the point of marginal utility is, of course, astonishing. Myshkin rejected that idea in the end, but he did so largely for practical reasons: marginal utility is an ineffective goal because it undermines maximum sustainable contribution. More good is achieved in the long run if we jettison the policy of giving

73 Compare footnote 28. I prefer to quote Uncle Joe, but the point is essentially the same.

to the point of marginal utility in favour of a policy of maximum sustainable contribution. But even this latter watered-down policy is extraordinary in its own way – requiring massive changes in the way we conduct our lives. So, we appear to have a moral ideal – maximum sustainable contribution – to which most of us will have difficulty adhering. No one said doing the right thing was going to be easy. But the question is not whether this ideal is too demanding. It is whether it should even be recognized as an ideal.

We can think of a moral saint as someone whose life is dominated by moral ideals. His or her life is dominated, completely, by the attempt to do what morality requires. Is this an ideal to which any of us should aspire? The question is not whether the ideal is one that most would find too difficult to adopt. That presupposes the ideal is a worthy one, and merely bemoans our inability to live up to it. The real question is whether this is a worthy ideal at all.[74]

Something that Myshkin missed during his moral calculations: it is not just his money he is obliged to give away. Moral sacrifice is not just a pecuniary notion. Put in terms of marginal utility, for example, you are required to give until the pain of giving outweighs the pleasure of receiving – but it says nothing about what you are to give. Maximum sustainable donation tells you to give this year only as much as will allow you to give the same next year – but, again, it does not specify the nature of the given. As Myshkin noted, the less he earns, the less he is able to give. The lives of those who might receive his money will be better if he keeps his high-salaried job. He plans to get out in two years but, whether we frame

74 Susan Wolf, 'Moral saints', *Journal of Philosophy*, Vol. 79, No. 8 (1982), pp. 419–39.

his moral obligations in terms of the idea of marginal utility or maximum sustainable contribution, the result is the same: he must stay where he is. He may hate his job, but it is far better than being one of the leprous mendicants that haunt his dreams. Changing his life in ways that are more agreeable to him is not compatible with a maximum sustainable donation to those in need.

It is not just his career: the same considerations would permeate every aspect of his life. He wants a family, or one day will – pricey! Think of all the lives he could transform if he took the money he would have put into a family and, instead, diverted it to the absolute poor. He might be unhappy, but any diminution in the quality of his life is more than compensated for by the augmentation in the quality of the lives he transforms. Perhaps he would like to take up a hobby – but this would consume time and resources he could be using to benefit the absolute poor. A family, a hobby, a holiday and anything else not directly related to the demands of morality could be justified on one ground only: they help him more effectively focus on the important business of helping the absolute poor. If a hobby, holiday or family keeps him sane, and so better at his job, for example, then it would be indirectly justifiable. But it is, ultimately, its beneficial effect on other people, and not on Myshkin, that supplies its justification.

If he followed this path, his life would be that of a moral saint, and perhaps one can already appreciate just how unattractive this life is. Everything that is commonly thought to make life worth living has been stripped away. There are no attachments he can ultimately cherish: all is subservient to the greater moral good. There is no room in this life for love or family or the things he does. The life of the moral saint is that of a tool, an instrument. And the lives of everyone around him – family, friends – are also instruments of the greater good. It is here, precisely at this point in logical space, where one can, for the first time, see the limits of moral calculation. For it is at this point that calculation encounters the incalculable. The unease we feel in the face of the moral saint is precisely the unease occasioned by someone who is willing to trade off the limitlessness of his or her life and the lives of those he loves.

It is one thing when we are dealing with money – and that is the way issues of redistribution are almost always discussed. The issue is framed, precisely, as an issue of redistribution of wealth, and wealth is understood as an exclusively fiscal phenomenon. Money is essentially calculable – that is, of course, its entire point. Your life, however, and all those things that go into making it something worth living, is not calculable. Your life is everything you have. The lives of those you love – these are everything they have. When you push the idea of moral calculation far enough you always, eventually, encounter the incalculable. Compassion, in its essence, is always about the incalculable, the limitless. Compassion without calculation may be blind. But calculation without compassion is empty.

Myshkin saw an echo of his own limitlessness in the little girl. That is why she haunted his dreams.

13

Rules

But how can a rule show me what I have to do at this point?

Ludwig Wittgenstein, *Philosophical Investigations*

'When I die, will I see my mum and dad again?' Just because the game stops, it doesn't mean the lies do too. Truth and reality are sometimes uneasy acquaintances.

The day my life changed forever had started off as a run-of-the-mill day in the world of high-stakes international finance. Yes, I was still doing that – five years and counting. I know what I said: two years and I was going to be out of there – prison, compensation. I said those things and I meant them. But the game will beat you in the end, because the benefits of self-deception are vast. The last five years had been ones dominated by a simple act of bad faith: I am a banker.

I knew this was a game, but if you want to get really good at a game, you have to be able to pretend it isn't one. Actually, it goes much deeper than pretending. You need to be convinced, and something you know is pretence will not work. It goes deeper, also, than the kind of suspension of disbelief required to enjoy a novel. In the moments you are engrossed in a work of fiction, it never occurs to you to doubt the reality of the characters. But, of course, as soon as you put the book down, you know they don't really exist. But suppose there were a book you could never put down, from which you could never, even for a moment, distance yourself enough to question the reality of the characters: that would be closer to the attitude that animated me during my years as a banker. Pretence isn't good enough, and neither is the suspension of disbelief you can turn on or off, as you pick up or put down a book. A suspension of disbelief that lies outside the bounds of volition, beyond the domain of caprice, there is a word for that: conviction.

Conviction is an interesting concept. A mere liar is in possession of the truth, and merely withholds this truth from others. Self-deception is entirely more interesting. The paradox of self-deception is that the one who lies and the one who is lied to are the same person. So, in self-deception, one withholds the truth from oneself. But, to do this, one must already be in possession of the truth. It is not often appreciated that the same paradox underlies conviction: it has the same basic structure as self-deception. I had to convince myself that I was a banker, thereby demonstrating that I was not a banker.[75] The one who convinces cannot be the one who is convinced. Conviction is, therefore, a complicated art, difficult to perfect. It involves holding something that one knows to be a lie as if it were not a lie: it is the art of the juggler who

75 The logic, here, is Sartrean – employed by Jean-Paul Sartre in *Being and Nothingness* – as my father, in effect, will acknowledge shortly. Sartre argued that the act of awareness could never be the same thing as the object of awareness. The one who sees can never be the same as the one seen, the one who thinks can never be the same as the one thought about. Once Sartre starts to make sense, you know you're in trouble.

keeps truth and lie always in the air, never touching one of them long enough to have to claim it as his own.

Influenced by Freud, we might be tempted to explain this in terms of some peculiar compartmentalization of the self. But I doubt that would help in my case. I didn't need the ministrations of a skilled analyst to allow me to discover that I was playing a game. I knew that: every time the lie passed through my hands, briefly brushing my fingers before vaulting once more into the sky, I knew it. For conviction to collapse, it is enough to stop juggling. That's why it pays not to linger in bed in the mornings, not even for a few moments, after the alarm has sounded. Get up, get moving, and keep moving. Don't stop: reflection is your implacable foe. I convinced myself for so long that I was a banker that I forgot what I was doing. I therefore became a banker. Sartre would say that I am suffering from bad faith. I, however, can't see anything bad in it. Thus, my days in the noble profession of international banking now number 1,685, with no end on the horizon.

Conviction of this sort also dominated my attitudes towards others as well as myself. At least, conviction provided the template, but there was one crucial difference. A stream of girlfriends – and others not yet elevated to that status – visit me in my apartment in Canada Water. I get them to like me by convincing myself that I like them. Mere pretence is not good enough: they will sniff that out with quick and ruthless efficiency. It is absolute conviction that is required. But, in this case, each time the lie momentarily drops into my hand I will hold onto it just a little bit longer, reacquaint myself with how it feels, remind myself of what it is. This conviction can't be allowed to run and run. We all know where that will end.

Rules

So there we have it: the truth. I'm an asshole. It's a truth
dressed up in a conceptual framework largely supplied by
Jean-Paul Sartre. But then, he was an asshole too.

Some, save the occasional brief and terrifying flash of
illumination, need never awaken from this game of conviction. For others, the game may come to a thunderous,
bruising halt. If conviction is a suspension of disbelief, then
the real must be the suspension of the suspension of
disbelief. My suspension of the suspension of disbelief took
the form of a telephone call, received as I was making my
way to the City of London Club – yes, my youthful flirtation
with Blacks has been consigned to history. 'I'm so sorry
Olga': I remember saying that. And those were the last
words I ever uttered in my old life. The words that ushered
in my new one were Olga's, not mine: 'Myshkin, we have to
talk.'

It's a story as old as time itself. Boy meets girl. Boy impreg-
nates girl, shortly before she returns to her Ivy League college
in America. Girl informs boy that she will 'take care of'
matter when she returns stateside in a few weeks' time. Boy –
being a really simple-minded boy – doesn't think twice about
this. Girl has a married sister unable to conceive. Girl proceeds with pregnancy, and in less than forty weeks' time
bequeaths her sister the baby. And sister, husband and baby
all live happily in upstate New York. But this is not happily
ever after: a few years of happiness are all they are allotted.
Sister and husband are killed in car crash. And boy becomes
a father – seven years after he really became a father – at the
ripe old age of twenty-seven.

My accession to known fatherhood was, thus, a rather
sombre affair. Far from the joyful, optimistic occasion I

would have imagined it to be – if I were the sort of person who imagines these things – my assumption of fatherhood was a ceremony conducted in whispers, tears and funeral dirges. To feel disappointed, even cheated, however, would have contravened the first rule of parenthood: it's not about you any more (and it never will be again).

Some of the associated phenomena were, however, entirely typical: some sort of time-dilation phenomenon is reliably distributed across new parents. It was as if someone had grabbed the TV remote of my life and started playing around with it. First, they pressed the rewind button. For a while, a few short blessed days, I was once again the twenty-year-old boy/man who believed in letting tomorrow take care of itself. Presumably this was the shock talking – startling me back into a previous incarnation. Standing in front of me was the concrete now, and in it the girl I loved. Stretching away in front of me was the exiguous future – its problems, possibilities and permutations merely insubstantial rumours. I know what you are thinking. Clearly, I was a man not averse to using someone else's tragedy to advance a personal agenda. I don't think you would be entirely wrong about this. But at the same time, there was another part of me that was motivated by the idea of doing the right thing. True: sometimes this part of me couldn't quite shake the feeling that I was still playing a game – a game of nobility, of doing what is right though the heavens fall. But I suppose games had been part of me for so long that this was hardly surprising. These different facets of me, doing different things, nevertheless all arrived in the same place. I proposed, and this time Olga accepted – no doubt that was the shock talking too.

*

Rules

The flirtation with the rewind button was brief, and from there the remote was flipped to fast-forward – a setting in which it would remain obstinately stuck for many years to come. I live in London; Olga lives in New York. One, or both, of us is going to have to move. Olga works in publishing, I in finance. I earn substantially more and my job is marginally safer. And so we agree that we should move to London. It means uprooting Nicolai[76] – yes, this is my son's name, and how strange that I haven't used it so far – but we both agreed that this couldn't be helped. And so it came to pass that I found myself with a son, a wife and a new life – all in the space of a few weeks. There was the hurried wedding in a county courthouse in upstate New York, and the flight to London with a confused and presumably terrified Nicolai.[77] I knew London was going to change. Obviously, the girlfriends were gone. But so too were my daily visits to the City of London Club. When I left in the mornings, Olga and Nicolai would both be asleep. If I wanted to see them at all – weekends aside – I'd have to run straight home afterwards. I knew all this. But I did still cling to the illusion that I might be able to hold on to my apartment in the Docklands. Our living arrangements were, however, a little cramped. What passes as a bedroom in the mind of a London estate agent qualifies only as a closet in that of his American counterpart. A few months later, I had bowed to the inevitable. I put the apartment up for rent, and we now lived in a smallish rented house in Wimbledon Village.

It was there one Saturday morning – Olga was out and

---

76 You can understand now why I was so animated about my parents' abortion deliberations.
77 Yep!

A Good Life

Nicolai and I were playing *Donkey Kong*[78] – when Nicolai looked at me and asked me the question, 'When I die, will I see my mum and dad again?' The nagging suspicion that I had carried with me, the feeling that I was playing a game – that everything is always and only a game – instantly disappeared. This was reality, cold and hard. But reality and truth have always had a troubled relationship.

Some people – I've met a few – believe you should always tell the truth, no matter how unpalatable it is. If this is right, it can only be because truth has a value that overrides any sort of heartbreak. People like this are emotional children, who misunderstand the value of truth. A liar, we sometimes say, is a person who has too little regard for the truth. This is, indeed, a vice, a character flaw. But there is also a corresponding vice of having too much regard for the truth. Perhaps there is a word for this vice: if there is I don't know what it is, and if there isn't someone should invent it. Words such as 'blunt', or 'candid' or 'forthright' aren't sufficiently specific. You might be blunt because you believe that, in general, little good is done by hiding the truth – but also willing to accept that, if unusual circumstances dictate, lying might be the right thing to do. The zealotry of someone who believes in the transcendent value of truth brooks no such exceptions.

The concepts of usefulness and benefit are the keys to understanding the value of truth. 'When I die, will I see my mum and dad again?' Those who think the value of truth trumps any other value believe I should say 'no' – for that is what they, and I, think is the truth of the matter. And if I acknowledge that I cannot, perhaps, be absolutely certain of

78 An unforgivable mistake! I'm certain it was *Super Mario Kart*.

this, then I should reply, 'Almost certainly not.' Such people think that truth is intrinsically valuable: valuable for what it is in itself. Moreover, this intrinsic value is of a magnitude so great that nothing should be allowed to override it. They are wrong on both counts. Truth has the value of an instrument or tool. The value of truth is like the value of money or medicine: valuable not because of what it is in itself, but because of other things it might allow you to have. Truth is valuable to the extent it allows you to live a better, happier or more fulfilling life.[79]

One reason why knowing the truth is often – probably even generally – a good thing is that basing your life on lies can lead to unhappiness or a wasted life (the two are not quite the same). Being repeatedly told, from childhood on, that you have a certain aptitude, you appropriately concentrate your efforts – shape your education and life choices – to develop it. But you were told a falsehood, and all your efforts will eventually be smashed on the cold grey rock of reality. You should have chosen another path, and might well have done so if you had been in possession of the truth. This may be the source of lasting regret and unhappiness. But even a happy life may be wasted. You come to believe a certain religious doctrine, join a commune, eschew the more usual sorts of self-development, career path, personal relationships and so on. The doctrine is palpable nonsense. But you never manage to work this out. Your life is a happy one – or as happy as the lives of most people. But it is still, arguably, a pointless

---

79 Interesting: if I were being uncharitable, I might speculate that the lying little boy in Mrs Maywood's office has grown up into a man able to rationalize and justify an innate lying streak. Happily, I'm in a charitable mood.

waste. Knowing the truth is usually a good thing. The truth helps guard against the twin evils of unhappiness and point-lessness. But this does not mean that truth is always a good thing. The truth can mess you up too.

The truth is often very unpleasant – shockingly so – and this may lead one to draw questionable inferences or leap to unwarranted conclusions. Tolstoy, when he first truly under-stood that he would one day die, and that the same would happen to everyone he loved, jumped to an unwarranted conclusion: nothing matters.[80] That life is a bitch and then you die is a hard truth, and it is easy to draw dubious con-clusions from it. And a life based on these conclusions can be just as unhappy, and just as pointless, as the life of someone gripped by nonsense. Unhappiness and pointlessness super-vene on the terrible: and the truth is often terrible.

Life is too slippery for rules. 'Always tell the truth': if it is to be remotely plausible, this rule must be followed by an indef-initely long list of exceptions. Unless your interlocutor is a mad axeman asking you where you keep your axe. Unless you are replying to your mother, in cancer treatment, who asks you whether the wig she is now obliged to wear looks 'natural'. Unless a child, grieving for the only parents he has ever known, asks you whether he will ever see them again. There are a range of circumstances in which telling the truth would not be a good thing to do, and a range of reasons why it would not be good. Sometimes this is concern for others, sometimes it is concern for oneself, and sometimes it is a mixture of the two.

---

80 I believe he is referring to Tolstoy's short essay, 'My Confession'. Tolstoy eventually found solace in faith.

Rules

The idea of a 'white lie' – a lie that is good, or at least acceptable to tell – is, in effect, an acknowledgement of the poverty of any general rule about telling the truth. But we can't avoid this proliferation of rules by inventing more specific ones, such as 'Always tell the truth unless it will hurt another's feelings.' Sometimes a truth is one that needs to be told: it is a truth that the other needs to hear, even if it 'hurts her feelings', perhaps even if it devastates her.

A grieving child has asked me whether he will ever again see his dead parents. I'm reasonably confident that he will not. But I am also confident that it would be monstrous of me to tell him this. Nevertheless, confidence can't be divorced from careful and considered judgement. If I say, 'Yes, Nicolai, you will see them again in heaven', do I believe that he will commit suicide – to hasten his reunion with his mum and dad?[81] Less dramatically, will he lose interest in the day-to-day business of life? Will he come to see this life as merely an inconvenient prequel to the most important part of his existence that will come later? If so, will this effect be more than temporary? If I suspect there is an affirmative answer to any of these questions, I will have to reconsider my initial impulse to dissemble. In all of this, careful judgement is required. The drawbacks of dissembling must be weighed against those of telling the truth. This weighing of consequences is a matter that calls for intelligent assessment and a certain amount of emotional detachment.

In all of this, rules are an afterthought. If we were so inclined, we might formulate my decision in terms of a rule: when a child's parents have died, and he is or has been exhibiting signs of immense grief, and he asks you whether

---

81 It was never on the cards.

he will one day see them in heaven, then tell him that he will, unless any of the following apply: (1) you suspect this might lead to his suicide, or (2) you suspect this might lead to loss of interest in life, and (3) you judge, with (4) a certain degree of probability, that the effect described in (2) will be of an unacceptable level of severity, and (5) permanent rather than temporary, and so on and so forth. But, as yet, I have merely scratched the surface of the possible exceptions and qualifications. Will (6) the lie I tell now lead to a damaging loss of trust further down the line, or will (7) Nicolai be capable of understanding its rationale? (8) How probable is this? (9) If my lie does lead to a loss of trust, is this acceptable given the heartache it will temporarily spare Nicolai? (10) Will the loss of trust – if real – be (11) merely in me, or will it (12) result in a jaundiced view of humans more generally, and so on. I am still just getting started. Even if we could formulate a rule that takes into account all the possible complications, qualifications and exceptions this would be pointless. Rules cannot be the basis of morality, because one already needs to be moral to understand them.

Once upon a time there was a dream shared, and pursued, by most moral thinkers. This was a set of rules that would, collectively, supply a moral decision procedure. These rules would show what was, in any given situation, the right thing to do. Moreover, these rules could be formulated in such a way that they could be understood, and applied, by any normal adult human being – even if he or she was not a good person and had no intention of following these rules.

This dream – or at least this kind of dream – was not peculiar to moralists. Cognitive scientists also dreamed of capturing intelligence in a net of rules. The rules would collectively specify how a person – an 'intelligent system', as they preferred – would behave in any given situation. The problem with the dream was not simply that any given situation had unforeseen levels of complexity. That didn't help, admittedly, but it was hoped this problem could be surmounted by dramatically expanding the number of rules. No, the real problem was that any rule that was devised had to be applied appropriately if it was to work. Sometimes the application of a rule is not appropriate. Sometimes it is empty-headed, idiotic, imbecilic – unintelligent. The fatal flaw now emerged: the application of a rule to any given situation is something that can be done intelligently or otherwise. This problem cannot be circumvented simply by introducing more rules – rules that specify how another rule is to be applied – for these further rules can be applied intelligently or not. Therefore, a hard truth slowly emerged: rules presuppose intelligence and therefore can't explain it.[82]

The idea that morality can be explained in terms of rules suffers from the same problem. The difficulty is not the moral complexity of real-life situations – although that doesn't help – but the fact that any moral rule can be applied well or badly. The application of a moral rule to a situation might, for example, be arrogant, brutal, calculating, callous, disloyal, feckless, grasping, harsh, hypocritical, incautious, inconsiderate, indiscreet, intolerant, irresponsible, lazy, mercenary, myopic, presumptuous, pusillanimous, reckless, selfish, tactless, uncooperative, ungrateful or vindictive. These terms all denote moral failings – moral vices. To avoid them, one would need to exhibit the corresponding moral virtue or, at

82 This is what is known as the 'frame problem', or, at least, it is one version of that problem. The problem emerged, slowly and uncertainly, from the work of Wittgenstein, among others.

least, be bereft of the vice. Therefore, rules will help only if the person who applies them is already morally virtuous, or at least not morally vicious. Rules cannot capture morality because, like those rules that tried to capture intelligence, they presuppose it.[83]

An alternative is to think of being moral as more like having a practical skill. Knowing how to ride a bicycle, for example, is not based on understanding rules: any rules, such as 'keep pedalling', would be far too incomplete and riddled with exceptions to be of much help. We learn to ride a bike by doing it. Things will go wrong, and when they do we can improve by thinking intelligently about why they went wrong. In this we need not be alone. We can seek out the advice of accomplished cyclists, and also watch to see what they do.

Aristotle thought of the ability to be moral in something like these terms. Whether you should tell the truth, withhold the truth or dissemble depends, crucially, on circumstances, and circumstances demand judgement. Judgement is a skill. Aristotle called it *phronesis* – 'practical wisdom'. Practical wisdom cannot be attained through the ingestion of rules. Rather, it is something acquired only through living: through being exposed to situations and trying to work out what is the best thing to do. Sometimes you will get it right, many times you won't. Practical wisdom involves not just the ability to get things right but also the ability to recognize when you have got them wrong, and, perhaps with the help of others, to think frankly, flexibly and intelligently about how to do

83 This sort of argument is associated with John McDowell. See, in particular, his 'Virtue and Reason', *The Monist*, Vol. 62, No. 3 (1979), pp. 331–50. See also Rosalind Hursthouse, *On Virtue Ethics* (Oxford University Press, 2002).

better next time. The practical wisdom thus attained is unevenly distributed. Some people have it in spades, and others seem to lack it completely. For most people it comes in varying amounts.

Practical wisdom might seem a somewhat cold, detached attitude. I must attempt to work out what is best to say to Nicolai – taking all relevant factors into consideration, working out probabilities, identifying the relative desirability of various outcomes and so on. It is a very calculative conception of morality. In the moral case, however – although this is an idea emphasized not by Aristotle but by Hume – there are strict limits on this detachment. My practical rationality must always be in the service of a single thought, paramount in its importance. What would it be like to be this seven-year-old child who has just lost his parents? How would it feel to be this child? How would I feel if I stood in the shoes of this child? This ability to put oneself in the shoes of the other is empathy. The ability to care about what you find when you do so is compassion. The ability to make this caring into something effective is practical wisdom.

Empathy is often confused with compassion, and it is useful to draw a distinction between the two. Empathy comes from the Greek *empatheia* – a compound of *em*, 'in', and *pathos*, 'feeling'. Empathy is, therefore, 'feeling in': an ability to project yourself into the mind and situation – the shoes – of the other and feel what he or she feels. The Greeks, however, distinguished *empatheia* from *sympatheia*. The latter derives from *pathos* combined with *syn*, 'together'. *Sympatheia* is, therefore, 'feeling together'. Empathy is, therefore, as different from sympathy as 'in' is different from 'together'. 'Compassion' is the ecclesiastical Latin translation of the Greek *sympatheia*. It derives from the Latin *cum*, 'with', and *passio*. The latter is the nominative noun form of the verb *pati*, to suffer or endure. Compassion is, accordingly, suffering with, or enduring with, the other.

Suppose I were to feel mere empathy for Nicolai. Then, in its pure form, I would feel what he feels. His desperate unhappiness, his inconsolable heartbreak, would be mine. Not only is this empathy, on its own, unlikely to do much good, it is not even a moral attitude – at least, as we ordinarily think of these. I will care about this unpleasant feeling I am now having – but care about it precisely because it is unpleasant for me rather than for him. To be a properly moral attitude, my caring must be directed towards him. I must care about, and want to mitigate, this terrible feeling because it is bad for him, not simply because I find its empathic echo unpleasant.

Compassion brings us closer to this idea. In compassion, I suffer with Nicolai, and so must recognize that he is suffering too. Moreover, while empathy for Nicolai would require that my emotions mirror his – what he feels I thereby feel also – this is not required for compassion. My compassion can take various forms. I feel sorry for his heartbreak not because I share it, but because I understand what he must be going through, and how horrible things must be for him. I recognize the heartsickness is his, not mine, and I sympathize with him for this reason. My compassion is built on empathy – if I had no empathy, I could not understand what he must be going through – but it involves having emotions that are, as we say, 'appropriate' to the other's suffering rather than ones that replicate that suffering. My compassion for Nicolai, therefore, requires empathy but also something more: I not only put myself in the shoes of this seven-year-old boy, but I care about what I encounter when I do so. And I care –

precisely – because the suffering is his. The heart of compassion is to care for the suffering of the other as the suffering of the other.

Compassion, however, is useless on its own. My emotional response must be channelled effectively. This is the function of practical wisdom: to allow me to choose the best course of action to help mitigate Nicolai's suffering. Compassion may be necessary for morality, but to be of any use it needs to be seeded with calm, detached, rational assessment. Compassion is, perhaps, the primary moral virtue. Intelligence is an executive virtue whose role is to make compassion effective. This combination of practical wisdom and compassion we might think of as intelligent compassion.

Intelligent compassion is the essence of morality. It is not rules: neither compassion nor intelligence can be captured by rules. Rules have their place only because some people lack intelligence, some people lack compassion, and some people lack both intelligence and compassion. Then rules can be very useful. But they are only ever imperfect approximations: life is too wayward for them to be anything more.

Nicolai was fortunate in only one respect. The timing was right. Even a couple of years before, I might have followed some unintelligent rule about people needing to know the truth and deal with its consequences – no matter how unpleasant these may be. *Rip the plaster off. Live in truth.* Romantically immature horseshit like that. But I suspect life had already started going to work on me, weakening me, allowing me to see myself as a vulnerable object in a world of similarly vulnerable objects. Compassion for others is often a mirror of one's own sensed fragility. Perhaps, also, I had picked up a little practical wisdom along the way. Whatever

179

the reason, by the time Nicolai asked me this question I was, I'm relieved to say, able to muster enough intelligent compassion to know how to answer: and to gauge my answer to the precise circumstances of the asking. This little vulnerable object in my world had only recently stopped believing in Santa Claus. And he had just lost his parents. I'm pretty sure Aristotle would have approved.

'Yes, you will. Of course you will, Nico.' For now, I will leave him with a little magic in his life. Life will teach him that I lied. The realization that he will never see his parents again will slowly seep into him as the years march on. But by then he will be stronger – strong enough to know that truth is not everything. Sometimes it is not even anything.[84]

---

84 It was a number of years before they told me that they were my biological parents. This is an omission, and depending on motives and consequences, can be as blameworthy or blameless as a lie. Again, a judgement call. Was it the right one? Maybe. I can't tell, because I have no alternative version of me to compare myself against. That's one of the annoying things about practical wisdom. Even if you have it, you can never be sure that you do. Overt confidence is often a sign of practical stupidity rather than wisdom.

14

Accidents

Now I can look at you in peace.
I don't eat you any more.

Franz Kafka

They say parenthood changes the way you look at things. It certainly changes the way you look at children. 'Looks horrible, but will probably grow up fine.' That's not what I said, but certainly what I thought when my brother showed me his new kid, a few years back, and his partner Stephanie said: 'Isn't she beautiful!' Babies were never beautiful until the moment Olga stuck mine in my lap a year or so before and told me to feed him. Congratulations to our (second) happy accident, Alexander, on being the world's first beautiful baby. This warping of perceived reality known as 'parent goggles' is, it goes without saying, a biological necessity, helping parents cope with offspring – mothers more likely to nurture, fathers less likely to leave – ever since there were such things as offspring.

I know it's just a biological phenomenon. Evolution needed a way to keep social groups together. With the insects, she formulated a complex language of chemical secretions. Perhaps recognizing that mammals wouldn't be able to handle anything as sophisticated as that, for them she devised a much simpler plan: emotions. Biology decrees that I shall love my children because this ensures the stability of the group, and through this stability increases the inclusive fitness of my sparkling genes. It doesn't always work out, but it's still the norm. I know all this: and I don't care.

The London plan, as you might have guessed, was doomed to failure. If we had known anything about children, or had listened to anyone who knew anything about children, we would have known it was asking too much of Nico: after everything he had already lost, to be deposited into a completely new culture, with strange accents, strange food, strange customs and months of unremittingly bad weather. After a little less than a year in London, we moved to New York. Olga planned to resume her role in publishing (she was a junior editor at a mid-size publishing house), and I had arranged for a transfer to our New York office.

I don't know what it was about New York, but I never really got the hang of it. I thought my London job was tough, but New Yorkers always have to take things just a little bit further. Then there was the expense: the monster Manhattan going to work on our bank account, chewing away at it day and night, like some enormous, ravening pecuniary rodent. My fiscally responsible suggestions of Brooklyn, or even Jersey, were rebuffed. Olga insisted that once you crossed any of the bridges, it would be nothing but albino kids playing banjos as far as the eye could see.[85]

85 I'm afraid I haven't a clue what he is talking about.

Accidents

But anyway, Olga had plans of her own: ones of her blood's devising. Olga is half-Latina. And no matter how much her dead father is in there, telling her to go off and live her life and do things no one else can do, there is also the pull of home. Latinas always go home in the end. Half-Latinas do too, just in a more diffident, half-hearted way. A good option for the time being, we decided. We moved to Miami.

Alexander – named after Olga's father – is a year old now. Nicolai – 'Nico' as he is now uniformly known, a suitably Latinized version of his name – is eight. We sold Nico on the move to Miami with the promise of a dog. He'd been asking for one for a while, but it had been impossible in the Docklands or Upper West Side. We made the rooky mistake of telling him he could choose the dog. A German shepherd – that is what we got, courtesy of an uncle of Olga's who bred them. Great protection for your children, he assured us.

Although Boss – we promised Nico he could name him too – is officially Nico's dog, he actually spends more time with Alexander. They are at home together while Nico is at school, time they spend engaging in mutual interests. Rooting around in cupboards is their favourite. Alexander opens a door, and they both climb in. You can always tell where they are from the cackles of delighted laughter and excited thumping of tail. More than their interests have converged: their intelligence has been developing neck and neck for the past year. A notoriously tricky thing to measure, perhaps – and it's not as if I've been administering IQ tests – but their abilities to respond to simple requests and to solve simple problems reveals no major gulf between them.

I do hope some daylight will open up soon, but it hasn't happened yet.

Dogs were a strange, alien life form to me. I didn't understand them and couldn't imagine why anyone would want to have them around, investing perhaps hours of every day feeding, watering and walking these things. Now I understand: they are, basically, just like us. More accurately, they are just like what we used to be before life got to work on our sense of wonder and made it just a little smaller every day. They remind us of a time when even the house we lived in was a series of adventures, a new one every day. They remind us of a time when the best thing in life was exploring new cupboards and wardrobes, new nooks and crannies: new lands, not of what is, but of what could be. They remind us of a time when we did things just to do them and not for any advantage that might accrue. Dogs remind us of when we were just like them. They remind us of our time in Eden.

If Eden was a time before good and evil, then Nico's time in the garden is coming to an end. The visit of a mobile petting zoo to his school, and his resulting acquaintance with a small pig, has convinced him that there really isn't much difference between Boss and the pig – certainly, not enough of a difference to explain why we love the dog and eat the pig. This is an inconvenient realization when you have at least one foot in a culture that uses every special, or even not so special, occasion as an excuse to stick an entire pig in the ground and cook it.

I had been having disturbing thoughts along these lines myself, although I came at them from a somewhat different direction from Nico. They began with a practical question:

what should I feed Nico and Alexander tonight? Yes, I'm a full-time daddy now. When we moved to Miami, I informed everyone that I was going to take some 'freelance work in the financial sector' – code for: I don't really have any idea what I am going to do. But I could hardly bring myself to worry. The prison-compensation model had worked out for me in the end – ironically, several years after I had abandoned it. On paper, at least, I was rather a rich man. And, after a few worrying years in the early 90s, the London property market had gone on one of its customary binges. I could have owned a chicken coop in the Docklands and still picked up close to seven figures. As long as I was careful with the money, I was in the enviable position of not having to work for a very long time. I was still doing a bit, to keep my hand in. But my opportunities were limited here: Miami is the gateway to South America – indeed, some think it is the capital of South America – and I speak neither Spanish nor Portuguese. Still, I picked up a little bit of work here and a little bit there, and thought of it largely as a hobby. Feeding Nico and Alexander was a lot more serious. The sort of question I would ask myself every day – 'What should I feed the boys tonight?' – gradually, over the days and months, became more and more abstract, culminating in: what should I feed my children in general? Disturbingly, one thing quickly became clear: the correct answer to this is 'not meat'.

'Well-planned vegetarian diets are appropriate for all individuals during all stages of the life cycle, including pregnancy, lactation, infancy, childhood, and adolescence, and for athletes.' So says the American Dietetic Association, the US's premier group of food and nutrition professionals. No one really knows how many vegetarians there are in the world. But the numbers are certainly huge – hundreds of millions, maybe billions.[86] It is not just that we don't need to eat animals for health. If health is what we want, then there are good reasons to refrain from eating them. With the protein meat supplies come other things – things we could really do without. The American Dietetic Association continues: 'Vegetarian diets are often associated with a number of health advantages, including lower blood cholesterol levels, lower risk of heart disease, lower blood pressure levels, and lower risk of hypertension and type 2 diabetes. Vegetarians tend to have a lower body mass index (BMI) and lower overall cancer rates.' Heart disease and cancer – between them they account for over 50 per cent of the annual deaths in the developed world. Think of it this way: there is a killer out there and – statistically – he is going to take one of my sons. However, this killer concentrates his efforts on people who eat meat. Abstaining from meat substantially reduces the probability that my sons will

86 This estimate would have been true in the first two decades of the twenty-first century. In 2010, for example, India was estimated to contain around 500 million vegetarians – 42 per cent of the country's 1.2 billion people. At the same time, in the USA vegetarians were estimated to comprise between 2.3 and 6.7 per cent of its roughly 311 million people (depending on how vegetarianism is defined – in India, for example, eating eggs disqualifies you). Studies in the UK at that time estimated between 3 and 11 per cent of the population were entirely vegetarian. Germany and Italy were each estimated to have over six million vegetarians. Even if one decides to take these figures with some caution, one fact is clear. In the early twenty-first century there were hundreds of millions of healthy vegetarians worldwide. Figures are somewhat different now, with the successful commercial introduction of in vitro meat in 2024. It doesn't taste great, in my view, but no one can remember what meat is supposed to taste like anyway. We gave up in vivo meat not because of some sudden episode of moral enlightenment, but because we effectively had no choice. That my father mentions none of this is, I assume, a symptom of the issues with time that I have detailed previously (see, especially, footnotes 59, 68 and 69).

attract the killer's attention. The conclusion is too obvious to need stating. How would I feel if I saw my son die of heart disease or cancer knowing that, in all likelihood, I had contributed to this because of my culinary efforts. The fact that I might not be around to see it would in no way mitigate my culpability.

I took Alexander to the paediatrician the other day. I'm still getting used to that – the fact that they have doctors that specialize in children over here, rather than the one-age-fits-all British option. It makes good sense, though. He had been pretty sick for a few days – a respiratory virus, probably. We sat that out – perhaps another legacy of my British upbringing, where a visit to the doctor when anything short of death's door would result in a dressing-down of the you-really-shouldn't-be-bothering-the-NHS-for-anything-so-trivial oeuvre. But the coughing didn't stop. Postviral infection, deduced Dr Myshkin, and I assumed that some antibiotics were called for, just to be on the safe side. Apparently not: the just-to-be-on-the-safe-side use of antibiotics has been consigned to history. Alexander would have to be near death before he'd get to see any antibiotics.

This is the result of an American Paediatric Association directive that discourages prescription except in cases of clear and overriding need. The rationale for this directive is increasing bacterial antibiotic resistance. Not completing a course of antibiotics can help promote antibiotic resistance. Indeed, even completing a course can increase the resistance of non-targeted bacteria. Therefore, reasons the APA, the fewer the courses of antibiotics prescribed, the lower the levels of bacterial resistance will be. Brilliant! Except that nearly six times as many antibiotics are being fed to animals as to humans.[87] This is because of the appalling conditions in which they are raised, which leaves them near-certain candidates for bacterial infections. To pre-empt this, farmers routinely add antibiotics to animals' feed – whether the animals are sick or not. Through one route or another, these antibiotics then find their way into the soil and water, where they encounter microbes that now have an opportunity to become resistant to them.[88] It's not as if no one predicted this would happen – scientists have been ringing the alarm bells since the practice became common in the 1960s. Their voices have been drowned out by the combined financial muscle of the animal and pharmaceutical industries. And so my son can't get antibiotics unless he is very ill, while the animals we eat will get them just in case.

I was fortunate enough to be born into the age of antibiotics. So were my children and almost everyone I know. My mother and father were not. My mother had a brother she

87 This estimate seems about right for the period in which my father is apparently stuck in this chapter. According to an estimate of the US Department of Agriculture made in 2012, 17.8 million pounds of antibiotics are given to animals in the USA each year, compared to around 3 million pounds given to humans. And that is an industry claim – other estimates are higher. For example, around the same time the Union of Concerned Scientists put the figure at 24.6 million. With the general demise of the animal-husbandry industry, this, of course, became far less of an issue. Nevertheless, widespread antibiotic resistance among microbes was endemic by this time. Occasionally, driven more by political than moral considerations, one or another of the Western powers – if they can still be referred to as such – engages in a drive to produce new antibiotics (the multinationals won't do it because there is no money in it, the laws on rapid replacement by generic drugs being what they are). But it is a very random stop-start affair.

88 According to the calculations of Jonathan Safran Foer, the intensive-animal industry was responsible for the production of 89,000 pounds of excrement per second. See his *Eating Animals* (Little, Brown, 2009). It is not as if this will be mitigated by the sophisticated waste-management structures built for human habitations.

never knew: he died of diphtheria before she was born. It is difficult for me to imagine how terrifying life must have been before antibiotics. We are talking, realistically, about the deaths of tens of millions each year.[89] And now the age of antibiotics might be coming to an end. If so, it has been significantly hastened by the animal-husbandry industry – one of the unacknowledged costs of eating animals.

I have to say: I love Miami. I took Alexander to the beach today, while Nico was in school. We live in the 'burbs – could be anywhere, really, and I sometimes forget. But when I drive over the Rickenbacker towards Key Biscayne, the Miami downtown skyline on one side of me, the twinkling blue waters of Biscayne Bay on the other, I am always struck by the same realization: I live here! It's not just the sea, it's the weather I love. People bemoan the heat and humidity. They don't bother me. Some people profess missing the seasons. Seasons are overrated. It's the utter predictability I love. For half a year, it doesn't rain. For the other half, you know exactly when it will rain. So, when I said to Alexander last night, 'We're going to the beach tomorrow', I didn't have to make this promise contingent on weather or other things that a one-year-old could not fathom. I knew both that and when we were going.

On the other hand, I have to accept that Miami is an affront to nature. Building a vast metropolis on land that never climbs more than a few feet above sea level was an act of

89 This is actually a conservative estimate. Hundreds of millions would be more accurate. If we take into account those whose lives were significantly shortened rather than straightforwardly ended by the systematic failure of antibiotics – by, for example, the inability to carry out formerly routine operations (knee and hip replacements, etc.) – the figure is more likely to be in the billions.

breathtaking optimism. It was never going to last, and Miami's days are numbered. Before we bought here, I had a chat with an old colleague of mine in London who specialized in environmental-risk assessment. It's only a matter of time for Miami, was his opinion – and, apparently, this is by far the majority view in his circles these days. He estimated 2025 as the year people start cottoning on and house prices start to fall. The sadness these thoughts occasion in me is always tinged with a strange, and no doubt selfish, sense of privilege. I do feel privileged to be here in the end times. To see Miami in her final, end-of-days, glory. I feel like I'm living in antediluvian Atlantis and one day will have grandchildren perched on my knee, saying, 'Wow! Tell us what Miami was like, Granddad.'

Miami will sink beneath the waves because we are putting too much carbon into the atmosphere, and have been for the last two hundred years. The earth has being doing its best to absorb it all, but indications are that its limits have just about been reached. The principal cause of this is not the Hummers and Ford F-150s that litter the roads in this part of the world. Nor is it the thousands of jets – glimmering in the blue sky above us – that wing people in and out of this paradise daily. These are serious problems, admittedly. But the primary cause has less to do with these and more to do with the barbecues that decorate Alexander's favourite beach today. The animal industry is responsible for more greenhouse-gas emissions than the entire transport sector combined – ships, planes, trains and automobiles.[90]

90 This was, in fact, correct. A 2008 study by the UN-sponsored Pew Commission argued that the animal industry was the largest single contributor to climate emissions. Globally, the animal industry contributed 18 per cent of greenhouse-gas emissions. The entire transport sector combined contributed 13 per cent. The animal industry, that is,

Accidents

When my sons are grown, Miami will never be anything more to them than a haunting, submerged memory. Most of Florida will live on only in their dreams and the dreams of children like them.[91]

South Florida is mostly coral rock. The chances of it making a comeback in the next ten thousand years or so are, therefore, not good. The number of living corals in the Great Florida Reef has been steadily declining – between 1 and 2 per cent a year – since they began to measure this in 1996. The causes are various – but they all stem from human activity in one form or another, and the animal industry is at the heart of things as usual. The animal industry is the biggest single contributor to rising temperatures in the oceans, which leads to coral bleaching. The warmer waters also help spread various coral diseases: coral pathogens either live better, spread better, or both, in warmer water. The increase in sea levels also reduces the salinity of the ocean, increasing the physiological stress on the coral. There is also acidification of the ocean due to agricultural run-off. It is a perfect storm. The

produced 40 per cent more climate emissions than the entire transport sector. According to the Commission, the farming of animals was also responsible for 37 per cent of anthropogenic methane, which is 23 times more powerful in trapping UV light than CO_2, as well as 65 per cent of anthropogenic nitrous oxide, which provides a staggering 298 times the global-warming potential of CO_2. The percentage was downgraded to 14 per cent in a subsequent report, but this still made the animal industry the largest single contributor to climate emissions.

91 My father didn't quite get the timeline right. But he wasn't far off. Miami is still there, but becoming emptier by the day. It is now a little like Detroit in the early part of this century – ever shrinking. Entire areas of the city have already been abandoned. Those who have not left are those with nowhere else to go. His colleague's estimate of 2025 for the year house prices crash was seven years premature. Small errors: they take nothing away from the overall picture.

Great Florida Reef has no future. In this, it is like coral reefs the world over.[92]

These problems are global. The malign fruits of our agency respect no boundaries. We live, as Bill McKibben puts it, in a post-natural world, a world where, for example, a polar bear is drowning, unable to find solid ice because, in part, of the proclivities of people on a beach in South Florida. No part of the world is now free of human touch, because what we have done has infected the air and the oceans. Anywhere my sons choose to live will have problems. Water – most of which we give to the animals we eat rather than drink our-selves – is going to become one of the leading sources of geopolitical unrest in the twenty-first century. Regions like South Florida, that are now agreeably subtropical, will become unliveably hot. Human greed and stupidity are behind all of this: stupidity beyond belief, the sort of stu-

92 Even by the early twenty-first century the population of Elkhorn and Staghorn coral in the Florida Reef had been almost eradicated by white-band disease – their numbers being reduced by approximately 95 per cent. The first great mass extinction event in the GFR occurred in 2022, and continued at roughly annual intervals after that. The GRF is now dead. My father knew this when he wrote these words. But instead, it is almost as if he is writing from the perspective of what he would have known at the turn of the century, when Alexander was a baby. This unsettling mixing of temporal perspectives is becoming more prevalent, and more striking, as this book proceeds. It is, I am now virtually certain, a symptom of the struggles he is having with time. The same is true of the arguments of the rest of this chapter. There is no mention of the commercial development of in vitro meat in 2024 – which unfortunately came much too late for the environment if not for the animals it replaced. This contrasts, however, with some of the other chapters, where his conclusions do not seem to be indexed to the period he is writing about. As I have noted before, it is as if he always has one foot in and one foot out of the time he is writing about, and is never really sure which foot is to carry the weight.

pidity that puts a climate-change denier in charge of the Senate Environment Committee.[93]

These are all prudential reasons for refusing to eat animals. On their own, they are clearly decisive. They do tend to mask, however, that there is another reason for this refusal, one just as good: eating animals is wrong – morally as well as prudentially. This moral consideration underlies the realization of Nico, inspired by the travelling petting zoo. We don't need meat to stay healthy – on the contrary, it is killing us and our planet. The only reason we eat it is that it tastes good. And that reason is nowhere near good enough.

I think almost everyone will agree that animals count morally. It's one thing to take a chainsaw to a living tree – no matter how regrettable that might be on aesthetic or broader environmental grounds – but it is quite another to take it to a living dog. Who is going to disagree with that? A few budding psychopaths, maybe, but no one else. This is why there are laws prohibiting cruelty to animals. If there were a moral club – a club made up of all the things that counted morally – then, I think most people would agree, animals would be in it. However, if they *are* in the moral club, it is hardly with the status of fully paid-up members. We do extraordinarily vicious things to them. Those animals we eat we first make live lives of barely imaginable

---

93 I assume my father is referring to James Inhofe, a notorious climate-change denier and/or climate-change advocate (it might benefit us, you know), who was appointed Chair of the Senate Environment and Public Works Committee following the Republicans' landslide victory in the mid-term elections of 2014 – perhaps around the time my father first began writing this chapter. One more nail in the environment's coffin.

misery, and then we kill them in ways that make the most twisted horror films we have ever seen look positively tame. We do all this to them because we like the way they taste.

Everyone is aware of the distinction between needs and wants. It is a distinction that, necessity dictates, you inculcate in children at a young age. No: you may want that unhealthy snack, or ridiculously expensive Lego set, but you don't need it. A need is something that must be met if you are to have anything like a fulfilling or happy life. Obviously, you will need things such as food, water and shelter – without these you will die, and you can hardly live a happy life if you are dead. So, life and the conditions of life are among one's needs. Also, if your life is to be remotely rewarding, you will need things like reasonable health and bodily safety and/or integrity. Your life is not going to go well if you are subject to repeated violent attacks. And life as a slave is not a decent one, and so you need the ability to pursue happiness – your conception of how you would like your life to go – free from unjustified coercion or restraint.

A want, on the other hand, is something that you would like to have but is not required in order for you to live a remotely happy, fulfilling life. After you have made your first billion, for example, it would be difficult to make the case that you now need to make the next. The same is true of the interest one might have in amassing mansions, yachts and Ferraris. If we assume that one can have a fulfilling, satisfying life without these things, then an interest in acquiring them expresses a want rather than a need.

A pleasure of the palate is a want, not a need. A nice taste in one's mouth may be desirable, but it is hardly a precondition of a fulfilling life. This claim seems indisputable. The case against eating animals is based on it.[94]

If the only reason for eating animals today – it might have been different in our distant past when sources of vegetable protein were difficult to find – is that they taste good, then in raising and killing animals for food we sacrifice their needs for our wants: we allow our comparatively trivial interests to override their most vital interests. There is a word for this: wrong. In fact, it is probably the most glaring case imaginable of a type of behaviour that is morally wrong.

Imagine if someone did this to you. Suppose this person decides to kidnap you, then harvest and sell your organs – all with a view to purchasing the Ferrari 458 Italia he has always wanted. He might want the car, but you need your kidneys. In elevating his wants over your needs, he is treating you as if you don't count morally. To treat someone who does count morally as if he does not count morally is, by definition, wrong. Therefore, also by definition, it should not be done.

Eating animals violates their most vital needs. In making their way to our stomachs, they live nightmarish lives and die horrific deaths. It does not promote any similarly vital human needs – indeed, eating animals, at least in the way we do it today, is incompatible with a vast swathe of vital human needs. Therefore, in eating animals, I violate their vital needs in order to promote a comparatively trivial want of my own.

94 Here, my father seems to be rehearsing an argument developed by Mark Rowlands in *Animal Rights: All That Matters* (Hodder & Stoughton, 2013). There are other ways of developing the case against eating animals, most of which are based on the concept of equal consideration and its implications. For some of these see Peter Singer, *Animal Liberation* (Thorson, 1975), Tom Regan, *The Case for Animal Rights* (University of California Press, 1983) and Rowlands, *Animals Like Us* (Verso, 2002).

In doing so, I treat them as if they do not count morally. But we have already established that they do count morally. Therefore, eating them is wrong and I should not do it.

Morality is not rocket science. It's not even a precise science. Often its premises and conclusions do not hang tightly together, in the way they must in a mathematical or logical proof. By the standards of the genre, the moral argument against eating animals is as unassailable as one could ever demand. There is no appeal to an otherworldly moral law that grounds a duty to animals. The argument appeals only to moral principles embodied in our culture. First: animals count morally. Second: elevating a want over a need is wrong (because it treats the one who needs as if he does not count morally). Together, these entail that eating animals is wrong. I understand this argument, I accept that it is as sound as a moral argument could ever aspire to be, and yet I am unable to divest myself of a nagging suspicion: the argument wouldn't be enough – not enough to make me change. I am not saying it should not make me change – if it is a valid moral argument it should, by definition, make me change – but that it would not. The argument is logically, but not psychologically, compelling. The statement this makes about my psychology is, no doubt, unflattering. But I am what I am. I fail to feel the visceral tug of the argument. A psychologically compelling argument has a certain feel: at the very least, it is a gentle current always pulling you in the same direction. And I just don't feel it.[95]

95 This is reminiscent of my mother's earlier point concerning the ineffi-cacy of moral arguments concerning wealth redistribution. Whether her remarks exerted any direct influence on my father's thoughts at this point is unclear.

Accidents

Far from a gentle current, the prudential arguments are more like the Indus in full spring flood. I imagine Nico and Alexander overweight, their arteries clogging, their bodies riven with cancer. I imagine them living in a world where death can beckon just beyond the next cough or cut. I imagine them as environmental refugees. I could not resist these arguments because they are grounded in love. But the problems of basing morality on love rather than logic are obvious. Given everything we know about where love comes from, we have to accept that it is going to be very restricted in its scope.

Love is, of course, not incompatible with evolution – on the contrary, it is a product of evolution. But, nevertheless, there is something about love that is inimical to the spirit, if not the letter, of the book of evolution. Before there was love, life rumbled interminably on and on – atrocity-by-atrocity – one living thing continuing to exist only at the expense of another. This was not ameliorable, but a requirement built into the fundamental thermodynamic laws of the world. The first law: energy can be neither created nor destroyed, merely converted from one form into another. The second law: the entropy of a closed system will always increase. Entropy is disorder, and complexity is order. To remain a complex system, one must acquire energy from somewhere else. Any resulting carnage is a simple consequence of these two laws. But then, after aeons of blind and bloody vendetta, love somehow insinuated its way into the picture. How? The love I have for Nico and Alexander is easiest to explain. If you love your offspring, they will be more likely to survive. If they survive, they will be more likely to pass on their genes – which are also your genes. It is the genes that are driving everything: love is simply a mechanism, designed by genes, to facilitate their continuance. Olga gets in there too, by proxy: my genes can't manage things on their own.

If this story is correct – and, while somewhat caricatural, the general contours of this explanation are widely accepted – it is easy to see why one's love would extend only as far as one's genes (or gene vehicles): where your genes go, your love follows. But then something strange and wonderful happened. An accident: a magnificent accident – perhaps the happiest, noblest accident in the history of the universe, but an accident nonetheless.

My genes, let us suppose, want me to love Nico and Alexander. Of course, my genes don't really want anything. They are not the sorts of things that can want – or think, or plan or design. Talking about them in this way is usually assumed to be harmless 'as if' talk. So, let's talk. How are they going to achieve that? It is not as if some vague, diaphanous feeling is going to be good enough. The point of my love is to get my genes – or, at least, roughly 50 per cent of them – into the next generation. To do that, my love must be precise and targeted. In particular, signs of distress in Nico and Alexander must be quickly and reliably acted upon. The strategy my genes developed was empathy: the ability to feel what they are feeling, or, in its more sophisticated forms, to imagine what they must be feeling. Threats to my gene line will be registered in me as unpleasant feelings – whether this gene line is located inside my body or that of my progeny. That was the strategy. The implementation of that strategy took the form of mirror neurons.

Mirror neurons, as one might surmise, mirror: that is their

function.[96] The basic idea is that the same neuron ensemble fires both when you are doing something and when you see someone else do that thing – although, in the second case, the activation threshold for action is not typically reached. The same principle applies when you see people acting on the basis of emotions. If you see someone angry, for example, then the neuron ensembles that would ordinarily make you angry are activated. You become angry as a result – although usually to a lesser degree, since the activation will typically be less.

If I see Nico or Alexander in distress, the neuron ensembles that would ordinarily cause me to feel distress are activated, and their distress is, consequently, transmitted to me. Mirror neurons, therefore, supply me with the most primitive form of empathy. This is a brilliant strategy because motivation is built into it. Why do I care about my offspring's distress? Because to see their distress is to feel distress also. I care about my distress – that's basic biological survival 101. Caring is built into empathy even though it is not, specifically, caring about the other as the other.

It is easy to see the evolutionary value of this. But it is not yet clear why this reaction would extend any further than my offspring. If Nico and Alexander's distress becomes my distress, this may indeed help get my genes into the third generation. But the same is not true of the distress of others who are genetically unrelated to me. And yet, feeling distress

96 Mirror neurons were first discovered in the early 1990s by Giacomo Rizzolatti and colleagues Vittorio Gallese, Giuseppe Di Pellegrino, Luciano Fadiga and Leonardo Fogassi at the University of Parma. Some thought they were among the most important discoveries ever for the understanding of morality. Others thought they were irrelevant. This disagreement says a lot about the state of moral philosophy in my father's lifetime. It's no better today.

at the distress of these others is neither unnatural nor unusual. If I see someone covered in blood and rolling on the ground in apparent agony, it would be abnormal if I felt nothing, and positively chilling if I felt pleasure – even if he were not genetically related to me. This phenomenon is not restricted to humans. It is possible to find examples of non-genetically based compassion in all the social mammals. You find it in the dog that rescues its canine friend from a busy highway after it has been struck by a car. You find it in the rhesus monkey who refused food for twelve days because it knew that acceptance would entail its companion receiving an electric shock. You find it in the gorilla that cradles in her arms the boy who has fallen twenty feet into her enclosure and lies there prostrate and unconscious. You find it in the elephant that protects her friend born with a withered leg.[97] Empathy is part of our animal nature, and does not seem to be restricted to our genetic kin.

This, then, is the puzzle of empathy: if the evolutionary rationale for empathy is explained in terms of the benefit it brings to my own genes, then why should my empathy at the suffering of another extend any further than these genes? Here is where we encounter evolution's glorious accident.

The accident is grounded in a fundamental feature of evolution: the relative desirability of false positives over false negatives. Suppose you are an animal subject to predation. As such, you have evolved a predator-detection mechanism,

97 For a good survey of the empirical evidence, see Marc Bekoff and Jessica Pierce, *Wild Justice: The Moral Lives of Animals* (University of Chicago Press, 2011) and also Frans de Waal, *Primates and Philosophers: How Morality Evolved* (Princeton University Press, 2006). For a philosophical treatment, see Mark Rowlands *Can Animals Be Moral?* (Oxford University Press, 2012).

designed to fire whenever a predator is present. Like any evolved mechanism, however, it is not going to be perfect: it will make mistakes. It might fire when there are no predators present: a false positive. Or it might not fire when there are predators present: a false negative. It is clear which error is going to be the most costly. If it fires when there is no predator present, then all it costs you is an unnecessary scare and whatever energy it takes you to flee from the non-existent threat. But if it does not fire when there is a predator present, you will likely be eaten. If you have two organisms, one prone to false positives in its predator-detection mechanism, the other to false negatives, it is clear which will likely survive longest. In the game of survival and passing on one's genes, false negatives are generally more costly and dangerous than false positives. Therefore, given that no mechanism will be perfect, natural selection will result in a bias in favour of false positives.

The same principle applies in the case of distress-detection mechanisms. A false positive will mean that I become distressed and tend to Nico or Alexander even when there is nothing wrong. A false negative will mean that I do not become distressed and so do not tend to them when there *is* something wrong. The first sort of mistake will lead to some unnecessary bother on my part. The second sort of mistake can lead to the demise of my gene line. If you have two organisms, one prone to the first mistake and the other to the second, it is clear which is more likely to pass on its genes into the third generation. 'Better to be safe than sorry' is one of the formative rules of evolution, and the first ingredient of the glorious accident.

The second ingredient is found in the targeted nature of empathy. If I detect distress in Nico or Alexander, it is always via some or other behaviour: screaming, groaning, weakness, torpor or one of many other behavioural indications. My distress-detection mechanisms are always proximally targeted at these sorts of things, for there is no other way of detecting distress. While the detection of distress or suffering is the goal of these detection devices, the target of these mechanisms is distress behaviour. This is the second ingredient in the accident.

The accident's third and final ingredient has to do with the conditions under which morality evolved: social groups. Empathy is, obviously, crucial in regulating relations between parents and offspring, and this is true whether the animal in question is solitary or social. But with solitary creatures there is no reason why empathy should extend beyond the boundaries of one's gene line – and there is little evidence that it ever does. When we look to the beginnings of morality, on the other hand, we find it in social groups, not solitary creatures. The social group is the necessary condition for the extension of empathy beyond the boundaries of one's genes.

Suppose I am a member of a group of social mammals. Which, of course, I am. But I have in mind a more primitive me, living at a time when the extension of compassion beyond one's kin was in its infancy. I have distress-detection mechanisms that have evolved for the purpose of protecting my gene line. But these mechanisms are heavily biased in favour of false positives, and work by targeting distress behaviour rather than distress itself. I am not, let us assume, going to be in direct contact with my offspring – proto-Nico, proto-Alexander, if you like – at all times. For example, I allow them to wander around within the confines of the group, for this is a necessary part of their socialization. Suppose also that while some members of this group are

Accidents

genetically related to me, others are not. That is, we have reached the point in human evolution where the extended family is being supplanted by the tribe, and the bonds of genetic relatedness are loosening.

Suddenly, I detect distress: a sound, a distinctive movement. Is it the distress of my offspring (or other genetically related infant) or that of someone else? I am not sure. A false positive means I will merely waste some time and energy, protecting genes that are not mine. But a false negative may have entirely more serious consequences. My bias in favour of false positives, instilled in me by natural selection, will ensure that, in these circumstances, I will have the sort of empathic reaction I would have had if I could be sure that the distress belonged to my offspring. Better to be safe than sorry.

Some think that the extension of empathy beyond those genetically related to you is the result of a mistake. My ability to feel empathy evolved in relation to your offspring or other genetic kin. Extending it beyond the boundaries supplied by my genes is a misfire: a misdirection of my empathy into a region in which it has no evolutionary justification. We might call this the Mistake Theory of Empathy.

The Mistake Theory is, I am now persuaded, mistaken. It is not a mistake but a happy accident that is driving outwards the boundaries of empathy. We might call this the Accident Theory of Empathy. What the Mistake Theory has overlooked is that the possibility of an outward drift of empathy is built into the way the empathy mechanism works. The outward drift of empathy, beyond the narrow confines of one's genes, is practically guaranteed by fundamental features of evolution. First, there is the heavy bias in favour of false positives. Second, there is the fact that distress-detection mechanisms can only work by targeting distress behaviour rather than

203

distress itself. Third, there is the fact that humans are social animals. If you combine these three factors, it is likely that empathy will generalize, moving slowly outwards, gently but inevitably slipping its genetic moorings and leaving them behind.

This is not what evolution had in mind. But, of course, evolution never has anything in mind. I can understand what motivates this thought. There is something about this expanding circle of compassion that is so inimical to – so contrary to the spirit of – the evolutionary pressures that produced it. I agree. Nevertheless, it exists. There are no real accidents, of course. This glorious accident that is so inimical to the spirit of evolution was nevertheless built into evolution, among the bricks and mortar of its foundational principles. The possibility of goodness lies there in us: the legacy of an ancient accident that lies coiled in the core of our biological being.[98]

---

98 My father does not cite any sources for the argument he develops in these pages. It may be that he regards this conclusion as merely an obvious consequence of three widely accepted premises. But it is also likely that arguments of this sort were 'in the air' at the time the chapter is based.

15

Love

*I can declare with unequivocal confidence
that I do not love my children more than other
children because I believe they are better.*

Harry Frankfurt, *The Reasons of Love*

American beer is hideous: a fact now accepted by most Americans. American beer commercials, on the other hand, are truly world-class (they need to be, given the product they have to shift). There is a classic I remember from years ago, when I used to get sent on business trips to NYC. I forget which unpalatable beer was being advertised, but that's not important. There's a group of men, doing manly things: for example, sitting around a campfire somewhere in the great outdoors. Then, one of the dudes turns to the others and says, with the ungrammaticality required by the genre, 'Boys, it just don't get any better than this.' I have these moments, from time to time. They cluster, conspicuously, around a rectangle that sits a few feet away from the back door of the house and is filled with chlorinated water.

Nico is ten years old; his brother Alexander is three. We

205

are playing the best pool game ever invented by boys aged three to ten: Hulk. Or, better: Hulk! This involves me pretending to be really angry, picking them up and throwing them as far as I can across the pool. How far this is varies significantly. Alexander sails across the pool like a missile. Nico's trajectory is less impressive – between my recidivist back, my questionable shoulder and Nico's burgeoning stature, I suspect the days of his involvement in the game are numbered. But, for the moment, it is an unceasing Sisyphean task: 'Again, Daddy, again!' – a constant background refrain augmented by Boss's frequent complaints. He is a shepherd: that is his nature. He likes all his sheep to be together. Conversely, he has a marked distaste for his flock being repeatedly submerged under water, and alternates between running around the pool howling, and jumping in to rescue them.

If it's ever been any better than this, I don't remember it. And if it is ever going to be any better than this, I can't imagine it.[99]

If things do not, in fact, get any better than this, it is because I have been infected by a love whose purity I couldn't have imagined in my childless days. I choose the word 'purity' carefully. You might assume that I don't love Olga as much as I love Nico and Alexander. But this is not what I mean. The purity of love is not the same thing as its breadth, depth or intensity. Romantic love is typically accompanied by various powerful distractions. Lust is the most obvious

---

99 My memory is somewhat different. I remember my father complained a lot: 'Oh my back! Oh my shoulder! Let me have a rest, I'm tired!' By the time I was ten it was me that was throwing Alexander across the pool. And my father didn't want any piece of me by then, believe me.

of these, and the things that lust brings with it: possessiveness in most cases, infatuation and obsession in some. Because of these distracting elements, romantic love does not provide a very good template for thinking about love in general.

The love I have for Nico and Alexander is a much purer form of love: an involuntary, inalienable identification of myself with them.[100] It is, of course, involuntary in the sense that it falls outside my control. Even if I were to try, I could not bring myself to not love them. This sort of modification, or restriction, of the will is an essential feature of all love. It is also inalienable in the sense that it cannot be transferred to another. My love is ineluctably personal, necessarily indexed to Nico and Alexander. If you love someone and then fall out of love, and eventually fall in love with someone else, this is not the old love transferred but a new love that has taken its place. Love does not transfer from one person to another, no matter their degree of similarity.

My love of Nico and Alexander involves identification with them. The purity of love is to be found in this multi-layered phenomenon. Part of what it means to identify with my sons is to value them in a certain way. I value them intrinsically in the sense that the value I see in them does not depend on anything else – on their serving some purpose, for example. If I thought of Nico and Alexander as a kind of insurance policy for old age – someone to look after me when age and infirmity are doing what they do best – then, morally speaking, I would be a real piece of work. Nor

---

100 As the chapter's epigraph will suggest, the general idea seems to owe a lot to Harry Frankfurt's *The Reasons of Love* (Princeton University Press, 2004), though some of the specifics are different. Frankfurt also thinks that romantic love is a poor template for love in general.

does the intended beneficiary matter. If I thought the value of Nico and Alexander was simply a matter of how useful they would be to society, I would scarcely be any better. If this were my attitude, then whatever I felt towards them certainly wouldn't be love. To love my sons is to value them for what they are in themselves, independently of whatever benefits they bring to me or to society more generally. This is what Kant had in mind when he said we must treat all people as ends-in-themselves rather than as means to ends. Seeing my sons as ends-in-themselves is a necessary condition of identifying with them.

This kind of valuing is, however, only the beginning of identification: it paves the way for what is truly important. In recognizing Nico and Alexander as ends-in-themselves – as beings with a value that does not depend on any ulterior purpose I, or anyone else, has for them – I understand that they have interests, hopes, goals and dreams of their own. These interests, hopes, goals and dreams matter to me – they matter as deeply, or more deeply, than my own. Consequently, I suffer with them when their hopes are dashed, and I revel with them when they prosper. To suffer with the others in their failures, and to delight with them in their triumphs, is precisely what it means to identify with the other. This is properly described as 'identification' with the other precisely because their interests, hopes, goals and dreams have become mine.

Love is an involuntary, inalienable identification with another. Identification is a matter of degree, and this is why love can vary in its purity. The distractions of romantic love – the possessiveness, infatuation, perhaps obsession – can inhibit the degree of identification. I recognize that Olga is an end-in-herself. I recognize that she has interests, hopes, goals and dreams that are hers. These matter to me. But if it were, for example, Olga's sincere, reasoned and consistently held dream to sleep with another man, then, I assure you, my powers of identification will go only so far. And this is even true – indeed, especially true – if she enjoyed the whole business or benefited from it. My love for Nico and Alexander may not be deeper, broader or more intense than it is for Olga. But it is, nevertheless, purer.

There is, at very least, a pronounced tension between the demands of morality and those of love. Love has always been a potential threat to morality. Morality is impartial – applying to all in equal measures, regardless of who they are. Increase the overall amount of happiness in the world: it doesn't matter who is made happy. Treat everyone as an end and never as a means only: everyone, and not just those you like. A preference for those you love, on the other hand, is an essential element of love. The happiness of Nico and Alexander counts more to me than that of others, and if it didn't, that would mean I didn't love them. Love, therefore, calls into question the authority of morality. Why, in any given situation, should I listen to the dictates of morality rather than the demands of love?

Some people have claimed that moral requirements are inherently motivating. If you understand, in a given situation, what is the right thing to do, you will be motivated to do it. And if you're not motivated – then you don't really understand that it is the right thing to do. Some go further: if you really understand what is the right thing to do, your motivation to do it will outweigh any conflicting motivation you may have. The good person knows what is right, and so he or she will always be motivated to do what is right. The truly good person can do no wrong.[101]

This idea is, of course, unfalsifiable: it is impossible to prove it incorrect no matter what evidence you gather. Any case of a person who fails to be motivated by moral considerations will be explained in terms of his or her not really understanding what morality requires. It is difficult to take seriously a view that cannot, in principle, be disproved.[102] But even putting this issue aside, the astonishing implausibility of the view, especially in its stronger form, will be evident to most. Perhaps some feel the visceral tug of morality more than others. Perhaps it is true that, for some, an action is right if it provides an automatic and unreflective reason to do it. For others there will be a discernible temptation to disobey. And for yet others it will always be an open question why, once a moral rule or principle has been established as correct, one should then go on and obey it. For those outside the first category, there is no obvious reason why morality should be the most compelling thing in their lives. But this is not just a question of human psychology. It is also a question of justification. It is not a question about what does motivate us but, rather, what should motivate us. What justification could there be for assuming that nothing can, in any circumstances, outweigh the demands of morality?

In most parents there is a serial killer, biding his or her time, waiting for his or her moment to come out and play. Parents, it goes without saying, have many disturbing aspects, but

101 This is a claim associated with Socrates, via Plato. It is a claim developed in several Socratic dialogues, especially *Gorgias*.
102 This is a theme famously developed by Sir Karl Popper, *Conjectures and Refutations* (Routledge, 1963).

this undoubtedly tops the list. It is a truth perhaps dimly grasped by the childless, one that underlies their – entirely justifiable – unease around those with children. There is a classic thought experiment, which I dimly remember from another life lived among the dreaming spires. Five people are tied to a railway track – don't ask why, they just are – and a runaway trolley is hurtling down the track towards them. You are in a position to pull a switch that diverts the trolley onto another track, but unfortunately there is another person tied to this. Should you sacrifice the one person to save the five?[103] Studies have indicated that a sizeable majority of people think that you should. A sizeable majority of the population, therefore, seem to be utilitarians, at least on this issue: the greatest good for the greatest number.

Interestingly, however, their opinions change in a variation on this thought experiment. As before, five people are tied to the track. There is, this time, no possibility of diverting the trolley, but standing on the bridge next to you is an extraordinarily fat man. Should you push him off the bridge – sacrificing him to save the five? That the man is morbidly obese is no indication that what we might call 'corpulophobia' – an unmotivated hatred of, or distaste for, the corpulent – runs rampant through the ivory towers of academe. The man is fat because only a fat person will have sufficient mass to stop the trolley. You'd sacrifice yourself, of

103 The trolley problem was first discussed by Philippa Foot in her essay 'The Problem of Abortion and the Doctrine of Double Effect', in *Oxford Review*, Vol. 5 (1967). It was also discussed by Judith Jarvis Thomson – of suppose-some-guy-hooks-himself-up-to-your-kidneys fame from my mother's discussion of abortion – in her 'The Trolley Problem', *Yale Law Journal*, Vol. 94, No. 6 (May 1985), pp. 1395–1495. See also Frances Myrna Kamm, 'Harming Some to Save Others', *Philosophical Studies*, Vol. 57 (1989), pp. 227–60.

course – bless you – but you are too slight to stop the trolley and so your sacrifice would be futile. The choice is essentially the same as it was before: sacrificing the one to save the many. Curiously, many people who think you should sacrifice the one person in the first scenario also think you should not do this in the second. If many people are utilitarians, they are utilitarians who don't like to get their hands dirty. This has led to much speculation about the way people reason morally – all of which is entirely irrelevant here.

The thought experiment – it's called, for entirely obvious reasons, the 'trolley problem' – is set up in a way typical in moral philosophy. Nothing is said about any of the unwilling participants – except that the man is fat, which is germane to his ability to stop the trolley. We are not told their ages, their sex, whether they are mothers, fathers, sons or daughters, whether there are others who love them or whom they love, others who rely on them or will miss them. We are not told what they want to do with their lives, what they think and feel, whether they cry during sad movies, whether they are nice to others, whether they have ever had their heart broken or broken the heart of another. We are told none of these things because, it is assumed, they are not relevant. At most, these are side effects. And we want to abstract from the side effects to get to the underlying principle. It is a question of the one and the many – of whether it is ever right to sacrifice one person to save many, or sacrifice few people to save more.

Some side effects might, of course, be relevant. If the five people were all murderous psychopaths who had been interrupted while on a killing spree and would resume this spree if untied, then we might be, justifiably, unwilling to divert the trolley to save them. Or, if the one person tied to the track

possessed, in her head, a cure for cancer, then we might, justifiably, be inclined to save her rather than the five. But these
suppositions merely replace one sacrifice-the-few-to-save-
the-many scenario with another. Now, our inclinations are
guided by the many we will save in future by saving the one
now.

Philosophers have a magical way of circumventing these
side effects via an enchanted phrase: *ceteris paribus* – all
things being equal. It is never entirely clear what this means,
largely due to the nebulous character of the terms 'all' and
'equal'. The general idea is that it means something like 'and
all the irrelevant things don't count.' Of course, if we assume
that irrelevant things, by definition, don't count, then this
appears to be nothing more than a tautology: 'All the things
that don't count don't count.' If you push for a little more
specificity and a little less tautology, you are likely to be told
that it is a highly contextual matter – the philosophical equivalent of an 'Out to Lunch' sign. I have always tended to think
of *ceteris paribus* clauses as a performative rather than a
descriptive expression: more like 'I hereby name this ship ...'
than 'This ship is big.'[104] A descriptive expression says something about something. But a performative expression does
something quite different. If I say, 'I hereby name this ship ...'
in the right circumstances – most obviously, I am authorized
to name the ship, and I say these words during an appropriate
ceremony, etc. – then I do something: I, in fact, name this
ship. The function of the *ceteris paribus* clause is also to do
something: to register that now we are playing a certain sort of
game. We are to assume, for the purposes of the game, that

104 For the descriptive/performative distinction see J. L. Austin, *How to
Do Things with Words* (Clarendon Press, 1962).

everyone involved in the trolley scenario is more or less the same: there are no mass murderers, no cancer-cure discoverers, everyone is more or less equal vis-à-vis the size of their family, the number of their dependants, their friends and so on. Everyone is more or less the same. Everyone is entirely average. The obvious fact that things are hardly ever equal, in this sense, matters not. There is an obvious – and I think crucial – question: why are we playing this game?

If he were faced with the trolley problem, someone like Aristotle would have been baffled by the *ceteris paribus* assumption. He would, instead, have been very interested in hearing about the *arete* – the types and levels of excellence – of each person tied to the track (and also of the fat man, although Aristotle would already have mentally convicted him of the character flaw of incontinence). Are the persons involved virtuous or are they vicious (in the sense of exhibiting vices)? Aristotle would have regarded answers to this question as crucial in determining who is to be sacrificed for whom. Today, we are driven by a very different ideal: not excellence but equality.

The Declaration of Independence, the document under which my sons and their mother were all born, states that everyone is born equal. If this were a statement of fact – a description of how things are – it would amount to the claim that genetics plays no role in determining the strengths and weaknesses of a person. This claim is clearly false. No one any longer takes seriously the old nature–nurture debate: both nature and nurture have a role to play in what a person turns out to be. And if we ask which is more responsible, our question has no clear meaning and therefore no clear answer. It varies from one factor, feature and ability to another, and from one person and one environment to another. But the idea that genetics plays no important role is no longer credible.

The claim that we are all created equal should not, however, be understood as a statement of fact. It is not a description of how people actually are, but a prescription for how they should be treated. The prescription is, roughly, for everyone to be given equal consideration. What this actually means, no one is quite sure. It is generally agreed that it does not mean treating everyone in precisely the same way. Different people, through the vicissitudes of birth and upbringing, often need different things, and some people need more than others. No one would advocate treating children and adults in precisely the same way, precisely because the needs of children are different. The same is true of people with various forms of impairment or disability. Differential treatment is perfectly compatible with equal consideration of interests. This shows that while morality is impartial, it need not be impersonal. Directing your efforts towards the specifics of people – their abilities, needs and interests and so on – is not only compatible with morality, it is often dictated by morality. Nevertheless, morality remains impartial in one clear sense. Needs and interests are to be counted equally, regardless of whose needs and interests they are.[105]

The pronounced shift of moral thinking in the direction of the idea of equal consideration is often represented as a triumph of reason: a manifest destiny of moral thinking. The circle of moral concern has gradually expanded from the

---

105 True: but one of the hardest problems in moral philosophy is working out what it is to treat people equally. The utilitarian, for example, has a very different conception of equal consideration from the Kantian.

family or tribe to encompass everyone.[106] Earlier, benighted thinkers such as Aristotle may have been led astray by the prejudice of their times, but we have left that all behind. These earlier, imperfect forms of morality were destined to be rejected in favour of this ideal, which comprises the most perfect form of morality yet devised.

I used to be a much more optimistic man.[107] I used to believe in moral progress underwritten by human reason. I'd like to think our reason is in the driving seat, but it is often difficult to distinguish reason from artefact, and I now suspect the latter's role was critical. In the small city-state – the *polis* – in which Aristotle lived, people knew one another. They were familiar with each other, aware of each other's likes and dislikes, strengths and weaknesses, virtues and vices. Today, we live largely anonymously. The circle of our acquaintances is limited to family and friends. We are all, by and large, strangers to each other. And so, where the morality of Aristotle's day was a morality for citizens who largely knew each other, the morality of today had to become something very different. Aristotle's morality was not exactly a morality for friends, but it was a morality for acquaintances. The morality of today is, and had to be, a morality for strangers. If most of the people who fall under the scope of our morality are people we do not know and will never meet, then impartiality will inevitably be our default assumption. This is why love has become such a problem for morality.

*

---

106 The expression 'the expanding circle' is associated with Peter Singer. His 1981 book *The Expanding Circle: Ethics, Evolution and Moral Progress* (Princeton University Press) was very influential.
107 True. Exhibit A: his dissertation on freedom of thought and expression.

Love

If Nicolai or Alexander were tied to a track, in the path of a runaway trolley, would I kill the fat man to save him? The fat man would be dead meat. I don't think anyone would blame me for that. Suppose I tried to make sense of this in moral terms. Impartially I reason: it's one against one. The ideal of equality gives me no basis for preferring one or the other: their interests should be considered equally. Therefore, I am, morally speaking, free to choose to save whomever I wish. There is something about this response that is so wide of the mark that it barely seems to be in the same postcode of what it is supposed to explain. If I got as far as thinking in this way – what the ideal of equality requires and does not require, the resulting permissibility of saving my son, and so on – then there would be something very, very wrong with me. This is one step too many.[108] My reasons should begin and end with one simple fact: he is my son.

But it doesn't stop there. Two fat men or fat women, or thin men or thin women: my response would be the same. I would kill any number of men or women to save my son. I'd have nightmares about it afterwards, but I'd do it nonetheless. If I had to murder the world to save my sons, I suspect I would do it. I would do it without hesitation, and my reasons would begin and end with a simple fact: they are my sons.

Oh yes, says the philosopher in me – resurgent, insistent, despite the gentle tide that has carried me away from Oxford – but what you would do is one thing and what you should do is quite another. Quite, quite – I know that. My

108 The one-step-too-many argument was devised by Bernard Williams, 'Persons, Character and Morality', in his *Moral Luck: Collected Papers 1973–1980* (Cambridge University Press, 1981), pp. 1–19. As Harry Frankfurt has pointed out, even citing the fact that 'he is my son' as a reason for his action may already be one step too many.

point concerns the authority of should over would. Why care about what I should do when what I would do clamours so much more insistently? I know that sacrificing an indefinite number of people to save Nico or Alexander would be wrong. Not only do I know that it is wrong, I understand why it is wrong. But I would do it nonetheless. If you put morality up against love, love will win every time. For Socrates, what is right conquers all – for those who truly understand. But those who truly love know this is not so.

The partiality of love versus the impartiality of morality, the challenge to the authority of morality that is posed by love: these are both just symptoms. At the very bottom of the rabbit hole, there is a fundamental inversion.

As it is widely understood today, morality is grounded in the idea of value or worth. The locus of this value can vary from one moral theory to another. In the tradition inspired by Kant, the locus of value is the human being, understood as an exemplar of normative self-government. Because they have certain features – rationality, reflection and autonomy – humans possess a distinctive kind of value. It is, therefore, morally incumbent on us to treat humans in ways that respect this value. Thus we arrive at Kant's primary moral imperative, at least in one of its forms: we are to treat all human beings never as a means only but always as an end. For utilitarianism, the direct locus of value is quite different. Value attaches to happiness (for the hedonistic utilitarian), or to satisfied preferences (for the preference utilitarian). Therefore, we are to act in ways that maximize what is of value – increase the overall amount of happiness or satisfied preferences in the world. Despite their disagreement concerning the locus of value, the advice of these two traditions converges, at least when looked at in a sufficiently abstract way: identify what is of value, and then promote and/or respect it to the best of one's abilities.

Love is the inversion of morality. I do not love my children because I perceive them to have some value which other children – or, for that matter, adults – lack. It is not as if they possess some worth that is independent of my love for them and decisively distinguishes them from all other people.[109] This gets things the wrong way around. I do not love my children because they are better, or more important, than other children. Rather, to me, they are more important than other children because I love them. It is my love that makes them more important. Those whom we love acquire value for us precisely because we love them. Our love does not respond to their value; it creates a value that they otherwise would not have had.[110] As an end-in-itself, the beloved already has a value that is intrinsic to her, rather than being a function of what she can do for other people. But I do not love all ends-in-themselves. Intrinsic value is no guarantee of love. All children are intrinsically valuable, but I love only two. Such value may be a necessary condition of love, but it is not sufficient. The distinctive value that my children have, a value that distinguishes them from all others, derives from my love for them, and not the other way around. Love comes first. The distinctive value of the beloved comes afterwards and as a consequence. Love, in this sense, has primacy over value. To

109 Frankfurt, *The Reasons of Love*, p. 39.
110 My father is here advocating what is known as the 'bestowal' theory of love, a theory that is opposed to 'recognition' theories. According to the latter, love is based on a response to the recognition of value in the loved. Both theories are problematic, each drawing as many opponents as advocates. This is as true now as it was in my father's time. We still have no idea what love really is.

the extent morality is based on the primacy of value, love is the anti-morality.

And yet, there is a well-known moral framework whose influence compares quite favourably to that of utilitarianism or Kant, and which seemingly grounds morality in love. It tells us to 'love thy neighbour as thyself'. Unfortunately, without some creative reworking of the idea of love, this seems too harsh and demanding a requirement – and this is so even if we overlook the fact that a non-negligible number of my neighbours have been asshats. Forget loving as I love myself – how can I love my neighbour when all my love belongs to two boys? And even if this were possible, it would hardly be desirable. Imagine what it would be like to follow this advice. You identify with everyone, and so you endure with everyone. You dream their dreams with them, suffer with them when those dreams are dashed, and rejoice with them when they are not. You are, in effect, in a state of empathic hyperarousal that is completely indiscriminate in whom it targets – a rapid and one-way journey to the nuthouse.

The inalienability of my love for Nico and Alexander means that it does not extend beyond them. The involuntariness of love means that I cannot extend it even if I wanted to. And the identification involved in love means that the attempt to extend it to all would be a bad idea anyway. Nico and Alexander are supermassive black holes. All my love returns to them in the end. But I can imagine a suitably watered-down version of this love: a weaker, diaphanous incarnation that can slip these gravitational bonds and so extend outwards to other people. This anaemic echo of love is called compassion, and it is all I have left for the world.

16

Juicing

Over himself, over his body and mind, the individual is sovereign.

John Stuart Mill, *On Liberty*

There comes a time in one's life when one's hypocrisy is revealed, once and for all, as having no limits. I received a text from Nico asking if we could skype. Unusual – both he and I detest the medium. He's in his senior year at Harvard, majoring in philosophy, and his old man couldn't be more proud. The subject of our conversation: drugs.

After our past indiscretions in India, among other places, I know both Olga and I were dreading the hypocrisy in which we would no doubt find ourselves engaging if the topic of recreational drugs was ever raised. Thus, you can imagine my relief when I discovered these were of the performance-enhancing, rather than recreational, variety. Neither of our children, stalwart members of Generation Wuss, has ever shown any interest in the latter. As far as we know, anyway.

Nico is a very serious, driven boy. He's also ambitious, and this has led him to his present predicament. His peers have been using cognitive enhancers to help them in their studies. I immediately thought of Ritalin and Adderall, but was informed that they are all very last-century, Granddad. He was then kind enough to provide me with a crash course in the emerging world of Nootropics: Piracetam was discovered in the 1960s. It's okay, moderately powerful, but no longer regarded as among the marquee cognitive enhancers. Pramiracetam is a more recent invention, but little use to him since it works primarily on the memory and what he's interested in – as an aspiring original thinker – is neural connections. The same is apparently true of Aniracetam. Phenylpiracetam is better. Best of all, perhaps, is Noopept, which has a nice stimulant effect as well as promoting the ability to see connections, analogies or isomorphisms between different things.

Nicolai wanted to know what I thought of these things. He felt, understandably, that in not using these substances he was losing an edge that he might otherwise have, one that might be crucial when you harbour ambitions of the *magna* or *summa* variety. What do you think, Dad? Given his apparently encyclopaedic knowledge of these substances and their effects, I couldn't help thinking that this request for advice had a distinctly ex post facto feel to it. But, anyway, I did what any self-respecting father would do in the circumstances: I told him I'd talk to his mother and get back to him. Unfortunately, this was a route he was not keen on exploring. He didn't want to worry her, he said. Curiously, he seemed to have little objection to worrying me – which, I suppose, is something I should think about when I find the time. Still, a kick into touch was required. Let me do some research, I tell him, and we'll talk again very soon.

This reaction – it is instructive to note – is quite different from what it would have been if the same sort of question had been asked of me by Alexander. The fun I've had with that boy over the years. Every week from September to January would begin with a barely noticeable frisson of excitement bubbling benignly just below the surface of conscious awareness, gradually reaching a crescendo on Friday nights. I thought I used to get nervous before big rugby games when I was young. But the butterflies of my youth were little Cabbage Whites, while those of Alexander's were enormous Queen Alexandra Birdwings flown in, especially for me – not him, he was a study in insouciance – from Papua New Guinea.

Alexander plays football, and he's not bad at it. He's been towering over me since he was fourteen. Some colleges are looking at him for a football scholarship, and if that's what he wants I'm more than happy for him. But I can imagine my reaction if he came to tell me he wanted to bolster his ambition with a little judicious steroid use: it would be visceral, dramatic and negative. Nico's question, on the other hand, I treated as an intellectual one: it required sifting through the available evidence and arriving at a warranted conclusion. It is unclear to me whether this divergence in attitude would be justifiable.

But I suppose the first reaction of most parents when they are asked, point blank, by one of their progeny, 'Should I use drugs?' is to immediately say 'no' and then thrash around in search of some justification: the stronger the better, but flimsy will do if that's all you have. The more I think about it, the more it strikes me that flimsy and conditional are all I am going to get.

The claim that performance-enhancing drugs are wrong is ambiguous. It could mean that it is morally wrong to use such drugs. Or it could mean that it is prudentially wrong. I'll take the moral case first. A category of drug can't, of course, be morally decried simply because it is performance-enhancing. At least, this is so if the performance in question is not itself morally iniquitous. If the performance were, for example, gunning down innocent civilians, then anything that aided in this performance would be morally question-able.[111] But navigating one's way through the intricacies of logical space or, for that matter, those of the football field, is not morally iniquitous. If the performance is not itself morally iniquitous, then we can't criticize a drug simply on the grounds that it is performance-enhancing. Indeed, men of a certain age – and women too, I gather – often make use of performance-enhancing drugs supplied by the dealers of Pfizer and Eli Lilly. I can't see anything wrong with that, and my opinion seems to be endorsed by a substantial proportion of the community, male and female, who have been joyfully blurring the distinction between recreational and perform-ance-enhancing drugs for quite some time. That an attitude is common does not mean that it is correct. But it does create a presumption in its favour. One can't just assume that per-formance enhancement is wrong. Some reason needs to be given in support of this.

As far as morality goes, there is also a sense, and I know this was part of my initial moral reaction, that performance-enhancing drugs are unfair: that they unacceptably tilt a

111 Speaking of hypocrisy: my father was always (a) vehemently anti-guns and (b) a serial gun-owner. He kept his pistol, usually a Glock, in a safe upstairs in his bedroom closet. He says it was for protection, and that is not unreasonable given the way South Florida became once the effects of climate change became evident. But if your goal is killing people, guns are, I suppose, a type of performance-enhancing substance.

previously level playing field. On reflection, however, I had trouble making sense of this idea. The playing field never was, and probably never will be, level.

Nico's high school advertised itself as the most academically rigorous in the state. (I am highly sceptical of this claim, but even if it were true, if you knew Florida you'd realize that this isn't setting the bar very high.) We always took an interest in his school work, helped him when we could, and sent him off to various advanced placement courses at the University of Miami from the time he was fourteen. It wouldn't have made any difference if he hadn't had the natural talent, of course. But given it was there, Nico was lucky to be in an environment that nurtured it. This is all luck. Even natural talent is a matter of luck. To the extent other kids have not been as lucky, the playing field was never even. Drugs might be a relatively cost-effective way of compensating for things you can't control, such as an environment that wasn't as helpful as the one in which Nico was raised. In these circumstances, condemning performance-enhancing drugs as unfair misses the point.

I know: two wrongs don't make a right. But this assumes that either of these things is wrong. And even if they are, what is the supposed method of rectifying them? There is a kid Alexander knows, Jamal, from West Perrine, a poor black neighbourhood a few miles away. Jamal is a running back, and a good one. He is going places. People say he is juicing: Alexander is not so sure, and I simply don't know. But suppose he were. He hasn't had the benefit of Alexander's lifetime of excellent nutrition. Instead of the gym membership we bought Alexander when he started becoming serious about athletics, Jamal has made do with a bench and a bar in his car porch. In the circumstances, saying that he can't have the one thing that he might be able to afford, at least every now and then – something that might compensate for his lack of fortune – seems to reek of hypocrisy. There isn't a level playing field, and without some truly unprecedented changes in the structure of society there isn't going to be one. Targeting those things within relatively easy reach of the disadvantaged seems grossly unfair.

Nevertheless, my failure to identify any moral case against performance-enhancing drugs notwithstanding, I still didn't like the idea of Nico using. So, I decided to explore the prudential case against their use – with, I think it is fair to say, mixed results. It would have been so much easier if it had been Alexander questioning me on steroid use. It's almost as if the two categories of drugs were designed by their principal target markets: cognitive enhancers by super-intelligent nerds, and steroids by muscle heads. It wouldn't have been necessary for me to delineate any of the serious distal effects: liver cancer, high blood pressure, heart and circulatory problems, psychiatric disorders, prostate gland disease. More pressing anatomical considerations would have done the trick: shrunken testicles, man boobs. Either of these would, I am certain, have been immediately sufficient to dissuade Alexander.

Cognitive enhancers, however, are an entirely different kettle of fish: no ball diminution or boob magnification issues with them, apparently. In fact, long-term health issues are not known because they simply haven't been around long enough or been used widely enough for the requisite studies to have been conducted. The studies that have been conducted suggest that the effects of at least some of the more popular cognitive enhancers – such as Ritalin and Modafinil[112] – are quite modest and variable. Some subjects clearly do respond, but others seem to show little or no benefit. It is not clear why this is the case, but some speculate that the effects of these sorts of enhancers at least might depend on the person's genotype and also on their baseline level of cognitive function. For example, several studies of dopaminergic (i.e. dopamine-related) drugs on working memory support the conclusion that those who benefit most are people who already have problems with working memory – for example, have a low working-memory capacity. Thus some drugs will improve working memory in people who have poor working memories but actually impair performance in people with good working memories.

In addition to the question of their efficacy, there is the question of long-term effects. No studies have, as yet, examined the long-term effects these drugs may have on health. Indeed, very few studies have even examined their long-term effects on cognitive performance. Therefore, as things stand, we have no way of accurately assessing the long-term costs and benefits of these drugs. They may be harmless to health and beneficial to cognitive performance, or they may be useless to cognitive performance and detrimental to health. The eventual answer will probably lie somewhere in between and will almost certainly vary from one drug to another.

The case I put to Nico was, therefore, this: given that their usefulness is unproven and their long-term effects unknown, the rational thing to do is to refrain from using them. They might not help you, and they might kill you. Health is more

---

112 My father's point here is about as relevant as pointing out that – to use the example of two other museum pieces – a gramophone is useless for playing music downloaded to a smartphone.

important than a vocation. I'm not sure how much of a case it is. I bought it, but I'm not sure if Nico did. It strikes me that, in its focus on the long term, in its elevation of caution over potential, there is something very old and dispiriting about this argument. I'm not sure it is the sort of argument to which a young person really should give credence.

My case, to the extent it works at all, is predicated on deficiencies of design and on the paucity of research into currently available enhancers. Who knows what the pharmacological industry will devise in the coming decades? Suppose there were a drug that did effectively and dramatically boost your cognitive performance, and was demonstrated to have no deleterious health effects. Suppose there were a substance that did spectacularly increase your atheletic ability – allowing you to build muscle more effectively, improving your power, speed and stamina – and also had no deleterious effects. Would there be anything wrong with these drugs?

The answer, I think, must be a qualified 'no'. This 'no' is qualified only in the sense that one might have worries about the effects on society if these drugs were very expensive. If they were, this would be yet another source of inequality, leading to society becoming even more two-tiered than it already is. But suppose they are relatively cheap and easy to acquire. It would be just like going into a pharmacy and buying paracetamol. Could these drugs be objected to in these circumstances? It is difficult to see what rational basis there could be for such an objection.[113]

*

113 There is, I suppose, a depressing inevitability to the way things turned out. New cognitive enhancers were, and continue to be, developed. No major systemic deleterious health consequences have yet been discovered, although there are health consequences for overuse, including,

Juicing

Suppose there was a drug – whether cognitively or athletically enhancing – that had dramatic short-term benefits but equally dramatic long-term drawbacks. And suppose Nico and/or Alexander were to say to me: 'I don't care about the long term. Tomorrow never comes. The now is what is important.' In effect, he/they would be making a value judgement,

notably, liver and kidney damage. Some unusually susceptible individuals die quickly and without warning, for reasons as yet poorly understood. But the level of mortality is judged by most to be within the bounds of acceptable risk. So we all use them now: those of us who can afford them, anyway. And society did become even more stratified as a result. They are not cheap, but well within the grasp of the average middle-class aspirant – a month's supply costs about as much as a premium Satellite TV subscription. The favourable cognitive outcomes are widely touted by the companies who develop these drugs, though, since few of us can remember what it was like before we started using, it is not clear how accurate these claims are (the research done in their support is untrustworthy: like all research done today, it is conducted by people who have a vested financial interest). The way things are, however, we just cannot take the risk of not using them.

These 'post-birth' forms of enhancement, however, pale into insignificance when compared to what we do to people before they are born. The real source of inequality lies in genetic embryonic modifications. It began with eliminating single-gene genetic disorders such as cystic fibrosis. But once the gene genie was out of the bottle, there was never any prospect that we would confine ourselves to disorders – not when there is money to be made. My father would no doubt condemn this on grounds of inequality. But his arguments could equally be used in support of the practice. Parents want the best for their children. That's why mine sent me to good schools, and looked after me in a myriad of others ways. Suppose you knew that by having a simple and safe procedure prior to, or after, conception you could immensely improve your child's prospects – giving him, or her, an advantage in the world comparable to the best education. What is the difference – the moral difference – between helping your child post-birth and helping him pre-birth? Moreover, suppose you knew that many others were already doing this. Thus, if you fail to follow suit, you will not only be failing to provide your child with an advantage, you will be actively disadvantaging him relative to others – and advantage and disadvantage are, of course, always relative (in the kingdom of the blind, etc.). You see the pressures? Everyone succumbed – if they had the money. I have to admit: I did. The result: our society is the most stratified, and least socially mobile, society in human history.

of the sort that Achilles once endorsed: a short and glorious life is better than a lengthy average one. Of course, Achilles was always ambivalent on this issue, and later came to rue his decision, and I suppose this is a point I might make, assuming I wanted to change his mind – which, it goes without saying, I would. But suppose my best efforts in this regard fail. What, morally speaking, am I legitimately entitled to do about it?

At the heart of the issue is the relation between welfare and autonomy – and something that has always had an uneasy relationship with autonomy, viz. parenting. A person's welfare is a matter of how well his or her life is going. This will be a function of many factors including how interesting or stimulating it is, how happy the person is, the relative amounts of pain and pleasure in her life, the extent to which she feels her life is worth living and so on. It is difficult to pin down with any precision what exactly a person's welfare amounts to, but it is the sort of thing we are after when we say to someone, 'Are you happy with life?' Autonomy, on the other hand, is a matter of the extent to which a person feels that her life is her own. Most of us have a conception of the way we would like our lives to be: the sorts of things we would like to do, where we would like to live, the sort of people with whom we want to live and so on. On the basis of this conception of our lives, we can make various choices and decisions about what to do – decisions that, we hope, will foster this desired life. That is, we have a conception of what would, for us, be a good life. And we have the ability to choose and act in order to promote, bring about, or make more likely, this good life. This ability is known as autonomy.

A person's welfare is obviously very important, but so too is their autonomy. Their autonomy can't be explained in terms of their welfare. Indeed, sometimes acting autonomously can be detrimental to one's welfare. We all occasionally, and many of us more than occasionally, make poor life choices: either because of a mistaken conception of goals, or because of mistakes in how we pursue them. How do we adjudicate between the often competing demands of autonomy and welfare? With which facet of the good life for humans do we side?

The idea that we always side with autonomy is not enticing. I remember, when he was young, I caught Alexander rooting through a kitchen cupboard (with Boss, of course) and emerging with a bottle of Drano, which he seemed intent on drinking. Clearly, I wasn't going to let considerations of autonomy trump those of welfare in this situation. Of course, it is not really meaningful to talk of autonomy at such a tender age. Nevertheless, suppose the topic of this week's conversation had, in fact, been Nico's to-ing and fro-ing over the decision to begin a heroin habit. Researching the pros and cons of heroin use would not have been high on my agenda.

On the other hand, giving absolutely no weight to autonomy doesn't seem to be tenable either. Suppose in the decade or so to come, it becomes clear that Nico is very poor at choosing a spouse. He's already had two, let's suppose, and they were both nightmares. Suppose, one day, I say to Nico: 'Hey Nico, I've found you a wife. I know you've never met her, but she's very nice, and my thorough investigation of both of you has convinced me, beyond reasonable doubt, that you will both be very happy together.' Then I force them to marry at gunpoint. Even if I was right about their future happiness, taking away a person's ability to make the most important decisions in his or her life doesn't seem to be right. The ability to make our own decisions – especially when they are the most important decisions of our lives – is one of the most highly prized features of the human condition.

It is tempting to suppose that we can bring autonomy and welfare into line by including in the idea of autonomy not only what a person actually wants, but also what he or she would want if he or she were suitably informed. Unfortunately, this won't work: if we do this, we are no longer talking about autonomy. In a situation where someone wants something – to take steroids, for example – but we think he wouldn't want this if he knew all the relevant facts, then all we can do is give him the relevant facts. If he still decides he wants to take steroids – man boobs and shrunken testicles notwithstanding – then there is nothing more we can do without infringing on his autonomy. If you claim, for example, that he doesn't really understand the facts or their ramifications, your claim may well be true. But if you then decide to physically stop him taking the steroids, you are still violating his autonomy. Autonomy is a matter of what a person actually wants, not what you think he would want in more ideal circumstances. Once we allow the latter, then any amount of intervention in a person's life could be justified on grounds of autonomy. This means that we are no longer talking about autonomy. In effect, you have replaced the idea of a person's autonomy with the idea of his welfare.

How to adjudicate the competing demands of welfare and autonomy is among the hardest problems in moral and political philosophy. The short answer is that no one really knows: no satisfactory answer to this question has ever been identified. It is unfortunate, then, that it is a problem every parent faces almost daily. In the end, you encounter a difficult realization: a realization so sad it almost makes you cry.

Juicing

There comes a time when it is no longer your job. All you can do is equip your child to think about these issues in the right way. But even what this amounts to is not really clear.

I have always, I suppose, been a Millian at heart – going all the way back to Oxford. Mill wrote: 'The only purpose for which power can be rightfully exercised over any member of a civilized community, against his will, is to prevent harm to others. His own good, either physical or moral, is not a sufficient warrant ... Over himself, over his body and mind, the individual is sovereign.' With a few qualifications here or there, I agree.

When I was young, I used to play against a local rugby club. It was rumoured that several of the players were juicing. Actually, it was more than rumoured: they clearly were. This was confirmed several years later – I was living in London by this time – when almost the entire first team, and many of the second, were arrested for illegal steroid use. My reaction, and I know several of my friends shared it: *But they were shit anyway!* Think about it. There you are – a mediocre player, playing for a mediocre team, in the sixth division of a regional rugby league. You are risking shrunken testicles, man boobs, liver cancer and a slew of psychiatric disorders – just so you can get to the fifth division! That is an example of poor decision-making. But there may be other circumstances in which you decide that the potential sacrifice to your health is worth the risk. You are on the cusp of the NFL and the multimillion-dollar contracts it involves, for example, and, since you possess few other talents, the alternative is a life of drudgery, as you see it. Your decision may still be unwise, and I'm not saying it is the right one. But it is not an obviously ridiculous decision in the way it was for these sporting journeymen.

A Good Life

The key to a healthy person, where welfare and autonomy have been appropriately integrated, is good decision-making. It is the ability to understand when a risk is worth taking and when it is not. And this is grounded in an appreciation of not only of what is important in life, of what you most want or desire in life, but also in the ability to realistically assess, in your current situation, how likely you are to get it. My most important function is like that of the state: not to tell Nico and Alexander what to do – even when I really want to. It is to make them healthy people capable of making good decisions.

When a life is new, questions of autonomy are unimportant. There is no real autonomy then. But its time is coming. As we get older – after a few glorious but essentially misleading decades of flourishing – our welfare will slowly start to diminish. Its decline is not linear, but it is discernible and inevitable. As welfare declines, autonomy becomes progressively more important: more and more it becomes something to be jealously guarded. There may even come a point in one's life where all one really has left is autonomy.

17

Crossroads

Death is a way to be, which Dasein
takes over as soon as it is.

Martin Heidegger, *Being and Time*

I have waited for evening. It's a little cooler. But, even so,
these are small margins. A degree or two of temperature
traded for more than that of acrid humidity. When I step out
of the house it's like being slapped about the face by a hot,
wet towel. For Boss II,[114] it must be much worse: he is wearing a thick fur coat. Sometimes he will just sit at the open
door: 'Nah, you go on, mate. It's not for me today.' But, today,
he enthusiastically agrees. I haven't taken him running for a
while. The mosquitoes will be out in force: vast gyrating
swarms. I come aerosol-protected, of course. By the time I
return, my face will be coated with a thick black shroud of

114 Boss II joined the family in 2010. Thus, the events my father describes
would have occurred no earlier than this. I suspect, in fact, that they
occurred a few years later. Boss II wouldn't have been ready for one of
my father's runs until he was at least a year old, and his reticence to
accompany my father suggests he was older than that.

them: dead, but still clinging determinedly – my eye sockets white from the covering of my shades, like an old World War I pilot returned from his mission.

I am running because there is something I need to know. There is a question that has been raised by the US medical establishment, but because of the arguably criminal vagaries of the US medical insurance system, it has yet to answer. Am I dying? I have been feeling unwell – perhaps the worst in my life – for a few weeks. I don't like going to see doctors, and I usually just sit out these sorts of things. But after a couple of weeks, my patience finally eroded. A few low-resolution CAT scans were done, and a mass was detected. 'Not a cyst,' the diagnosis continued – which, in the medical profession, is a way of saying: 'Oh shit, could be cancer.' It gets worse. This not-a-cyst is located in my liver. Which means that if it is cancer, it's going to be the sort that definitely kills me, and will do so in weeks or months, not years. The follow-up liver function and liver enzyme tests were inconclusive – gnomically straddling the borderline of normal.

If I hadn't been feeling so ill, I probably wouldn't have worried so much. And if it were just the illness without the unexplained masses, I wouldn't have worried either. But I was both sick and worried. 'Worried sick' is an entirely accurate expression. There is a substantial overlap between the symptoms of terminal cancer and those of extreme anxiety. Loss of appetite: check. Significant weight loss: check – but covered by aforementioned loss of appetite. Nausea – check, but in the absence of food, that stomach acid will really go to town on you. Weakness, fatigue: both of those. Happily, I couldn't convince my skin to turn yellow – which would have been the final, and decisive, indication. That gave me hope.

Crossroads

I needed a high-resolution CAT scan or, better, an MRI to adjudicate the issue. But my extraordinarily expensive insurance which, every month, I had been paying on time for fifteen years said: Fuck you – we don't cover those. They do cover them – I've read the policy – but dealing with a US insurance company is a complex negotiation. Denial of coverage is the opening gambit. They hope you will then go away. Or die before you get the coverage to which you are entitled. As a consequence, the MRI that would either exonerate or condemn my liver was still a few weeks away.

I've tried running through this illness: Walk it off, Myshkin. I've tried a paltry three-mile circuit around my house that, on my healthy days, I follow only when I am at my most attenuated or time constraints are most unrelentingly stern. Now, by the time I'd reached a mile, the world would be spinning dramatically, and it was all I could do to bumble and stumble my way home. But today I am feeling stronger. There is a clarity to my thoughts that has, I realize, been missing for some time. And, today, I am going to do everything I can to run this circuit in the fastest time I have ever run it. I am going to run as if my life depended on it – because, in a sense, it does. I know that if I run this circuit the fastest I've ever run it, I can't possibly be dying. Can I?

I turn my iPod to my six-minutes-per-mile songs. The Chemical Brothers' 'Hey Boy, Hey Girl', Saliva's 'Click, Click, Boom', and keep running as fast as I can. Boss II – he insisted on coming, and I'm glad he is here – is more than a little chagrined when I refuse to permit him the customary stops to mark his territory, and is almost certainly regretting his decision to run today with this mad, driven version of me. I keep going, slamming down one foot in front of the other, through the lurching, spinning streets of suburban Miami, through burning lungs and mute lactic agony. Dragging the long-suffering Boss behind me for most of the second one-and-a-half, I come home in just over eighteen minutes. I've never been able to even get close to that time again – not even within a minute. I am much stronger now. Not dying after all, the MRI will later confirm – a harmless congenital condition. I was, in all likelihood, suffering from nothing more than a long and tenacious virus. But I am nowhere near as fast as I was that day. I am no longer running for my life.

I wouldn't want to overly dramatize the episode I have described. It's the sort of thing most people will go through at some point in their lives, and for many there will be no happy resolution. For me, one might think it would be a turning point: an event that allows me to put all the minutiae and assorted meaningless drivel of life into perspective. 'Don't sweat the small stuff,' my father used to say. You would think it is the sort of thing that would allow me to both identify the small stuff and then prevent the unnecessary perspiration. But that's not quite how it turned out.

The paradox of death is that one both runs away from and, simultaneously, runs towards it. I have spent much of my life running from death. My death is something I neither want to talk about nor even think about. I know it's there, that it will happen, but I know this as an abstract possibility: as something that will happen to someone, somewhere, sometime down the line, and it just so happens – a pure contingency – that this someone is me. But in the cool, pale hours of the morning – after I have awoken but before I have arisen – there is a voice that whispers to me that my death is so much more than this. And in those moments I think I really do understand that I shall die. But this quickly fades with the sun, dissipates like a dream, and I can never quite remember what it is I understood in those moments. Sometimes life provides you with an opportunity to remember.

We often think of life in terms of turning points or crossroads. That was the moment – that was the event: the one that set me on my current path, and made me the person I am today, for good or for ill. It is not clear how much of this is after-the-fact rationalization, and it probably varies from case to case. But that doesn't matter. Far more interesting is what the possibility of a turning point in someone's life says about that life. A turning point is a moment in someone's life where that life can be illuminated, and seen, at least for a while, as what it is. Life is a goal-structured edifice: where one thing is done for the sake of another, which is in turn done for the sake of something else. We run through life on a course that is charted by the goals we pursue. A turning point is a clearing in a man or woman's life when the goal-structured character of this life shows itself. A turning point occurs when one realizes that the goals one has been pursuing were not as important as one thought, and so one now, consequently, turns to a new set of goals.

A turning point, in this sense, is still just more small stuff – one set of goals is identified and merely replaced by another. But there is another sort of crossroads, quite different in character and significance. This is the turning point that calls into question the possibility of turning points. The idea of a turning point is a temporal one. It presupposes a future – you need a requisite amount of time to continue along your new path, the one towards which you have been turned. The biggest turning point is the one that heralds the end of turning points. Or does so possibly, one can never be sure, and that is part of the point. The biggest crossroads in life is when one is no longer confident enough to see one's life in terms of crossroads. Then you start to think that here, where you are right now, is precisely where you are going to end up. The idea that I am no longer travelling, that I might just have arrived at wherever it was I was going, this idea fills me with a nameless terror.

Arrival terror – the horror of the destination – is a common complaint. It is the terror that accompanies knowing what lies at the end of every goal. A turning point in the first sense reveals the course: a course determined by the goals you pursue. By allowing you to understand the course, it allows you to change it if you so choose. But a turning point in the second sense reveals the destination. This crossroads that calls into question the possibility of crossroads thereby reveals what is at the end of every course, every goal, every road. That end is death. Whatever road I choose, and no matter how often I change it, I have always been running towards death. But, on this occasion, death was waiting for someone else.

18

Olga

Alexander didn't recognize me. He's in college on the West Coast, and we won't let him fly back every weekend, not unless there is some decisively unfavourable development – which I suppose there has now been. It's only been three weeks, but I'm not really surprised at his lack of recognition. My skin is pallid, waxy parchment stretched over small and brittle bones. Three weeks ago, I had been sitting up talking to him, and still looking more or less like the mother he knew, still playing the part of a mother. (Yes, I have one more contribution, something I've been working on these last weeks in hospital. It will, undoubtedly, be my last intervention in Myshkin's story.)[115] Today, however, I'm up to my gills in morphine, prostrate, but more aware than they real-

---

115 I discovered the material that made up this chapter in a file on my mother's laptop that, I was astonished to discover, still worked after all this time. It has been some years since my mother passed. Those years scarcely made the job of reading these pages less painful.

ize. I can't really see much any more, but I still know things. I was aware of them when they came to the door. I could hear Alexander's panicked exclamation: 'No, Dad, we're in the wrong room!' he said, his eyes darting wildly from the bed to the door, before alighting again on me. Another look, and then a terrified realization slowly crystallizing on his face – something I could feel rather than see. Another look: recognition, consent. I knew Myshkin hugged him, I could feel it. 'It's okay, Alexander,' he said. The trembling in his voice showed it was anything but.

You don't come back from stage-four pancreatic cancer. There is no hope. You are going to die, and die soon. I knew this as soon as the diagnosis was in. The pain I would have been feeling has been kept to a reasonable level by the morphine that has been pumped into me over these last weeks. There may come a point when the morphine they need to give me to keep the pain at bay will be enough to kill me. I will fall asleep and my heart will stop. In many ways, I long for this to happen. At the same time, I have expressly forbidden it. I'm torn: my public displays of conviction didn't capture my lack of self-unanimity on this matter. Worst of all is that I know how hard this must be on them, on the three people I love most: for them to watch my gradual corruption, each day a little worse than the one before, until finally the worst day of all arrives. I hate it, and I want it to end. But what I want least of all is for the last memory these men ever have of me to be a memory of me giving up.

The way we die can be one of the most important things we ever do. There is a lesson – an ethical lesson – contained in it. The hardest moments of one's life leave the deepest scars, and these scars are memories of a certain sort, but memories you don't even know are memories. These memories assert themselves not in the familiar way of most memories. They are not episodes of conscious recall. They are to be found not in your mind but in your life and the way you live it. They are to be found in a certain outlook, a certain attitude, a certain demeanour, sometimes even, if you are lucky, as a certain swagger. These are the memories that have become part of your blood, as Rilke once said, memories nameless and no longer distinguishable from who you are.[116] The course and quality of the lives of those you leave behind can be inextricably tied to the way in which you bid them adieu. I will leave them with a lesson about fighting, about never giving up, even when everything is hopeless. I did explain this to Myshkin, early on, but I don't think he understood. He may never understand that my parting wish was a lesson. But it can still be one.

In Catholic Miami, the doctors are very keen on the idea of 'double effect'.[117] Suppose you are considering doing something that has two different consequences. One of those consequences is good, while the other is bad. You really only want the good consequence. If you could arrange things so only the good consequence ensued, you would be delighted. But you can't and so are stuck with both. According to the doctrine of double effect, you can legitimately pursue your proposed course of action, knowing both consequences will result, as long as you intend only the good consequence. So, I

116 Rilke talks about this sort of memory in his only novel, *The Note-books of Malte Laurids Brigge* (1910).
117 The doctrine of double effect emerged from the writings of medieval Catholic philosophers, Aquinas in particular. More precisely, since there was no Catholic Church as such – the split with Protestantism had not yet happened – I should say it emerged from medieval philosophers who would later be adopted by the Catholic Church.

could ask them to pump me full of morphine, knowing my death would result, as long as I only intend to relieve my pain rather than die. This idea would provide a way out for all of us – allow me to keep my parting wish and also spare us a protracted goodbye. It's a pity, then, that it is a crock of shit.

Aquinas first introduced the idea of double effect in the context of a discussion of the right of self-defence. I may legitimately kill someone in self-defence as long as I only intend to save my own life rather than to kill my assailant. Knowing that he is out to get me, I may not try to have him poisoned beforehand, for that is simply seeking his death. But killing him in self-defence involves me merely seeking to defend myself, even if his death were another consequence. But this is a hopeless analogy, largely because the self-defence scenario is too vague. In particular, there are two possibilities. The first is that my assailant's death is not known to be a certain or even probable consequence. If I kill him with a punch, for example, given that punches do not typically result in death, his death would be an unlikely consequence. If, on the other hand, I shoot him in the face at point-blank range with a large-calibre handgun, his death does seem to be a near-certainty. But, precisely because of this, it seems more apt to describe what I do as saving my own life through the killing of another. When the death of my assailant is a near-certainty, it seems nonsensical to say that I intended only to save my life and not cause his death. Don't misunderstand me: if someone is trying to kill me, then, as far as I'm concerned, I'm well within my rights to kill him first. But, let's be honest, this has nothing to do with intending only to save myself rather than killing him. On the contrary, I intend to save myself by killing him.

Suppose I flip a light switch, and the lights come on. Can I say that I intended only to flip the switch and not turn on the lights? There are situations in which it makes sense to say this. I might not have known that the switch was the light switch. Or I might know that faulty wiring makes it very unlikely the lights will come on. But these are not like double-effect scenarios. There, the consequence of what you do is certain or near-certain. Can I legitimately claim that I intended only to flip the switch and not turn on the lights if I know that the turning-on of the lights is a near-certain consequence of flipping the switch? The more the turning-on of the lights is a near-certain consequence of flipping the switch, the less it makes sense to say that I can intend to flip the switch without intending to turn on the lights. The doctrine of double effect relies on the idea that you can intend to do X without intending to do Y, even though you know that Y is an overwhelmingly likely consequence of X. This assumption is risible. What the doctrine of double effect can sometimes be, however, is a bad reason for doing the right thing.

Our attitudes to euthanasia are confused. Years ago, Boss also made his own way into the long goodnight, at the hands of a vet. He was an old dog, and had also acquired cancer. I agonized over the timing. Even now, I still agonize: was I a day too soon? Was I a day too late? And I'll never be sure I got it right. But one thing I never questioned was the absolute necessity – and absolutely moral rightness – of having Boss euthanized. When it would be the right thing to do was a good question. That it was the right thing to do was beyond question. Humans are apparently too valuable to be afforded even this simple act of kindness. Someone I once knew had a severely brain-damaged daughter, a result of her being born with meningitis. She wasn't expected to make it past her fourth birthday, but somehow she got as far as twelve. Then, a botched operation intended to alleviate some of her suffering left her unable to move and in constant pain. All agreed – parents and doctors – that she must die. How was this achieved? The doctors 'withdrew fluids'. That is, they let her die of thirst. This is standard practice. It took her two weeks to pass. That this is morally abhorrent would, you'd think, be obvious to everyone.

The problem is that medical orthodoxy – and medical law – still see a vast moral gulf between 'active' and 'passive' euthanasia. Active euthanasia is the killing of a patient. Passive euthanasia is merely letting that patient die. While it is not acceptable to actively kill a patient who is suffering intensely, it is morally acceptable to let her die. Indeed, more than morally acceptable, it is often morally required to let her die. To not do so would be morally wrong. You can see the sense in this idea. If someone's death is inevitable, and her suffering unpleasant, then why bring her back from the dead merely to suffer for a few more days? Far better to just let her go. Like most patients in my situation, I have a DNR – Do Not Resuscitate – note in my file. Letting a person in my circumstances die is the right thing to do. I may have decided to go out fighting, but I'll be damned if I'm going to be brought back from the dead to fight some more.

However, this is where the confusion sets in. If it is right to allow a patient like me to die, then why is it wrong to hasten him on his way – as we did for Boss? Obviously, the circumstances have to be right. I have in mind someone in my situation: someone for whom there is absolutely no hope – someone who is going to die, will die soon, but before this happens will suffer significantly. But the person I have in mind is unlike me in one crucial respect: she has said that enough is enough. She would like to die now, be killed rather than merely wait for death to arrive in its own good time. Let's suppose, finally, that the person in unable to take her own life. What could justify the moral difference between the two cases? In one case we act to end a persons' life. In the other, we fail to act to save a person's life. The ultimate consequences are the same: the patient dies. If there is a moral difference between the two cases, therefore, it can only be because there is a moral difference between acting and failing to act – a difference between acts and omissions. In other words, if one thinks there is a vast moral gulf between killing someone in these circumstances and merely letting her die, then this is only because one must tacitly believe in the acts-and-omissions doctrine.

The acts-and-omissions doctrine, you might remember, first made its way into our lives through Myshkin's reflections on our obligations to the absolute poor. According to the doctrine, there is an intrinsic moral difference between acting and failing to act. That is, there is a difference in the moral status of an act and an omission that cannot be tied to any difference of intentions or consequences. The acts-and-omissions doctrine is false. If you fix the intentions, and fix the consequences, then an act and the corresponding omission are morally equivalent. A murderous uncle might drown his nephew in order to acquire an inheritance. But he might also, having gone to the pond with the intention of drowning his nephew, merely decline to save a nephew who is already drowning. The intentions are the same: to see his nephew dead. The consequences are the same: the child is dead. In these circumstances, there is no moral difference between what the uncle did in the first scenario and what he failed to do in the second. His action and his omission are morally equivalent.

*

247

The fall of the acts-and-omissions doctrine spells trouble for the idea that there is any moral gulf between passive and active euthanasia. Assume that medical orthodoxy is right: the policy of not resuscitating terminally ill patients is morally correct. Intuitively, this does seem right. The idea that there is a moral difference between passive and active euthanasia will be true only if one of two conditions is met. The first is that there is some difference in intentions or consequences between the two cases. The second is that the acts-and-omissions doctrine is true.

In the case I am envisaging there does not seem to be any difference with regard to intentions or consequences. Whether the doctors merely fail to resuscitate the person or actively take steps to speed her on her way, the consequences are the same: the patient is dead. And the intentions are also the same in each case: to spare her further suffering (by killing her – let's be clear). Both the intentions and consequences are, therefore, the same for both the act and the failure to act. In other words, there are no extrinsic differences between the act and the failure to act.

Therefore, in these circumstances, the only way there could be a moral difference between active and passive euthanasia would be if the acts-and-omissions doctrine were true. But the acts-and-omissions doctrine is false. The conclusion is obvious and inevitable. If the policy of DNR – declining to resuscitate terminally ill patients – is morally right, then so too must be a policy of active euthanasia. If a person really is in such bad shape that not resuscitating her is the morally right course of action, and if she has requested death, then speeding her on her way must also be the morally right course of action.

*

That case is the easiest one – voluntary euthanasia, where a person requests her own death. Euthanasia comes in different forms. All of these forms differ from assisted suicide. This, technically, is not euthanasia at all. Assisted suicide is, precisely, suicide aided by someone else. The patient kills herself with the help of someone else – for example, a doctor who provides her with the substances and the apparatus to do so. Voluntary euthanasia is the first category of euthanasia proper. This occurs when a patient indicates that she wants her life to be ended, but is sufficiently incapacitated to be unable to commit suicide, assisted or otherwise. Instead of pushing the button, literal or figurative, she must ask someone else to do this for her. If a person were in the sort of shape that would make a DNR notice morally justifiable, then, I have argued, voluntary euthanasia would be similarly justifiable.

The next category is morally trickier: non-voluntary euthanasia. This occurs when the patient is unable to express a wish one way or another. Euthanasia, if performed, would be done in her interests. Someone I knew once, an eighteen-year-old friend of mine, fell down a flight of stairs at a party. She – Christina – was paralysed from the neck down, unable to speak. She could communicate only through eye movements, and that was not a reliable method as her eyes were usually filled with tears. Mercifully, in my view, she died soon after. Imagine someone like her, but whose ability to communicate has been entirely, rather than almost entirely, destroyed, and you have a candidate for non-voluntary euthanasia. Non-voluntary euthanasia is more difficult to justify than its voluntary counterpart, as we are unable to find out the patient's preference. Nevertheless, you can imagine someone like Christina, condemned to a life of discomfort, hopelessness and boredom verging on madness, and you can understand the pull of the idea that non-voluntary euthanasia can be morally legitimate in some circumstances. I know her parents, brothers and sisters shared this view, and this had nothing to do with callousness or selfishness on their part. If we accept that a DNR order is justified in Christina's case, then it is difficult to escape the conclusion that non-voluntary euthanasia is also morally justifiable. Once again, rejecting the acts-and-omissions doctrine leads to an unequivocal conclusion: if a person is in such bad shape that not resuscitating her is the morally right course of action, then we are already tacitly conceding that death would be the best thing for her. Assuming she has not expressed a wish to the contrary, and assuming she really is in as bad a shape as we think, then I think the default assumption must be that non-voluntary euthanasia is also the morally correct course of action.

I, however, fall into another category: I have expressed a wish not to be euthanized. Any euthanasia performed on me would, therefore, be involuntary, and there is a crucial difference between this and other forms. In neither of the other cases of euthanasia are we contravening the known preferences of the patient. Involuntary euthanasia, however, does override a person's expressed preferences. This is a game-changer.

When you take decisions regarding another, there are two factors that are immediately relevant: that person's welfare and her autonomy. In a case of non-voluntary euthanasia, the patient has expressed no wish. Therefore, all we can base our decision on is her welfare. The failure of the acts-and-omissions doctrine means, in effect, that in the protection of a person's welfare there is no intrinsic moral difference between acts and failures to act. Therefore, if circumstances are appropriate, we are licensed to promote her welfare either by failing to save her or by the positive act of killing. In the case of involuntary euthanasia, however, the patient has expressed a preference. This means that we cannot, now, consider only the patient's welfare. We must also take into account her autonomy.

Involuntary euthanasia is, in effect, homicide and, as with homicide in general, there are circumstances in which it might be justifiable. Cormac McCarthy imagines a possible scenario in *The Road*. You and your young son are about to be captured by cannibalistic killers. You have one bullet left in your gun. Not enough for you, unfortunately, but enough to spare your son the horror that will surely follow. He, however, doesn't agree. In extreme circumstances such as these, there may be a case for involuntary euthanasia. But most circumstances are not extreme. In most cases, there is little more justification for involuntary euthanasia than there is for murder.

Murder and involuntary suicide are both cases of killing that override a person's autonomy. There are circumstances in which one might justifiably override a person's autonomy in favour of her welfare. But these are usually tied to the idea of future welfare. Myshkin whisked the bottle of Drano from the eager hands of Alexander – a violation of his autonomy, perhaps, if he had any at this young age: but, nevertheless, justifiable because of the inordinately detrimental effect this would have on his long-term future welfare. For those like me, whose welfare extends no more than a few hours or days, violations of what little autonomy we have left are almost always indefensible.

Thus, I believe I should be allowed to exit this life in the

manner that I choose. For better or for worse, I am determined to exit by way of a lesson. And that, therefore, is how
morality dictates I should be allowed to go out. I did choose
this, and were I still capable of speech, I would reiterate my
choice. But it's a hard choice, nonetheless. What makes it
hard for me is what makes it hard for them, my three boys. It
is a hard thing to be powerless in the face of someone's
wishes, and it is a hard thing to wish for something when you
know it will impart so much sorrow to those you love. I exit
this life grateful to Myshkin for ensuring that my wishes were
respected, and that my last act in this world was not rendered
meaningless. But I exit also with a bitter taste on my tongue,
knowing how much my lesson will have cost him. There is a
bad end in store for all of us, and sometimes nothing you can
do is good; there are just various shades of bad.

19

Confession

Can you do it? When the time comes?
When the time comes there will be no time.
Now is the time.

Cormac McCarthy, *The Road*

I always thought it might come down to this in the end: a room, a table, a chair, a bottle of Jack Daniels, a Glock 9mm. And me. Albert Camus once argued that the fundamental question of philosophy is suicide. Why not end this mad game of existence? Suicide, Camus argued, is fundamentally a confession: an admission that life is no longer worth the trouble. My blood has form. There was a time for my grand-father when he stood before life, stared it in the eye, and confessed. Don't think badly of him. It seems like every day you read the newspaper and some kid, with an entire lifetime in front of him, kills himself because he has become so unbearably miserable and he can't see a way out. There is always a way out. Except when there is not. My granddad was an improbably tough old man. Or so I'm told. You know the only thing I can remember of him? A bald, brittle man, wearing his pyjamas in the middle of the day, sitting on the settee in the living room of his little two-up, two-down, watching wrestling on TV – we would visit on Saturday afternoons and wrestling was the standard offering on the BBC in those days. Mick McManus, a short, rotund Londoner of presumably Irish descent, was the rather unlikely king of British wrestling. I remember more of Mick McManus than I do of my poor granddad. He had spent most of his waking life beneath the ground, a collier – a cutter of coal. A collier, not a mere haulier: the strongest of the village crop, among the best of its sons. By the time I was able to remember him, he spent most of his remaining hours coughing up his lungs into a red bucket, the closest thing he had to a companion during these times. This coughing, disgorging and discharging continued relentlessly for nearly ten years. Until one day he ended it. Or, at least, so I am told, in and by various whispers and murmurs that were never permitted to grow into anything more: the deafening testimony of the known but unsaid.

In my grandfather's case, his confession was fundamentally a judgement. Or, rather, it was three of them. First, his life was no longer of a quality sufficiently high to make its continuation an attractive proposition. Second, things were not going to get any better. Third, there was no less drastic course of action, short of suicide, that might be adopted to mitigate his plight. From what I remember of his condition, I would not be surprised if his judgement was sound in this instance. If so, I have to conclude that he did the right thing.

When a suicide is not the right thing – and in so many cases it is not – this is because of a failure of judgement. Matters are not as bad as they seem. Or, if they are, there is every reason to suppose they won't always remain this bad. There was a boy in school, a year or two younger than me. Seemed like a happy kid – always in trouble, but his mischief was never malicious. I liked him. One day he hanged himself off a bridge. A few years on, there was another guy I knew, in his twenties – good guy, handsome, smart, about to graduate from university, had his whole life in front of him – hanged himself from a tree at a party. I was actually at that party, but had gone home before this happened. I would never want to belittle the suffering of these two young men. I have some idea of what was behind the second suicide, but no idea about the first. Until recently, I couldn't even begin to imagine the sort of psychological state someone who would do this could possibly be in. But, in the first case I have to suspect, and in the second case I know, these acts were based on flawed judgements.

The tragedy of suicides such as these is that they are based on a misrepresentation of how bad things are, unjustifiably pessimistic predictions of the future, or the failure to consider less drastic, non-lethal means of ameliorating one's predicament. I suspect we are never, any of us, very reliable in our assessments of our own quality of life. We are, if anything, even worse at predicting the future. And many of us do have a tendency to be rather blinkered once we have decided that this is how things have to be. Failures of judgement happen all the time. The big difference with suicide is, of course, that this failure is irrevocable.

As a general rule, therefore, intervention is almost always justified. If I saw the schoolboy preparing to hang himself from a bridge, or the college student preparing to do the same from a tree, then of course I would intervene. And when I say that I would intervene, I don't just mean rational persuasion:

I would use physical force to restrain them if necessary. Non-intervention, in these circumstances, would be monstrous. This is an invasion of the person's autonomy, and in general I'm opposed to that. But intervention is merely temporary. The person is being given a chance to think again, to judge again. And if his judgement remains consistently the same, he will always have another opportunity to end his life. But if his judgement is flawed, and he is permitted to proceed, he will never have an opportunity to judge better.

There is, however, a world of difference between the troubled man or woman who, in a time of enormous emotional distress and upheaval, makes a decision to end his or her life, and my grandfather who, after suffering for years with a progressively worsening condition that had drastically diminished the quality of his life, decided that enough was enough. What if I could travel back in time, and I walked in on my grandfather's suicide, just before he hanged himself (for I believe that is also the method he employed). Would I stop him? More to the point: should I stop him? Given what I know about him, and the disease that was turning him into a skeleton, would my intervention have been justified? I don't think so.

My current circumstances are, unfortunately, more akin to my grandfather's. I have dementia. Dementia is a syndrome: a group of symptoms. Underlying the syndrome is a disease. The most common cause of dementia is Alzheimer's disease, which accounts for 60–70 per cent of dementia cases. My doctors are, accordingly, 60–70 per cent certain that this is what I have. Autopsy is the only way to definitively identify the underlying pathology. They could perform a battery of other tests that would raise their certainty to around 90 per cent. But, really, I can't be bothered. I have only so much time left, and I'll be damned if I'm going to spend any of it in a doctor's office worrying about 20 per cent. Dementia is going to get you in the end, whatever its underlying cause.

Forgetting – I've been there for a while. I have been misplacing things too. I shall, in the not too distant future, forget how to perform basic tasks, such as tying my shoelaces. Eventually I'll forget how to wash and dress myself. I have increasingly common episodes of confusion to look forward to: and with this confusion will come fear, distrust, irritability and delusions. This is not going to be a slow or graceful degradation of my psychological faculties. It's going to happen fast and get faster and faster as the disease progresses. And at the end of it all is the loss of me. I shall no longer be there. My physical body will still be there. But this living, breathing organism will no longer be me.

That is probably how it will end – how I will end – unless I take the appropriate action. There are more optimistic scenarios. There is a cancer that has been growing in my prostate for some time, and there's always the chance that this will end me first. But, unfortunately, it appears to be a rather sluggish, apathetic cancer, and it's taking its own sweet time over things. And that, I think, tells me all I need to know. When you are hoping that cancer will hurry up and kill you – keeping your fingers crossed for cancer – then I think you have to accept that it is time to stand before life, as my grandfather once did, and admit that it is no longer worth the trouble. Nevertheless, there is the issue of irrevocability to consider. And if my life has stood for anything at all, it has been for thinking: accruing evidence, identifying what follows from it and what does not, the balancing of judgements, intuitions, opinions and viewpoints. It would be disappointing if I should exit the world in a way entirely orthogonal to these principles. I must pause. And think.

I think we can quickly dispense with religious arguments against suicide. There is an idea that suicide takes away God's right to choose the time and place of a man or woman's death. This idea is hopeless – and it's hopeless even if you believe in God. If killing yourself were wrong, because it takes away God's right to choose your demise, then so too would be taking steps to save yourself. Stepping out of the way of a speeding car would be denying God's will. One can't reply that stepping out of the way was God's will – because He didn't intend you to die in that way after all. Because then you could make an analogous case for suicide: killing yourself is God's will after all – that is how He intended you to die.

Some claim that suicide is selfish. It is true that among the factors that have to be considered when considering suicide is the effect on other people. To the extent that other people are not considered, or the welfare of the suicidal person is elevated to a level that eclipses relatives' and friends', an act of suicide can be a selfish act. In the suicides of young people – such as the two dead boys I used to know – the lives of family members are permanently and irrevocably blighted. I am not saying that their suicides were selfish acts. But the effect on others is something that needs to be taken into consideration.

I have thought long and hard about this issue, and these considerations do not seem to be so obviously applicable in my case. Olga has gone. I agonize about the effect on Nico and Alexander. I do worry that my suicide will put a permanent psychological blemish on their lives. I also worry that this will stain the way they remember me. This is not necessarily a selfish worry. I'm not worried about how posterity views me so much as I worry for my children. One of the greatest things any parent can do for his or her children is to leave them with good memories.

Let's for a moment, then, consider the alternatives. The first is that I decide not to kill myself and just let nature take its course. Eventually, I am hospitalized. How long could I survive in a hospital? Three years? Five years? Ten years? The costs for my children would be astronomical, and for what? The living carcass sitting there would no longer be me. I wouldn't know who they were, and I wouldn't know who I was. They might still feel an obligation to visit this breathing corpse that I have become – costly regular visits that will be extraordinarily upsetting to them, and perhaps also to my husk. At least part of the reason I am sitting here with a handgun is to save my sons the financial and emotional burden of looking after my breathing bodily remains. I don't think a charge of selfishness has any merit in these circumstances.

There is another alternative. I tell them what I am planning to do: I talk to them, and explain to them my reasons. This course of action has much to recommend it. At least they would understand why I did what I did, and so hopefully wouldn't interpret it as some failing on their part. On the other hand, it does have some rather crushing drawbacks. Suppose I tell them. What then? I remember Boss. I loved that dog. Towards the end of his life, when he was slowly dying of cancer, he became incontinent. Apart from that he seemed okay. He didn't appear to be in pain. His appetite was fine and he still seemed to enjoy his walks. Every morning, and usually several times a day, I would have to mop up after him. He had a favourite part of the house in which to void his bladder – under the dining room table. The legs of the table were slowly starting to rot, at their base. Suppose he was able to talk, to say to me: 'You don't have to do this any more. It's okay: I can go now.' I wouldn't have even entertained this suggestion for a second. As long as he was free of pain, and he could still enjoy some of what life had to offer, I would happily have gone on mopping up that floor forever.

If I were to tell Nico and Alexander, they could either agree or not agree. If they didn't agree then we would be back to square one. Even worse, they would be down here watching over me like hawks to make sure I don't off myself. But it's the possibility that they agree that really scares me. I couldn't have them around while I kill myself. The laws on assisted suicide being what they are, this would compromise them legally. And so there would inevitably come a moment when they would have to say to me: 'Okay. Goodbye, Dad. You do it now.' This is the hardest thing anybody could ever have to say to someone they love. I could never have said that even to Boss: it was too hard for me to think. And I know they would never be able to say this to me. I want to spare them this heaviest of all burdens.

The course I have decided on is not ideal. It has its drawbacks. But I think it is the best course, all things considered. Explaining my reasons would be a good thing. But that is what suicide notes are for. Think of this book as one long suicide note, if you like.

Another objection – which, in effect, inverts the charge of selfishness – is the idea that if suicide is encouraged then old, infirm people (people such as I, in fact) will feel under pressure to end their lives so as not to become a burden to their children or society as a whole. I just want to end my life because I don't want to be a burden, you say. Well, yes: that's it precisely. At least, that is part of the story. It is my wish, thought out at great length and freely entertained, not to be a burden to my children. That is one reason why I want to die. What is wrong with that? I think this is a perfectly legitimate preference of mine, and in acting on it I am exercising my autonomy – in the short time it remains to me. When you have no meaningful welfare to look forward to, all you have left is your autonomy: and this is my autonomy speaking. I am not being pressured by anyone. My sons know nothing. I'd feel the same even if keeping my carcass alive were all paid for by the state. Now, believe me, if I thought I had a chance of a remotely good life, I don't think being a burden on the state would bother me too much. I mean, I think I would be able to live with myself. But it is pointless. There will come a time when I am no longer there, a vegetable as they say – a vegetable that costs several hundred thousand a year to keep alive. What is the point?

I wouldn't want to underplay the dangers in suicide becoming a mainstream option. And so let me reiterate: I am not defending suicide as a general policy, still less as some-thing to be encouraged. I am not a Kantian: I don't believe that if it is the right course of action for me it must be the right course of action for everyone in the same circum-stances. What I am saying is that for me, given the specifics of my situation and my prognosis, suicide is the right thing.

Part of the problem, part of the reason why my death is going to be so messy, is because I can't say to my doctor: 'Look, when the following circumstances obtain – when I no longer know who I am, when I no longer recognize the faces of those I love, when I am no longer able to perform basic tasks – just slip something in my drip, would you, and end me. When exactly these circumstances obtain: that's your call.' Nor can I make a living will requesting this. The reasons why are less than convincing. There is, some say, a danger of a slippery slope. It's true: mistakes will be made. But, when you look at the alternative, I think it's worth the risk.

The alternative is that I am going to have to put a gun to my head and pull the trigger. It is not only messy, but it will rob me of at least some days of a life worth living. Yes, I forget things and get a little confused. It's going to get worse fast. But at the moment, my life is still worth living. The problem is, given my disease's aetiology, by the time my life is not worth living I shall no longer be capable of ending it. I need someone to do it for me. But there is no one. And so I am going to have to end myself prematurely. Some say it is unfair to doctors to ask them to kill their patients. But this isn't fair either.

And there is one final twist of life's knife, as if I needed it. I'm certain this is the dementia talking already. But it's part of what I am now, part of what is left of me. For those like me – those who will one day stand before life and confess – there were two things that grew in their mother's womb. There was the person they shall become and also, because of this, the confession that they shall one day make. Death, my shadowy friend – my umbral companion – has been keeping me company all these years. It's been good to have him around since Olga went. But I picked up enough Spanish during my years in Miami to know that *umbral*, in Spanish, means 'threshold'. If you have read these pages, then you know that I am not a religious man. Any hope I place in an afterlife would be merely a stunted parody of a dream. If I put the Glock to my head and pull, then my chances of waking up in another life are, I accept, so devastatingly low as to be not worth mentioning. But still, I also have a healthy respect for the fundamental ignorance of human beings, which, I suspect, is profound and incurable. So, I can't dismiss the possibility. And think of what I would gain if this possibility were real. I would wake up to see Olga's face again. Who could resist odds of slim to none when the potential prize is so high?

Herein lie the seeds of my damnation. If there is an after-life, then there is probably a God. And He or She may take a dim view of my efforts at life truncation, and may send me to one of the less desirable post-life locales. So, I would have seen Olga, if only I hadn't been so eager to do so. Conscience makes cowards of us all? Not true: hope makes cowards of us all. I am damned by a faint, irrational, baseless hope. I hate myself for it. I know – I really do know – death is the end. I know it but don't really understand. Hope is a symptom of this failure to understand. My hope is my damnation.

So, what do I do? I piss about. I prevaricate. I clean my Glock. I know I have taken out the magazine. I know I have cleared the cartridge from the chamber. I know these things. And yet I still find myself putting the barrel to my head and pulling the trigger in the faintest hope that I have not. God couldn't blame me, surely, if I sincerely but mistakenly believed I was not killing myself?

It seems I am not going to do it today. That's okay: I have a little more time. I don't know how much, but who of us does know that? I have been marked, for better or for worse, by Olga's desire to die her death as a lesson. Your life is your argument, as Albert Schweitzer once put it. So too is your death. Perhaps nothing lives on more vividly in the lives of those who stay behind than the way you die. And it seems the lesson of my grandfather is the one that stuck. My grandfather didn't die because he felt sad and hopeless and couldn't see an end to, or way out from, this misery. My granddad was a collier. Misery warranted a shrug of the shoulders, nothing more. He died at his own hand because he understood something, and succeeded in conveying this understanding to me. When going out is inevitable, it is best to do this on your own terms. A wise man will live as long as he ought, not as long as he can. I used to know who wrote that, but I can't remember now. It doesn't matter any more.[118]

118 It was Seneca the younger: *Moral Letters to Lucilius*, letter 70. I apologize: for reasons that may be apparent, I felt unable to comment on this chapter. Enough years have passed since my mother's death for me to be able to muster a half-hearted comment here and there. But, with this chapter, I simply couldn't.

20

Limitless

To see the world in a grain of sand,
And heaven in a wild flower,
To hold infinity in the palm of your hand,
And eternity in an hour.

William Blake, 'Auguries of Innocence'

Some moral theories claim that it is acts that are, fundamentally, right or wrong, and these should be judged by their consequences alone. No, say others, it is not the acts themselves that are right or wrong but the rules they instantiate. On the contrary, say others, it is neither acts nor rules that in themselves are right or wrong, but only the motives of the person who acts or follows the rules: it is only a will that can be truly good or bad. Whether it is frasmed in terms of acts or rules, consequences or motives, intentions, duty, obligations, happiness, preferences, any moral theory will inevitably be smashed on the rock of one irrefutable fact. Seen from one perspective, the difference between 18,635,843 deaths and 18,635,842 deaths is inconsequential. If, on some arbitrary scale of value, a human life had a value of 1, the value of this difference would be 1:18,635,843. But, from another perspective, that of the one saved, the difference is limitless: it is the difference between everything and nothing.

Like all humans, I am a broken creature. A fissure runs through me, neatly dividing me into two irreconcilable things. I am the nominal subject of two stories, and while I know both of these can't be true, I can't stop believing either of them. On the one hand, there is a story told from the inside. In this, I am the central character: the hero around whom the plot wends and weaves its serpentine way. In this story, I matter. I have goals, dreams, aspirations, problems, hopes and fears. And these matter too. Indeed, they are what the story is all about. Will my dreams be fulfilled or crushed, my aspirations satisfied or stymied? There will, for sure, be twists and turns of plot: conflict, crisis and then crushing resolution. Or not. But whatever happens in it, the story is about me.

There is also a story told from outside my life, and whose natural expression lies in the third person. In this, far from being the central character, I am little more than a faceless extra. I differ in no significant way from anyone else, and my dreams and aspirations are no more important than those of any other. My contribution to this evolving story is minimal. I live, I die, I disappear and am erased: my dreams and aspirations, the hopes and fears that dominated my life excised with me, changing nothing, leaving no trace that they were ever really there.

My life – the life I have lived and I have experienced – has no end in the way my visual field has no limit. I remember it was Wittgenstein who said that.[119] I cannot see the

119 *Tractatus Logico-Philosophicus* 6.4311. 'Death is not an event in life: we do not live to experience death. If we take eternity to mean not infinite temporal duration but timelessness, then eternal life belongs to those who live in the present. Our life has no end in the way in which our visual field has no limits.'

limit of my visual field. If I could, it would be part of, and so could not limit, this field. The limit of the visual field must always lie just beyond what can be seen. Similarly, my death is not, and can never be, something that occurs in my life. My death is the limit of my life and so must always lie just outside it. I cannot, therefore, understand my death. The deaths of others I can understand without too much difficulty – for these deaths are, unlike my own, events in my life. These events will vary dramatically in their impact: most are unnoticed, many more barely register – a passing flicker and no more in my consciousness. And then there are the deaths that desolate and mutilate. Olga's death was an existential evulsion: I could merely shuffle sadly in its wake, a little less substantial, a little more ethereal, than I was before. But whatever else it is or may be, the death of another is an event in my life: and no matter the extent to which it blinds the soul, the intellect remains untouched. The death of someone else can always be thought. It can always be understood, no matter the complexity of its aetiology or mechanics, and no matter the severity of its consequences.

I have an outside too. My death, too, will be an event in the lives of others, as easily intelligible to them as theirs is to me. But from the inside my life stretches away towards eternity. I look at this old map of the world on my bedroom wall, and think: soon, there is nowhere on this map that I shall be. This is not a thought but a skin, a surface that hides waters too deep to fathom: and in these caliginous depths lurks a formless and dizzying horror.

In the face of this horror, moral rules, principles, doctrines and theories reveal themselves as what they are: paltry, risible existences, impotent under the gaze of the limitless. A morality that is worth anything at all can deal only in life. Only when acts and rules, intentions and consequences, motives, will, happiness, preferences, duty and obligation are all woven together, seamlessly, into the fabric of a single life do we have anything that can be understood and evaluated. In the end, it is only a life that can truly be judged.

The resurgence, in recent decades, of virtue ethics – a federation of views grounded in the work of Aristotle – was in large part a response to the failure of the rule-based understanding of morality. Morality cannot be based on rules because rules can be applied well or badly – in some cases, morally or immorally – and so you already need to be a moral person in order to understand how to apply the rules. In virtue ethics, the fundamental moral injunction is to become a good – a morally virtuous – person. This will undoubtedly have implications for how we are to act. But what is the right thing to do in any given circumstance is not decided by rules, duties or obligations. Instead, the overriding questions are always the same. What would a virtuous person do in this situation? And why would they do it?

This appeal to the person has its strengths but also its weaknesses. The focus on the person, rather than on concepts such as rule, duty and obligation, does capture an important truth. Only when entwined in the fabric of a life do these concepts have real significance. Understood in isolation from a life – under the harsh glare of the philosopher's dissecting table – they are ineffectual contrivances that we can't understand unless we are already good. It is significant that one of the people who brought virtue ethics back to the consideration of philosophers, Iris Murdoch, was both novelist and philosopher (and far more of the former than she was of the latter).[120] The currency of literature is life: ideas in motion. The focus, characteristic of virtue ethics, on the whole person – on what a person is rather than what rules she should follow – is a tacit acknowledgement of the superiority of literature to philosophy.

Nevertheless, this new centrality of the person is ironic, for it comes just as other disciplines are, rightly or wrongly, administering its last rites. While evident in several disciplines, this contemporary assault on the self or person is being led by the neurosciences. There is no self or person – so say many of the more philosophically inclined neuroscientists – instead there are just neuron ensembles, systems and sub-systems, either competing with or complementing each other. The idea of the self is an illusion that emerges out of this activity.[121] This attack on the self is illuminating – not because it is true but because of what it reveals about the sort of thing the self or the person would have to be if this attack were to be true. When neuroscientists, and philosophers influenced by them, say there is no self or person, what they mean is that there is no central executive. There is no organizing focal unit through which the activity of the various neuron ensembles is filtered. There is nothing that brings all this activity together in one place and weaves it into a single unified whole. Their implicit assumption: if there were a self or person, that is the sort of thing it would have to be. As Ryle has shown, this view of the person is unsubstantiated.

120 Iris Murdoch, *The Sovereignty of Good* (Routledge & Kegan Paul, 1970).
121 Daniel Dennett, *Consciousness Explained* (Little, Brown, 1991), is a good example.

1.

*My father does not explain this point. Indeed, the remainder
of this final chapter is simply a collection of jumbled
remarks. Neither the significance nor the meaning of these
remarks is always apparent. I am confident, however, that I
know what he means when he refers to Ryle.*

*Gilbert Ryle explained what he came to label a 'category
mistake' through the example of a foreigner being shown
around Oxford University.[122] He is shown the various
colleges, the sports fields, the administration buildings and
so on. At the end of his tour, he asks, 'But where is the university? I have seen the colleges, sports grounds,
administrative buildings, but you have not yet shown me the
university!' The 'category mistake' lies in misunderstanding
the sort of thing the university is. It is not something separate
from the colleges, fields and administration buildings.
Rather, the university consists of precisely these things, all
related in appropriate ways. To think of the self as something
over and above a dense network of related psychological
states – as something to which these psychological states
attach, for example – is to fall victim to the same sort of category mistake.*

2.

*In these closing pages, my father also frequently mentions
Buddhism. The contemporary attack on the idea of the self is
nothing new. In explaining their rejection of the idea of the
self, the early Buddhists often used the analogy of a chariot.
We might think there is such a thing as a chariot, but in reality all that there is is a collection of simpler things: wheels,*

122 Gilbert Ryle, *The Concept of Mind* (Hutchinson, 1949).

axle, felly, yoke, pole and so on. These simpler things can be broken down into simpler things: a wheel, for example, is broken down into a rim, spokes and axle housing. In the same way, the Buddhists claimed, while you may think you are a self – and this you understand as something that thinks, feels and experiences – all there is, really, is a network of related psychological states and processes. One thought gives rise to another, which occasions a certain feeling, or quashes another, and so on. Your sense that you exist – that these thoughts, feelings and experiences happen to you, that they belong to you – is simply a matter of further thoughts: namely, the thoughts that all these things are happening to you or belong to you. There is no you, there are just thoughts that a 'you' exists. You can never get behind the thoughts to anything – a self or person or soul – that supposedly has them.

3.

The guiding assumption, common to these ancient Buddhists and their shiny new scientific descendants, is this: if a self or person were to exist, it would have to be something quite different from, and separate from, activity – whether mental or neural. If it exists, a self would have to be something that binds this activity together. No doubt this is a common understanding of the person. But there is no reason to suppose it is true. Why must we conclude, from the Buddhist's reflections on the chariot, that there is no such thing as a chariot? It seems just as reasonable to conclude that there is a chariot, and this is what it is – a system of related elements. The one who denies the existence of the chariot is in the grip of a certain picture of what the chariot must be. The chariot must be something separate from these parts and their *relations. It must be another thing – something that binds these parts and relations together, a principle of unity in this diversity of parts. Similarly, the Buddhist and scientific rejection of the self is predicated on a certain picture of what the self must be: something that binds together mental and neural activity, a principle of unity in psychic and neural diversity. But there is no more reason for thinking of the self in this way than there is for thinking of the chariot in this way. The denial of the self, just like the denial of the chariot, is grounded in a category mistake.*

The view of the self or person implicated in the Buddhist and scientific attacks – the self or person as something lying behind our thoughts, feelings and emotions – we might, adopting my father's expression, call the 'executive' sense of self. The other view of the self that sees it simply as a network of appropriately related psychological and bodily processes we can call the 'minimal' sense.

To feel compassion is to endure together. But what does 'together' mean? You suffer and I suffer. We are both located in the same vicinity: I am here and you are just over there. We thereby suffer together – in one sense of together. But the connection between our respective sufferings may be stronger than this. Your suffering moves me: I suffer because you suffer. The relation between our sufferings is not merely one of spatio-temporal proximity: it is a causal relation. A knife and fork are together in the kitchen drawer in the first sense. Smoke and fire come together in the stronger, causal sense.

There is, however, another – a third – sense of enduring together. When your suffering causes mine, or mine causes yours, there are two distinct episodes of suffering – one in you, the other in me. Causation is, as Hume correctly noted, a relation that holds between 'distinct existences'. But suppose two people are playing a game together. If I am playing a game with you it is not as if I am playing one game and you another, and the one causes the other. There is only one game that we are both playing 'together'. The game is, we might say, shared between the two of us. In other words, the word 'together' is multiply ambiguous. There is the 'together' of spatial proximity. There is the 'together' of causal connectedness. And there is the 'together' of sharing.[123]

The essence of love is identification. True identification cannot be achieved without sharing: causal connectedness or spatial proximity is not enough. If I know Nico is suffering, then I suffer too. But his suffering does not merely cause mine: it becomes mine. There are no two things here – his suffering and mine. Rather, his suffering and mine are one and the same episode – his-suffering-for-him and his-suffering-for-me. If Alexander has a dream, a consistent, fervently held dream, his dream can become mine: there is his-dream-for-him and his-dream-for-me. The suffering of Nico is my suffering. The dream of Alexander is my dream.

---

123 My father is employing what is known as a *type-token* distinction. Types are kinds. Tokens are individual exemplars of those kinds. The cup of coffee I drink is one token of the type 'cup of coffee', and the one you drink is a different token of the same type. In the same way, if I am suffering and you are too, then it is common to think that there are two different psychological episodes occurring – one in me, the other in you – two tokens of the same general type. A game that we play together is not like this. It is not as if there are two different tokens that fall under the same type. Rather, there is only one token episode – a game that you and I are both playing. The suggestion that we can suffer together in the same way in which we can play a game together entails that we can share the same token experiences, and not merely share experiences of the same type. This is, to say the least, controversial.

We share these things as we might all share in a game. The indexicals are, admittedly, different. Nico's suffering is still his, and my suffering is still mine: but they are one episode in the way that 'here' and 'there' can denote the same place. This is what identification with another really is: not spatio-temporal coincidence, not causation, but the sharing of a mental life. This sharing is always partial and ephemeral. But if love exists, this sharing exists too because that is what love, in its essence, really is.

Love is our only real template for compassion. Compassion is the spectral echo of love, sufficiently diaphanous to slip its gravitational bonds. Compassion comes in moments only: a laconic enduring together. To endure together, in its highest sense, is to share something, and to share is ultimately to see. To endure with the other is to see – not think, but see, however briefly, however inadequately and incompletely – your own limitlessness in the other. To endure with the other is to see the boundlessness and immensity of your own life in theirs. The attack on the self is misguided but welcome.

1.

The final sentence of that section was somewhat cryptic. We can express what I think my father meant in terms of the distinction between the executive and the minimal interpretations of the idea of the self. There is a certain way of enduring together that is only possible for the minimal self. The substantial executive self is what we might call 'impermeable'. If you represented such a self as a circle in a Venn diagram, then this circle might touch others, but could go no further than this: there would be no overlapping circles. An executive self stakes a claim on a little corner of reality, and from this excludes all other selves – as a solid object excludes all other objects from the same space. Consequently, the possibilities for enduring together available to executive selves are restricted: these possibilities are restricted by their impermeability. Executive selves could never endure together in the way that two people might play a game together. They can only ever endure together in the sense of being located in the same general vicinity or standing in certain causal relations – which is to say they can only ever really endure apart.

2.

The implications are reasonably clear, if controversial. If love is identification with the other, and identification is enduring together – in the sense of sharing the same dreams and disappointments, the same hopes and sorrow, the same joys and agonies – then love is only truly possible for a minimal self. And if love is our only real template for compassion, and compassion lies at the living core of morality, then morality is only possible for a minimal self. This claim is strong, I think implausibly so. My father needs only a weaker claim. There is a certain kind of goodness that is possible only for the minimal self.

It is instructive to note that all the major religions – if they accept the idea of salvation at all – identify an ethical path to salvation. (I trust you will forgive me, in my current circumstances, these brief thoughts of salvation.)[124] What is it about the ethical that makes it peculiarly amenable to soteriological concerns?

---

124 In much of his book, not just the present pages, I am struck by just how much of my father's 'Christian' education in a state school in a small industrial town in Britain is still there, shaping his outlook whether he likes it or not, even though he has long since publicly and privately repudiated it.

The ethical comes in both calculative and compassionate forms, the former accentuating the difference between persons, the latter effacing it. This distinction is reflected in religious conceptions of salvation.[125] Some themes in Christianity, for example, reiterate the importance and distinctness of the self. Basic ethical prescriptions – love thy neighbour as thyself, turn the other cheek, and so on – are overwritten by multiple layers of mythology that reinforce the importance of the self: the purpose of being good is to ensure that you – the very same you – will enjoy, rather than suffer, eternity.

One suspects that this reiteration of the importance of the self was precisely the opposite of what was intended. When Jesus told us to 'turn the other cheek', this has more to do with letting go of the self than reiterating its centrality.[126] It is, indeed, typical for the mythology to sully and distort a religion's underlying ethical message. In Buddhism, for example, we again find a collection of ethical prescriptions: one must engage in right speech, right action and right livelihood. Then, however, as with Christianity, the subsequent centuries superimpose a mythology on these prescriptions. We are asked to believe there are many realms or dimen-

---

125 At this point in the text, my father has made some scrawled notes, difficult to decipher. His general point seems to be that religions are not monolithic enterprises, and any single religion typically comprises distinct, and often mutually incompatible, strands. An admonition against the dangers of overgeneralization, then: and the focus of his comments, accordingly, seems to be on strands of thought within religions rather than religions in toto.

126 This was, in fact, Nietzsche's interpretation of Christ (whose teachings he clearly distinguished from the religion of Christianity). In Nietzsche's view, *turn the other cheek* was the foundational precept of Christ's teachings, and its aim was to free the person from the pernicious effects of what Nietzsche called *ressentiment*. Jesus emerges as a kind of proto-Freudian.

sions, each a possible locus of rebirth. One's actions in this life determine where one will be reborn in the next. The thoroughly despicable end up in hell. Those whose lives are dominated by greed are reincarnated as hungry ghosts of swollen bellies and tiny mouths, never able to assuage the terrible desires that consume them. So far this all sounds very Christian.

However, this mythologized version of *samsara* – the eternal wheel of suffering and rebirth – is incompatible with the teachings of the historical Buddha. Suffering results, first and foremost, from clinging to an illusion: the illusion of the self. There is no self, there is no person: not if we understand this as something different from thoughts, feelings and experiences – a central executive that has these things. There are simply *skandhas*: thoughts, feelings, experiences, bodily and psychological occurrences that arise from preceding causes, exist for a time, and then pass away, never to return, becoming themselves causes of further psychophysical events. There is nothing to which *skandhas* attach – no self, no person, no subject and no soul. Neither is there a body. There are only the *skandhas* themselves. But, if there is no self, then what is it that is nailed to the wheel of *samsara*?

The world is only *skandhas*. It is, therefore, these that are reborn. Suffering begets more suffering. Malice begets more malice. Hate begets hate. Love begets love. Karma is not a divine punishment visited on a transgressing self. There are no individuals to suffer or enjoy the karmic consequences of their previous actions. Hate is not my hate. Love is not my love. There is no me and there is no you. The self has all been a dream. There is only love and there is only hate: love and hate, and all the other *skandhas* that make up this world. These *skandhas* are the words in which this world is written.

Put them together, and you will find the story of reality. In the end, it is words that are nailed to the wheel.

1.

The conclusion that we are all words brings us back, full circle, to my father's opening ruminations. What is the relation between a character in fiction and one that is, as we say, 'real'? What is the relation between a character and what we call a man or woman's character? There are words written on a page and words written in bodily and neural tissue. This is a difference, and a not insignificant one. But it masks something shared and equally important. The creation of the pen and the creation of the world are both founded upon the deep contingency of limits.

2.

A fictional character seldom emerges fully formed from the mind and pen of an author, like Venus from the waves. Slowly he or she takes shape, the product of writing and re-writing, of multiple drafts superimposed one on another. The birth of a fictional character is protracted and painful, and the outcome of this process is always uncertain. Perhaps it is not until a little cone-shaped head emerges from the page that one is really sure there will even be a character. Once he does exist the possibilities are limitless, and before the writing continues one will never know which will be actualized. But once the book is finished, you might think, that is it: the character is now complete: determinate. All possibilities have now collapsed into the concrete actuality of the page. That, as we say, is all she wrote.

But none of this is true. The writing need never be complete. What did Sherlock Holmes have for supper on the evening of

21 October 1885? If Conan Doyle did not address this matter in any of the pages of the Sherlock Holmes corpus then, it is thought, any answer we give to this question can be neither true nor false. But perhaps he did indeed address this matter in some as yet undiscovered manuscript? Or suppose someone else were to continue building on this corpus and, in so doing, address this very question? On what grounds, then, could we deny that there is an answer to this question? But this new Holmes would not be the real Holmes, one might object. (The real Holmes? Really?) What is meant, I assume, is that this new Holmes would not be the creation of Sir Arthur Conan Doyle. As far as fictional characters go, we might think authorship confers reality of a sort. The 'real' Holmes is the one created by one and only one person. Any Johnny-come-lately Holmes would be 'fake', because he would not be the creation of the right person. But why must we think this way? Once created, why is the reality of Holmes tied only to one person?

This is not how it is with words. Plato, rightly, regarded the advent of the written word with great suspicion. His argument: when put into written form, one's words become orphans. They are now out in the world. One can no longer do anything to protect them and they must make their own way, stand or fall on their own merits. Others can twist them, wilfully misunderstand them or employ them for their own questionable purposes. But they can also support them, refine or augment them. All rests on the vicissitudes of fortune. This is the way of the written. Thus, once consigned to the page, why is Holmes not also an orphan? Why does the strange cult of ownership hold sway in the case of fictional characters? The author's identity confers ownership of his characters, or so we are tempted to suppose. But what if the author is also just more words? If an author writes a book about a person who is writing a book, we are not tempted to say that the ownership of the characters in the latter book is tied to the fictional character creating them. The fictional creator is just more words, and as such cannot own anything. Now it becomes clear: underlying the cult of ownership is the idea of the executive self.

3.

Why is literature a superior art form to philosophy? Why are its ideas living rather than moribund items laid out for dissection? Why is all great literature essentially an invitation to compassion? The answer is that literature allows us to glimpse – briefly, uncertainly, fallibly, to be sure – our own limitlessness in the life of another. It does this because it allows us to grasp the deep contingency of limits. We understand that it is a deeply contingent fact that Conan Doyle never addressed the matter of Holmes's late-evening dining arrangements on 21 October 1885 – if he did not, in fact, address this. We understand that this omission is something that can be easily written in, a gap in Holmes's life that can easily be bridged, whether by Conan Doyle or another, and if it is not, then this, too, is simply chance. A life, as it is lived, is essentially open-ended: that it should encompass some events and not others, and that it should end at all, is a curiously, indeed unthinkably, contingent fact. Literature is an invitation to compassion because it takes the contingency of limits that we apprehend all too well in our own lives – that is why we cannot, truly, understand our own deaths – and, for a moment if no more, transfers this to the life of another. In moments, and only moments, we can see our own limitlessness in the life of another.

*

Love is possible only if the self is like a rope. A rope is nothing more than the strands that comprise it. There is nothing else to which the strands attach: they attach only to each other. A self, in the minimal sense, is nothing more than mental and bodily events, states, processes bound together in the right way. There is nothing else to which they attach: they attach only to each other. In this minimal sense, a self is the same thing as a life: a single track through space and time, beginning at a certain point and ending at another, a track cut by a human animal. A life is not impermeable. Lives intersect, they mingle with each other: they can fundamentally shape each other's course and character. When two lives encounter each other, when each is still relatively new, still soft and pliable, not overly stiffened by life's salt wind, then the strands that make them up can become intertwined. There may still be discernible ropes, but with multiple knotted points of contact. Or, in the end, there may be only one rope.

1.

My father employs the analogy of a rope. At the beginning of the book, he talked instead of a musical composition constructed from distinct melodies – an analogy that I believe he owed to Kundera. But perhaps the best analogy has been staring me in the face for the past three hundred pages. Think of a person as akin to a text. Suppose someone were to discover a manuscript written by someone very dear to him. The author dies before its completion and, perhaps as a tribute of sorts, the discoverer decides to attend to the manuscript. If this self-appointed editor is peculiarly unambitious, he may confine his efforts to footnotes. A little more sanguinity – or hubris – might see him attempt to address

any obvious plot issues, perhaps fill in a few of the characters, explain the writer's reasoning where he feels it needs
explaining. Suppose also that he finds someone else has
been commenting on the manuscript too – perhaps unbe-
known to the author, perhaps not. Finding these comments
insightful, the self-appointed editor decides to incorporate
these comments also, injecting them into the storyline as
seamlessly as possible, changing the primary voice to
acknowledge and interrogate the secondary, and so on. Now
who is the author of the manuscript? The answer is clear:
they all are. The resulting text is a product of multiple drafts,
written by multiple people. In time, perhaps others may join
in, adding new drafts, exploring new avenues of interpretation. And if they do, or if they do not, either way that is a
deeply contingent fact.

2.

If a person were akin to a text of this sort, there would, as my
father put it, be more to that person's life than is immured
within the spatial limits of his body and the temporal limits
of his birth and death. It is a deeply contingent fact that I discovered my father's manuscript and my mother's comments.
It is, similarly, a matter of deep contingency that the ocean
did not swallow his writing before I found it. But if I had
never discovered my father's writing – and if my mother had
decided to keep her thoughts to herself – that would also
have been a deeply contingent fact. Discovered or not, com-
mented on or not, edited or not, the manuscript would still be
the product of multiple drafts, written by multiple people.
The promise of limitlessness is contained within every
memory. In every memory there is an invitation to revision,
redrafting, expansion and excision.

The anachronisms that have meandered into my father's writing demonstrate this conclusively. Memories are always multiple drafts written in different words. In any memory, there is the event recalled, but also the act of recalling it. These are not the same and can have very different features. I can remember with fondness an event I found devastating at the time. I can remember with sorrow and regret an event that, at the time it happened, filled me with happiness. We can distinguish the properties of remembering and the remembered but we cannot, as a practical matter, keep them apart. Our memories are never stable records of a past, engraved in the stone tablet of the mind. In the act of recall, our memories are always updated – restructured and re-defined to bring them into line with our current concerns, moods and interests. This Janus-faced feature of memory underlies its anachronistic character.

When my father remembered the face of his father – flitting between him and the TV screen, confusion turning to incredulity to resignation – it was the face of an old man that he recalled, even though when the remembered event took place his father would have been no more than thirty years old. The memory has been rewritten.[127] *A new draft has been*

127 The anachronistic character of memory is, in fact, both obvious and endemic in all autobiography. Consider just one example, this childhood memory of Tolstoy: 'I am sitting in a tub surrounded by a new and not unpleasant smell of something with which they are scrubbing my tiny body.' This passage is from Tolstoy's notes, and in his biography of Tolstoy A. N. Wilson argued that Tolstoy must have been confabulating. If this was a genuine memory, then he would not have remembered his body as tiny: a child does not see his own body as being tiny. Wilson is mistaken, or at least there is no evidence of confabulation in this case. Anachronism is quite different: a real memory is overwritten and updated by way of a perspective that could only have come later. See Peter Goldie, *The Mess Inside* (Oxford University Press, 2012), for lucid discussion of this case.

superimposed on the old. This is always the way of memory.[128] *Every act of recall changes the memory recalled, in ways either subtle or dramatic. Any memory is always a composition: a structure made of more than one draft. If our memories make us who we are, then we are all the products of multiple drafts.*

3.

I find it curious, and somewhat amusing, that the footnotes in the preceding paragraph were footnotes to myself: curious, perhaps, but nevertheless entirely appropriate. Perhaps the safest general characterization of each and every one of us is that we are a series of footnotes to ourselves. Some people think we are all narratives – each one of us is a story we make up to explain ourselves to ourselves. I think this idea is too vague to be very helpful. If we are narratives, we are certainly not good ones. Did my father's life contain a flaw, one that gradually developed into a conflict, escalated into a

128 For a detailed defence of this conception of memory, see Mark Rowlands, *Memory and the Self* (Oxford University Press, 2017). One of the most significant discoveries ever made by the sciences of the mind was the discovery of the phenomenon of reconsolidation by K. Nader and colleagues in the early years of this century. It had long been known that when a memory is first made, it must undergo a process of consolidation. Nader and colleagues discovered that when a memory is accessed is must be reconsolidated. Thus, if you are injected with a chemical that blocks protein synthesis, any memory that you subsequently try to recall will be lost forever. The conclusion these researchers drew was correct: remembering is not the accessing of a stable memory trace, but is, at least in part, a process of reconstruction and updating. This provided neurological confirmation of a phenomenon that had been documented for some time: the extraordinary unreliability of memory. See K. Nader, G. Schafe and J. LeDoux, 'Fear memories require protein synthesis in the amygdala for reconsolidation after retrieval', *Nature*, Vol. 406, pp. 722–6 (2000). Also K. Nader, 'Memory traces unbound', *Trends in Neurosciences*, Vol. 26, No. 2, pp. 65–72 (2003).

crisis, and then, finally, admitted of a crushing resolution? Not at all: he was born, he died, and a few things happened in between. That's the way it is for me too, and I suspect for most of us. For many people, most of the time, life is just one damned thing after another. The time to tell stories about oneself is a luxury afforded to few.

Nevertheless, there may be a grain of truth in the idea that we are narratives. Or, rather, there are grains – and these are our memories. Any memory, in its very nature, invites composition: it calls out to be built upon by what is new, what is novel, what could not have been present in the remembered event. And every time a memory is recalled, it will indeed be augmented in this way. Each time my father remembered, his memory was reconstructed anew, updated to reflect what happened only later in his life. The consequences of this are profound: each person is defined by a kind of openness. The very nature of our memories – the memories that make us who we are, a different person from anyone else – invites others to build on us. Anachronism litters my father's writing, just as it litters the lives of each of us, precisely because any memory is always a composition. Sometimes this composition takes place within the confines of a single track through space and time – a single life – and sometimes it is the result of multiple tracks meeting, overlapping and perhaps travelling with each other for a time. The differences, in the end, are not as important as we think. If our memories make us who we are, then the boundaries between us are minimal. This pathway that I am through space and time, this product of multiple compositions, is never truly separate from all the other pathways. Any separation is a deeply contingent fact. This is what makes love possible, for it underwrites the possibility of genuine identification with the other. This is what

285

makes compassion possible, since it underwrites the possibility of enduring together rather than enduring apart. It is our openness that makes true human goodness possible.

Words written on words, superimposed on words: accentuating or challenging, underlining or refuting each other. These words are the book of the real. The boundaries between us are not real. Your pain can be my pain. Your delight can be mine also. There is no writer behind the written. We are all just words somewhere. You have to be careful in my condition. It may be the amyloid plaques, the tau-protein clumping or the loss of neural connectivity. Perhaps it is these that are doing the talking. But these are now as much part of the written as anything else.

The self, this glittering prize of my younger days, does seem like a dream to me now. Growing inside of me is a sense, as yet amphibological but nevertheless discernible, that somehow I am the victim of a bizarre joke. It is not that I don't recognize this face when I look in the mirror. That I can understand. Rather, it is that behind this very face are those memories that call themselves mine. That these fading memories – which, still, defiantly proclaim they span more than eight decades – should all belong together in the same single pathway through space and time, that they belong to my life rather than the life of someone else: this, to me, is a progressively surreal discovery. It is as if someone were trying to tell me about a time before I was born, or a land to which I have never been.

A land: perhaps that is it. Most of our moral problems come from the fact that we could not bring ourselves to love the land as much as we love ourselves, never suspecting that we were always the land. There is something that happens to the best thinkers when they become too old. No one finds

286

them convincing any more. Some would say, they're losing it: they can't do it any more. Perhaps this is correct in some cases, but in others something else is happening. A person is a land that exists not in physical space, but in the space of logic and the imagination. After many years of travel, the person comes to know this land better than anyone else ever could. He knows, immediately and effortlessly, which direction of travel is permitted in logical space, and where any turn of the imagination will lead to from any given place. Because he knows it so well, the land becomes impenetrable to anyone else, and his attempts to chart the terrain for another are doomed. These attempts always presuppose too much knowledge of the land: he is like an old country peasant giving directions to a stranger, ones that he couldn't possibly follow unless he already knew the land. You have become a land that makes no sense to anyone else: if you have not already lived there, it is too profuse and extravagant for you to understand. But this is just the beginning of the end. The complexity of the land is built on, successively, layer by layer, until in the end it becomes too much even for you: the sweep of the land too extensive for you to encompass; its slopes too steep to climb, and its depths too tenebrous to plumb. Then, in this dream that you have become, the deep truth of your existence reveals itself. There never was you, there only ever was the land. And the land is more fertile and more variegated, more beautiful and more confused – more wonderful – than you could ever have been.

Acknowledgements

I would like to thank peerless Max Porter, one of those rare editors with whom it is not just enjoyable to work, but exciting. Max was kind enough to believe in this project when it was nothing more than a perfunctory 'What do you think of this idea?' email, and then wise enough to provide indispensable advice along the way. Without him, this book would never have been written. My thanks to Amber Dowell for her excellent – and refreshingly painless – copy-editing. My thanks also to Sue Phillpott for proofreading.

I am grateful to Picador for granting me permission to use a quotation from Cormac McCarthy's *The Road*: Copyright © Cormac McCarthy, 2006. I am grateful also to Faber and Faber, for permission to use a quotation from Milan Kundera's *The Unbearable Lightness of Being*: Copyright © Milan Kundera, 1984.

My greatest thanks are to the best things that ever happened to me: to my sons, Macsen and Brenin, and to my wife, Emma. This book is dedicated to them.